Gluten-Free
GROCERY SHOPPING
GUIDE

2007 EDITION

Dr. Mara Matison
Dainis Matison

D1311141

Kal-Haven Publishing

Cecelia's Marketplace
Gluten-Free Grocery Shopping Guide

by Dr. Mara Matison & Dainis Matison

Kal-Haven Publishing
P.O. Box 20383
Kalamazoo, MI 49019 U.S.A.

ISBN 978-0-9794094-0-0

First Edition 2007

Printed in the United States of America
Cover illustration: Lilita Austrins

CONTENTS

About the Authors

The co-author of this book, Dr. Mara Matison, received her Doctor of Dental Surgery degree from University of Detroit Mercy, and her Bachelor of Arts degree in Psychology from Villanova University. Her husband and co-author, Dainis Matison, received his Master of Science degree in Information Technology and Bachelor of Arts degree in Finance from Ball State University. They are both members of the Gluten Intolerance Group, a nationwide organization that supports people with celiac disease, gluten intolerance, and other gluten sensitivities.

Cecelia's Marketplace was established by both Mara and Dainis in 2006, soon after Mara was diagnosed with celiac disease. The couple struggled with Mara's major lifestyle change, which included adhering to a strict gluten-free diet. Shopping trips to the grocery store were very frustrating. Spending time calling food manufacturers to find out if products were gluten-free seemed like a daily routine. They knew there had to be an easier way, so they decided to compile a gluten-free grocery shopping guide.

Thanks to *Cecelia's Marketplace Gluten-Free Grocery Shopping Guide*, grocery shopping now has become easier for not only Mara and Dainis, but also their family and friends that prepare gluten-free meals.

Preface - Note to the Reader

Cecelia's Marketplace Gluten-Free Grocery Shopping Guide has been written to help people that are in search of gluten-free products. Whether you are on a gluten-free diet, prepare gluten-free meals for yourself or others, or just enjoy eating gluten-free foods, this book is for you. It will help guide you to easy grocery shopping and eliminate the frustration and headaches that you've experienced trying to find gluten-free products. This guide is also great for restaurant owners, chefs, dieticians, family members, husbands, wives, friends, and others that shop for, or prepare gluten-free foods. For those that are not familiar with gluten-free cooking, we have included two special sections in the front of the book: What is Gluten and Gluten-Free Kitchen Tips.

We have alphabetized our *Gluten-Free Grocery Shopping Guide* to help you quickly find brand names of the products you are looking for. The guide is easy to use: just pick a product, look it up, and you'll have gluten-free brands at your fingertips. The book is small enough so that it can be carried with you to the grocery store when searching for products. Use it anytime, anywhere. In addition to the *Gluten-Free Grocery Shopping Guide*, there is also a section in the back of the book that lists gluten-free over the counter (OTC) medications. Gluten-free shopping has never been easier. Treasure this book and enjoy all the gluten-free foods that are available!

Due to periodic changes in ingredients and new products, *Cecelia's Marketplace Gluten-Free Grocery Shopping Guide* will be updated annually. Look for the new edition every spring.

Cecelia's Marketplace - "Making Gluten-Free Living Easy!"

Dr. Mara Matison
Dainis Matison

Acknowledgments

There are many people that have contributed to the creation of this book. The support from our family and friends has made this journey more enjoyable. Lilita A. for hours of data entry, editing, cover illustration, and all the gluten-free meals that kept us going; Mik for editing, critiquing and successful business strategies; Ray for all the reference materials and guidance to becoming successful entrepreneurs; Ligita for supporting us and all the delicious gluten-free recipes along the way; Lija for online advertising and marketing; Lilita M. for showing us 'The Secret'; Liana and Lauma for the wonderful laptop; Velta and Ilga for believing in us; Jonnie Bryant for all the publishing advice and knowledge; Dr. Heidi Gjersoe for all the recommendations, diagnosis, and support; Tisha Pankop for editing; Larisa Kins for page layout & cover design; Jeff Matson/Creative Group for logo design; Dr. Arnis Pone, Dr. Jason Ham, Kal-Haven Publishing, Color House Graphics, and all our fellow "celiacs" for all the support.

Warning - Disclaimer

What is Gluten?

Gluten is a special type of protein that is most commonly found in wheat, rye, and barley. It is comprised of two main protein groups: gliadins, and gluteins. People that have celiac disease (also called celiac sprue, gluten intolerance, gluten enteropathy, or commonly known as a gluten "allergy"), may suffer from chronic digestive problems when ingesting foods that contain gluten. Gluten is found in most cereals, breads, pastas, soups, and pizza crusts. It may also be hidden in foods such as seasonings, salad dressings, additives and natural flavors. Maintaining a strict gluten-free diet is the only treatment. After gluten is eliminated from the diet, the digestive tract begins to heal and the symptoms normally start to disappear after a few weeks.

Approximately 3 million Americans are affected by celiac disease (1 in 133 people), making it almost as prevalent as Type I diabetes.[1] It is known to be more common in people of Northern European descent. Celiac disease is diagnosed through blood tests and a biopsy of the small intestine lining. If left untreated, it may lead to serious health complications, some of which may be fatal.

[1] www.mayoclinic.org/celiac-disease/

Gluten-Free Kitchen Tips

It is very important prior to preparing a gluten-free meal, to clean the surrounding area including, pots, pans, utensils and any other items being used. Bread crumbs, flour particles or other gluten containing foods left in the cooking area can potentially contaminate a gluten-free meal.

Here are some tips to help prevent gluten contamination:

- Use an uncontaminated sponge to wash all working surfaces with soap and water.
- Clean and inspect pots, pans, utensils, cutting boards and other kitchenware for gluten residue.
- Use clean kitchen hand towels.
- If grilling, place aluminum foil over the grilling area.
- Use squeeze bottle mayonnaise, mustard, ketchup, peanut butter, jelly/jam, butter/margarine or other condiments that can easily be cross-contaminated.
- Avoid using wooden utensils. Gluten residue can stay embedded in wooden utensils and cutting boards.
- Use a separate toaster for gluten-free bread, rice cakes, etc..
- In commerical kitchens, if using latex/rubber gloves, make sure the gloves are not coated with powder (starch).
- Do not deep fry foods in contaminated oil (i.e. from breaded chicken wings, breaded chicken tenders, mozzarella sticks).

This book is dedicated to:

All those in search of gluten-free products.

Gluten-Free
Grocery Shopping Guide (A-Z)

A A

Acorn Squash... see Squash

Alfredo Sauce
> **Bertolli** - Regular
> **Mayacamas** - Regular
> **Safeway Select** - Light Alfredo

Almonds... see Nuts

Amaranth
> **Bob's Red Mill -** Amaranth Flour
> **Nu-World Foods -** All Varieties

Anchovies
> **Crown Prince -** Flat Anchovies

Angel Hair Pasta... see Pasta

Animal Crackers
> **Mi-Del** - Arrowroot Animal Cookies

Antipasto
> **B&J -** Antipasto Mixed Vegetables In Oil

Apple Butter
> **B&J** - Apple Butter
> **Eden** - Apple, Apple Cherry, Cherry

Apple Cider... see Cider

Apple Cider Vinegar... see Vinegar

Apples... *All Fresh Fruits & Vegetables Are Gluten-Free*

Applesauce
> **365 Organic Every Day Value** - Cinnamon Applesauce,
> Unsweetened
> **Albertsons** - Applesauce
> **Applesnax -** Applesauce
> **Authentic Food Artisan** - Ela Family Farms Organic Applesauce
> (Gala, Just Jonathan)

1

A

Baxters - Applesauce

Beech-Nut - Applesauce (Stage 1 Fruits, Stage 3 Fruits)

Eden - Apple, Apple (Cherry, Cinnamon, Strawberry)

Hy-Vee - Applesauce, Cinnamon, Natural Style

Marsh Brand - Applesauce

Midwest Country Fare - Applesauce, Home Style, Natural, w/(Cinnamon, Peaches, Raspberries, Strawberries)

Mott's - Applesauce, Fruit Blends

Safeway Brand - Cups, Natural, Sweetened

Spartan Brand - Applesauce (Cinnamon, Natural, Peach, Raspberry, Regular, Strawberry)

Stop & Shop Brand - Applesauce (Chunky, Cinnamon, Mixed Berry, Natural, Strawberry)

Trader Joe's - All Flavors

Wegmans -

　　Applesauce (Cinnamon, Mixed Berry, Peach Mango)

　　Applesauce w/Calcium & Vitamin C (Cinnamon, Regular, Sweetened)

　　Chunky Sweetened Applesauce (Chunky, MacIntosh)

　　Natural Applesauce (Chunky, Regular)

Whole Kids Organic - Cinnamon, Mixed Berry, Organic Apple, Peach, Strawberry Banana, Unsweetened

Winn Dixie - Unsweetened

Apricots... *All **Fresh** Fruits & Vegetables Are **Gluten-Free***

Albertsons - Canned

Del Monte -

　　Canned Fruit (All Varieties)

　　Fruit Snack Cups (All Metal & Plastic Containers)

Hy-Vee - Unpeeled Halves

Meijer - Halves Unpeeled In Pear Juice, Tropical Fruit Blend

Stop & Shop Brand - Heavy Syrup, Island Apricots In Light Syrup, Splenda

A
B

Wegmans - Canned Halves

Artichokes... *All Fresh Fruits & Vegetables Are Gluten-Free*

365 Every Day Value - Artichoke Hearts

B&J - Imported Marinated Artichoke Hearts

Birds Eye - All Frozen Vegetables *(Except With Sauce)*

Native Forest - Artichoke Hearts (Whole, Marinated)

Trader Joe's - Artichoke Hearts In Water

Wegmans - Artichoke Hearts (In Brine, Marinated & Quartered)

Asparagus... *All Fresh Fruits & Vegetables Are Gluten-Free*

365 Organic Every Day Value - Organic Asparagus Spears

Albertsons - Asparagus

Birds Eye - All Frozen Vegetables *(Except With Sauce)*

Del Monte - All Varieties

Green Giant -

Canned Asparagus Spears

Cut Spears Asparagus (50% Less Sodium, Regular)

Simply Steam w/ No Sauce (Asparagus Cuts)

Laura Lynn - Cut Asparagus

Marsh Brand - Whole Asparagus

Native Forest - Green Asparagus Cuts & Tips, Spears (Green Asparagus, White Asparagus)

Nature's Promise - Organic Asparagus Spears

Stop & Shop Brand - Asparagus (Spears, Tips & Cuts)

Wegmans - Cut Green Spears & Tips

Avocado... *All Fresh Fruits & Vegetables Are Gluten-Free*

Avocado Dip... see Guacamole and/or Dips

B

Baby Food

Beech-Nut -

Stage 1 Fruits
  Applesauce
  Chiquita Banana
  Peaches
  Pears
Stage 1 Meats
  Beef & Beef Broth
  Chicken & Chicken Broth
  Lamb & Lamb Broth
  Turkey & Turkey Broth
  Veal & Veal Broth)
Stage 1 Rice Cereal
Stage 1 Vegetables
  Butternut Squash
  Tender Golden Sweet
  Potatoes
  Tender Sweet Carrots
  Tender Sweet Peas
  Tender Young Green Beans)
Stage 2 Cinnamon Raisin Pears w/Apples
Stage 2 Desserts
  Dutch Apple
  Mango
Stage 2 Dinners
  Chicken & Rice
  Homestyle Chicken Soup
  Macaroni & Beef w/Vegetables
  Pineapple Glazed Ham
  Vegetables & Beef
  Vegetables & Chicken
  Vegetables & Ham

B

Stage 2 Fruits
  Apples & Bananas
  Apples & Blueberries
  Apples & Cherries
  Apples & Pears
  Apples w/Mango & Kiwi
  Apples w/Pears & Bananas
  Apricots w/Pears & Apples
  Banana w/Apple & Pineapple
  Peaches & Bananas
  Pears & Pineapples
  Pears & Raspberries
  Plums w/Apples & Pears
  Prunes w/Pears)
Stage 2 Rice Cereal
  w/Apples
  w/Cinnamon
  w/Golden Delicious Apples Instant
  w/Island Fruits
Stage 2 Vegetables
  Carrots & Peas
  Corn & Sweet Potatoes
  Country Garden Vegetables
  Mixed Vegetables)
Stage 3 Country Vegetables & Chicken
Stage 3 Desserts
  Banana Pudding
  Fruit
Stage 3 Fruits
  Apples & Bananas
  Applesauce

      Bartlett Pears

      Chiquita Bananas

      Peaches

   Stage 3 Rice Cereal & Pears

   Stage 3 Turkey Rice Dinner

   Stage 3 Vegetables

      Carrots & Peas

      Sweet Potatoes

   Toddler Meals

      Turkey Stew w/Rice

      Vegetable Stew w/Rice

Bright Beginnings - Pediatric Drink (Chocolate, Vanilla)

Del Monte Nature's Goodness Baby Food

   Stage 1

      Applesauce

      Bananas

      Carrots

      Pears

      Squash

      Sweet Potatoes

   Stage 2

      Apples & Blueberries

      Apples & Chicken

      Apples & Pears

      Applesauce

      Apricots w/Pears & Apples

      Bananas

      Bananas w/Pears & Apples

      Corn & Sweet Potatoes

      Mixed Vegetables

      Pears, Plums w/Apples

B

> Squash
> Sweet Peas
> Sweet Potatoes & Turkey
> Stage 3
>> Bananas & Strawberry w/Tapioca
>> Bananas w/Tapioca
>> Sweet Potatoes

Earth's Best Organic Baby Food -
> Stage 1
>> First Bananas
>> First Peas
>> First Sweet Potatoes
> Stage 2
>> Apples
>> Apples & Apricots
>> Apples & Blueberries
>> Apples & Plums
>> Apples & Raspberries
>> Bananas
>> Corn & Butternut Squash
>> Green Beans & Rice
>> Pears & Raspberries
>> Peas & Brown Rice
>> Sweet Potatoes

Gerber Baby Food-
> 1st Foods
>> Applesauce
>> Bananas
>> Carrots
>> Green Beans
>> Pears

B

Peas

Prunes

Sweet Potatoes

2nd Foods

Apple Strawberry Banana

Apples & Cherries

Applesauce

Apricots w/Mixed Fruit

Pear Pineapples

Banana (Apple Dessert, Mixed Berry, Orange Medley, Plum Grape, w/Apples & Pears, Yogurt Dessert)

Bananas

Carrot Apple Mango

Carrots

Dutch Apple Dessert

Fruit Medley Dessert

Garden Vegetable

Green Beans

Guava Dessert

Mixed Vegetables

Papaya Dessert

Peaches

Peas

Prunes w/Apples

Squash

Sweet Potatoes

Sweet Potatoes & Corn

Tropical Fruit Medley Dessert

2nd Foods Dinners

Apples & Chicken

Beef & Beef Gravy

B

Chicken & Chicken Gravy
Chicken & Rice
Pears & Chicken
Sweet Potatoes & Turkey
Vegetable Chicken
Vegetable Beef
2nd Foods Cereal (Rice Cereal w/Applesauce)
3rd Foods
Applesauce
Banana Strawberry
Bananas
Carrots
Fruit Medley Dessert
Green Beans w/Rice
Hawaiian Delight Dessert
Peaches
Pears
Squash
Sweet Potatoes
3rd Foods Dinners
Vegetable Beef
Vegetable Chicken
Vegetable Turkey
Gerber Organic Baby Food -
1st Foods
Applesauce
Bananas
Carrots
Pears
Sweet Peas
Sweet Potatoes

2nd Foods

Applesauce

Apple Strawberry

Bananas

Butternut Squash & Corn

Chicken & Wild Rice

Green Beans

Squash Corn & Chicken

Sweet Potatoes

3rd Foods (Tender Harvest Savory Carrots Potatoes & Beef)

Mini Fruits

Apple Strawberry

Banana Mango

Whole Grain Rice Cereal (Box)

Bacon

365 Every Day Value - Uncured Center Cut Bacon (Low Sodium, Smokehouse)

Applegate Farms - All Varieties

B&J - Sliced, Thick Sliced

Black Label

Dietz & Watson - Bacon (Canadian Style, Premium Imported)

Dorothy Lane Market - All Varieties Uncured Bacon

Food Club - Sliced, Thick Sliced

Hormel - Canadian Style, Fully Cooked, Microwave

Hy-Vee - Fully Cooked

Jennie-O - Extra Lean Turkey

Old Smokehouse - Bacon

Oscar Mayer - Center Cut, Low Sodium, Regular

Range Brand

Red Label

Shaw's - Hickory Smoked

B

     Shelton's - Turkey Breakfast Strips

     Stop & Shop Brand - Bacon (Center Cut Sliced, Lower Sodium, Maple Flavored, Regular Sliced)

     Tops - Hardwood Smoked

     Trader Joe's - Uncured

     Value Brand - Sliced

     Whole Foods - Sliced

     Yorkshire Farms - Canadian Style Uncured, Seasoned Uncured, Uncured Maple Syrup, Uncured Sliced

Bacon Bits

     Hormel - Bacon Bits & Pieces

Bagels

     Enjoy Life - Bagels (Cinnamon Raisin, Classic Original, Toasty Onion)

     Glutino - All Star Glutino Sesame Bagel, Cinnamon Raisin Bagel, Plain Bagel, Poppy Seed Bagel

     Jo-Sef - All Varieties

     Trader Joe's - Gluten-Free Bagels

Baking Bars

     Baker's - German Chocolate Baking Squares

     Ghirardelli - Milk, Mint & Dark Chocolate Squares

     Nestle - Chocolate Flavor (Semi-Sweet, Unsweetened), Premier White

Baking Chips

     365 Every Day Value - Chocolate Chips

     B&J - Semi-Sweet Premium Chocolate Chips

     Baker's - Bitter Sweet, Milk, Semi-Sweet, Semi-Sweet Chocolate Flavor, Unsweetened, White

     Ener-G - Chocolate Chips

     Enjoy Life - Semi-Sweet Chocolate Chips

     Ghirardelli - Chocolate Chips (Double, Milk, Semi-Sweet)

     Hershey - Chocolate (Semi-Sweet Baking, Semi-Sweet Chips, Unsweetened Baking)

baking decorations & frostings

B

Hy-Vee - Butterscotch Chips, Milk Chocolate Chips, Semi-Sweet Chocolate Chips

Lecour's - Real Chocolate Chips

Meijer Brand - Chocolate Chips Semi-Sweet

Midwest Country Fare - Chocolate Flavored Chips

Nestle - Choco Bake, Milk Chocolate Morsels, Peanut Butter and Chocolate Morsels, Premier White Morsels, Semi-Sweet Chocolate (Chunks, Mini Morsels, Morsels)

Price Chopper - Butterscotch Baking Chips

Safeway Select - Butterscotch Chips, Chocolate Chips (Milk Chocolate, Real Chocolate, Semi-Sweet)

Spartan Brand - Baking Chips (Butterscotch, Chocolate, Chocolate Semi-Sweet, Milk Chocolate, White Chocolate)

Stop & Shop Brand - Semi-Sweet Chocolate Chips

Tops - Semi-Sweet Chocolate Chips

Trader Joe's - Chocolate Chips (Milk, Semi-Sweet, White)

Tropical Source - Semi-Sweet Chocolate Chips

Wegmans - Chocolate Morsels Semi-Sweet

Baking Cocoa

Equal Exchange - Organic Baking Cocoa

Hy-Vee - Baking Cocoa

Price Chopper - Baking Cocoa

Spartan Brand - Cocoa Baking Chocolate (Can)

Stop & Shop Brand - Baking Cocoa

Watkins - Baking Cocoa

Baking Decorations & Frostings

Betty Crocker - All Bottle Decors (Chocolate Sprinkles, Rainbow Sprinkles, Nonpareils, Sequins, Sugars)

Almond Paste

Candy Cards

Decorating Gels (All Colors)

Decorating Icing (All Colors)

B

Easy Flow Icing (All Colors)

HomeStyle Frosting Mix (Fluffy White)

Marizpan

Neon Decorating Gel

Parlor Perfect Ice Cream Topping

Rich & Creamy Frosting (Dark Chocolate, Coconut Pecan)

Cake Mate - Decorating Gels (All Colors), Decorating Icing (All Colors)

Cherrybrook Kitchen - Frosting (Chocolate, Vanilla)

Dagoba - All Varieties

Duncan Hines -

Caramel

Chocolate Buttercream

Classic Chocolate

Classic Vanilla

Coconut Supreme *(Except Coconut Pecan)*

Cream Cheese

Dark Chocolate Fudge

French Vanilla

Lemon Supreme

Milk Chocolate

White Chocolate Almond

Edward's & Sons - Let's Do Organics Chocolate Sprinkelz

Ginger Evans - All Frosting Flavors *(Except Coconut Pecan)*

Laura Lynn - Sprinkles (Chocolate, Rainbow)

Let's Do...Sprinkelz - Carnival, Chocolate, Confetti

Meijer Brand - Frosting Ready To Spread (Lemon)

Safeway - Sprinkles (Easter, Halloween, Holiday, Sand Sugar Party, Valentines)

Trader Joe's - Frosting Chocolate

Baking Powder

B

    Barkat
    Bob's Red Mill
    Clabber Girl
    Davis
    Durkee
    Ener-G - Double Acting Baking Powder
    Featherweight
    Glutino
    Hearth Club
    Hilltop Mills
    Hy-Vee - Double Acting Baking Powder
    KC
    Kinnikinnick
    Kraft - Calumet Baking Powder
    Laura Lynn
    Marsh Brand
    Rumford
    Spice Islands
    Tone's
    Tops - Double Acting Baking Powder
    Watkins
    Wegmans - Double Acting

Baking Soda
    Albertsons
    Arm & Hammer
    Bob's Red Mill
    Durkee
    Hilltop Mills
    Hy-Vee
    Laura Lynn
    Meijer Brand

B

Price Chopper
Spartan Brand
Spice Islands
Stop & Shop Brand
Tone's

Banana Chips

365 Organic Every Day Value - Organic Sweet Banana Chips
Hy-Vee - Dried Fruit (Banana Chips)

Bananas... *All Fresh Fruit & Vegetables Are Gluten-Free*

Chiquita
Dole

Barbeque Sauce

Annie's Naturals - Organic (Hot Chipotle, Original, Smokey)
Bone Suckin' Sauce - Hiccuppin' Hot, Hot (Original, Thicker Style), Original, Thicker Style, Rib Rub
Consorzio Marinades - Organic BBQ (Original, Spicy)
Daddy Sam's - Medium Ginger Jalapeno, Original Recipe
Deep South - Regular
Hy-Vee - Hickory, Honey Smoke, Original
Isaly's - Original, Spicy
Lea & Perrins - Bold, Original, Spicy
Midwest Country Fare - Hickory, Honey, Original
Mr. Spice - Honey BBQ
Old Cape Cod - BBQ & Grilling Sauce (Honey Orange, Lemon Ginger)
Pappy's - BBQ Sauce
Safeway Select - Hickory Smoked, Honey Mustard, Honey Smoked, Original
Saz's - Original, Sassy
Stop & Shop Brand - Hickory Smoke, Original
Sweet Baby Ray's - Hickory, Honey Sweet, Hot 'N Spicy, Original
Trader Joe's - Kansas City, Original

Walden Farms - Original, Thick & Spicy

Wegmans - Memphis Style, Tropical

Wild Oats - BBQ Sauce (Carolina, Kansas City, Texas)

Wild Thymes - Spicy Island BBQ Sauce

Winn Dixie - Regular

Bars... (includes Breakfast, Energy, Fruit, Protein, etc.)

365 Organic Every Day Value -

Dark Chocolate Bar (Regular, w/Almonds, Organic Swiss (w/Coconut Flakes, w/Mint Crisps))

Organic Honey Roasted (Hemp & Flax Bar, Mixed Sesame Bar)

Aller Energy Bars - Apple Cinnamon, Blueberry, Cherry, Chocolate Chip

Alpsnack -

Apricots & Cranberries

Coconut/Mango & Pineapple

Fair Trade (Dark Chocolate, Espresso Chocolate)

Plums & Currents

Arico - Cookie Bars (Almond Cranberry, Chocolate Chip, Double Chocolate, Peanut Butter)

Atkins - Advantage Bar (Almond Brownie, Chocolate Coconut, Chocolate Peanut Butter, Mocha), Cinnamon Bun Breakfast, Endulge Bar (Chocolate)

Balance Bars - Almond Brownie, Chocolate, Chocolate Raspberry Fudge, Mocha, Yogurt Honey Peanut

Boomi Bar -

Apricot Cashew

Cashew Almond

Cranberry Apple

Fruit & Nut

Healthy Hazel

Macadamia Paradise

Maple Pecan

B

Perfect Pumpkin
Pineapple (Ginger, Regular)
Pistachio
Protein Plus (Almond, Cashew)
Walnut Date

Bumble Bar -
Chai w/Almonds
Chocolate Crisp
Lushus Lemon
Original Flavor
Original Flavor w/(Almonds, Cashews, Hazelnuts, Mixed Nuts)

Carb Safe - Sugar Free Chocolate Bars (Dark, Milk)

Clif Nectar -
Cherry Pomegranate
Cinnamon Pecan
Cranberry Apricot Almond
Dark Chocolate Walnut
Lemon Vanilla Cashew

Dagoba - Chocolate Bars (All Varieties)

Eat Natural - Bars (All Varieties)

Ecco Bella - Health by Chocolate Bar, Women's Wonder Bar

Ener-G - Chocolate Chip Snack Bar

Enjoy Life - Caramel Apple, Cocoa Loco, Very Berry

GeniSoy -
Bars (Chunky Peanut Butter, Creamy Peanut Yogurt)
Low Carb Crunch Bars (Chocolate, Chocolate Chip, Lemon, Peanut Butter, Raspberry)
MLO (Brown Rice Protein, Milk & Egg Protein)
MLO Xtreme (Chocolate, Chocolate Mint, Cookies & Cream, Peanut Butter)

Protein Crunch Bars (Chocolate, Chocolate Chip, Lemon, Peanut Butter, Raspberry)

Gertrude & Bronner's Magic Alpsnack - Cookie Bars (Almond Cranberry, Chocolate Chip, Double Chocolate, Peanut Butter)

Glutino - Breakfast Bar (Apple, Blueberry, Chocolate)

Gopal's - All Varieties

Govinda's Blissbar - Cosmic Combo, Heavenly Hazelnut, Macadamia Madness, Walnut Date The Great

Heaven Scent Natural Foods - Marshmallow Bar (Chocolate Chip, Original, w/Soy Protein)

Larabar - All Varieties

Maya Chocolates - Chocolate, Chocolate (Coffee, Mint, Orange)

MLO Xtreme Bars - Chocolate, Chocolate Mint, Cookies & Cream, Peanut Butter

Meijer Brand - Xtreme Snack Bars

Nature's Path Organic - Crispy Rice Bars (Cheetah Berry, Koala Chocolate, Peanut Butter)

Neeco - Clark Bar, Skybar

Newman's Own Organics -
   Chocolate Bar (Espresso Sweet Dark, Milk, Orange Sweet Dark, Sweet Dark)
   Milk Chocolate w/Butter Toffee Crunch Bar
   Peanut Butter Cups (Dark, Milk, Peppermint)

Nutiva Bars - Flax & Raisin

Odyssey - Caramel Nut Bar

Omega Smart Bars - All Varieties

Organic Fiber Bars - All Varieties

Organic Food Bar - All Varieties

Orgran -
   Choc-Bar w/Hazelnuts
   Fruit Bars Fruit Medley

B

Fruit Bars w/(Banana, Figs)
Fruit Filled Bar (Apricot, Blueberry, Cho-Cherry)
Oskri Organics - Sesame Bar w/(Date Syrup, Molasses)
Ruth's Hemp Power -
　CranNut Flax
　Hemp & Trail
　Maca (Chocolate Ginger, Ginger Almond, Lemon Hazelnut)
　Tropical Flax
　Very Berry Flax
Schar - Snack, Solena Bar
Seitenbacher -
　Choco Apricot Bar
　Energy Bar
　Fitness Bar
　Natural (Cereal Bar, Energizer, Sports Bar)
thinkGreen -
　Blueberry Noni
　Chocolate Chip
　Cranberry Apple
　Peanut Butter Chocolate
thinkOrganic -
　Apricot Coconut
　Cashew Pecan
　Cherry Nut
　Chocolate Coconut
　Cranberry Apple
　Tropical Nut
thinkThin -
　Brownie Crunch
　Chocolate (Fudge, Mudslide)
　Creamy Peanut Butter (Chunky, Creamy)

Dark Chocolate

White Chocolate Chip

B

Tiger's Milk - Peanut Butter, Protein Rich

Whole Treat - Chocolate w/Almonds, Organic Dipped Bars
(Chocolate, Vanilla)

Basmati Rice... see Rice

Bean Dip... see Dips

Beans... *All Fresh Fruits & Vegetables Are Gluten-Free*

365 Every Day Value -

Cannellini

Frozen Cut Green

No Salt Added (Black, Cut Green, Garbanzo Beans,
Kidney, Pinto)

Refried Beans (Black, Black w/Roasted Red Jalapenos,
Fat Free Pinto, Pinto w/Roasted Chile & Lime,
Vegetarian Pinto)

365 Organic Every Day Value -

Baby Lima

Cut Green

Organic (Bag, Baked, Black, Garbanzo, Kidney, Pinto)

Albertsons - Green Beans (Canned, Frozen)

Amy's - Organic Refried Beans (Black, Black Light In Sodium,
Traditional, Traditional Light In Sodium, w/Green Chiles,
Vegetarian Baked)

Arrowhead Mills -

Adzuki

Anasazi

Black Turtle

Garbanzo (Chickpeas)

Green Split Peas

Lentils (Green & Red)

Pintos, Soybeans

B

B&J - Frozen Cut Green Beans

B&M Baked Beans - Baked Beans w/(BBQ Flavored, Bacon & Onion, Country Style, Maple Flavor, Original, Vegetarian)

Bachelor - Baked Beans

Birds Eye - All Frozen Vegetables *(Except With Sauce)*

Bush's Best -

Barbeque Baked

Black

Bold & Spicy Baked

Boston Recipe Baked

Cannellini

Country Style Baked

Garbanzo

Great Northern

Homestyle Baked

Honey Baked

Kidney Dark Red

Maple Cured Bacon Baked

Microwaveable Cup Original

Onion Baked

Original Baked

Pinto

Refried Beans (Traditional)

Vegetarian Baked

Cascadian Farms - Organic Green Beans Almond

Del Monte - All Varieties *(Except Del Monte Savory Sides Green Bean Casserole)*

Eden -

Organic (Aduki, Baked w/Sorghum & Mustard, Black, Black Eyed, Black Soybeans, Butter, Cannellini, Caribbean Black, Garbanzo, Great Northern, Kidney, Navy, Pinto)

Refried (Black, Blacksoy & Black, Kidney, Pinto)

B

Rice & (Cajun Small Red, Caribbean Black, Garbanzo, Kidney, Lentils, Pinto)

Small Red

Spicy Refried (Black, Pinto)

Fantastic World Foods - Instant (Black, Refried), Hummus Garbanzo

Freshlike - Frozen Plain Vegetables *(Except Pasta Combos and Seasoned Blends)*

Giant Brand - Pork & Beans, Vegetarian

Grand Selections - Fancy (Cut Green, Whole Green)

Green Giant -

Canned Cut Green Beans (50% Less Sodium, Regular)

Canned French Style Green Beans

Canned Kitchen Sliced Green Beans

Canned Three Bean Salad

Frozen Baby Lima Beans & Butter Sauce

Frozen Cut Green Beans

Frozen Select w/No Sauce Whole Green Beans

Frozen Simply Steam w/No Sauce Green Beans & Almonds

Simply Steam w/No Sauce (Baby Lima Beans)

Haggen Brand - Black, Green French, Kidney, Refried

Halstead Acres - Great Northern, Pinto, Pork & Beans

Health Market - Organic (Baked, Black, Cut Green, Dark Red Kidney, Garbanzo, Pinto, Refried)

Hormel - Microwave 10 oz Trays (SW Style Black Beans & Rice)

Hy-Vee -

Baby Lima

Black

Blue Lake Cut Green

Butter

Chili Style

Chili w/Beans

B

Cut Green
Fat Free Refried
Frozen Baby Lima
French Cut Green
Frozen Cut Green
Frozen French Cut Green
Great Northern
Home Style Baked
Large Lima
Lentils
Light Red Kidney
Navy
Onion Baked
Original Baked
Pinto
Pork & Beans
Red
Red Kidney
Traditional Refried
Whole Green

Joan of Arc - Black, Butter, Dark Red Kidney, Garbanzo Great Northern, Light Kidney, Pinto, Red

Kid's Kitchen - Beans & Weiners

Laura Lynn -
All Dried Beans,
Canned Beans & Franks
Canned Kidney
Canned Lima
Chili
Cut Green
Fat Free Refried

    French Style Green

    No Salt Cut Green

    Polo

    Pork & Beans

    Refried

Marsh Brand - Pork & Beans, Yorktown Chili Style, Yorktown Green Beans

Meijer Brand -

    Canned Green Beans Cut

      Blue Lake

      Chopped Pork & Beans

      French Style Blue Lake

      French Style No Salt

      No Salt

    Canned Beans

      Black

      Butter

      Fat Free Refried

      Garbanzo

      Great Northern

      Mexican Style

      Pinto,

      Red

      Vegetarian Refried

    Canned Kidney Beans (Light Red, Dark Red)

    Frozen Green Beans (Cut, French Cut, Italian Cut)

    Frozen Lima Beans (Baby, Fordhook)

Midwest Country Fare - Chili Style, Cut Green, Fare Pork & Beans, French Style Green, Frozen Cut Green

Nielsen-Massy - Whole Vanilla Beans

Pictsweet - All Plain Vegetables (Frozen)

B

Price Chopper - Kidney Beans (Canned)
S&W - All Bean Products
Safeway -
  Canned
    Black
    Black-Eyed
    Chick
    Dark Kidney
    Green
    Light Kidney
    Lima
    Pinto
    Pork & Beans
  Dried
    Baby Lima
    Black
    Black-Eyed
    Great Northern
    Green Split
    Large Lima
    Lentils
    Light Red Kidney
    Navy
    Pink
    Pinto
    Small Red
    Small White
  Refried Beans
Shaw's - Baked, Pork & Beans, Refried Fat Free
Spartan Brand -
  Dried Bean Bags

Barley Pearl
Black
Black-Eyed Peas
Great Northern
Kidney
Lentil
Lima Baby
Lima Large
Navy
Pinto
Dried Beans 16 Soup Mix Bags (Chicken, Chili, w/Ham)
Refried Beans (Fat Free, Regular)

Stop & Shop Brand -

Baby Lima
Beans
Black
Brown Sugar & Bacon Baked
Dark Red Kidney
Fordhook Lima
Garbanzo
Golden Cut Wax
Green Beans (& Wax, Cut, French, Italian, No Added
   Salt, w/Garlic, Whole)
Homestyle Baked
Italian
Kidney Light
Lima
Organic Green
Pink
Pinto
Red

B

Romano

Vegetarian Baked

Thrifty Maid - Great Northern, Green, Kidney

Tops - Canned Chili Beans

Trader Joe's -

Black

Cuban Black

Fat Free Refried Black Beans w/Jalapeño Peppers

Garbanzo

Organic (Baked, Black, Garbanzo, Kidney, Pinto)

Red Kidney

Vegetarian Refried Pinto-Salsa Style

Wegmans -

Baked Beans (Homestyle, Original, Vegetarian)

Black

Butter

Cannellini Beans Italian Classics

Cut Green Beans (No Salt, Regular)

Dark Red Kidney (No Salt Added, Regular)

French Style Green Beans (No Salt, Regular)

Garbanzo Beans Italian Classics

Great Northern

Light Kidney

Lima

Pinto

Pork & Beans In Tomato Sauce

Seasoned Chili

Veggi-Green Cut Green

Wax

Wild Oats Label -

Green Beans

B

    Organic
        Black
        Dark Red Kidney
        Garbanzo
        Great Northern
        Lentils
        Pinto
        Red
        Soybeans

Beef... *All Fresh Meat Is **Gluten-Free (Non-Marinated, Unseasoned)***
    Albertson's - Corned Beef Hash
    Always Tender - Flavored Fresh Beef (Non-Flavored, Peppercorn)
    Applegate Farms - Roast Beef (Organic, Regular)
    Boar's Head - All Varieties
    Butcher's Cut - Corned Beef, Corned Beef Brisket
    D&W Vac Pack Meats - Roast Beef
    Dietz & Watson - Italian Roast Beef, London Broil Roast Beef, Prime Rib of Beef, Roast Beef
    Hormel - Fully-Cooked Entrees (Beef Roast Au Jus, Deli Sliced Seasoned Roast Beef, South West Shredded Beef)
    Hy-Vee - Corned Beef, Quarter Pounders
    Isaly's - Roast Beef
    Lloyd's - Beef Ribs w/Original BBQ Sauce
    Pacific Natural Foods - All Natural Beef Steak Chili w/ Beans
    Spartan Brand - Canned Meat Corned Beef Hash
    Trader Joe's - Fully Cooked & Seasoned Prime Rib of Beef
    Winn Dixie - Beef, Ground Beef (All Varieties)

Beef Jerky... see Jerky

Beef Sticks... see Jerky

Beer
    Anheuser-Busch - Redbridge Beer

B

    Bard's Tale Beer - Dragon's Gold Gluten-Free Lager

    Lakefront Brewery - New Grist Sorghum Brewed Beer

    Ramapo Valley Brewery - Honey Passover Beer

Beets... *All **Fresh** Fruits & Vegetables Are **Gluten-Free***

    365 Every Day Value - Sliced

    Baxters - Beetroot Pickled

    Del Monte - All Varieties

    Haggen - Beets Sliced

    Hy-Vee - Diced , Shredded Sliced

    Laura Lynn - Cut, Sliced

    S&W - Pickled

    Stop & Shop Brand - Sliced No Salt Added

    Wegmans - Harvard, Sliced (No Salt, Pickled, Regular), Whole (Pickled, Regular)

Berries... *All **Fresh** Fruits & Vegetables Are **Gluten-Free***

    Del Monte -

        Canned Fruit (All Varieties)

        Fruit Snack Cups (All Metal & Plastic Containers)

    Meijer Brand - Frozen Berry Medley, Frozen Triple Berry Blend

    Spartan Brand - Frozen Berry Medley

    Stop & Shop Brand - Frozen Berry Medley

    Wegmans - Berry Medley

    Wild Oats - Organic Frozen Berry Blend

Biscuits

    Aproten - Chocolate/Hazelnut Biscuits

    Dr. Schar - Chocolate Covered Biscuits, Savoiardi (Savory Biscuits)

Bittermelon... *All **Fresh** Fruits & Vegetables Are **Gluten-Free***

Black Eyed Peas... see Peas

Blackberries... *All **Fresh** Fruits & Vegetables Are **Gluten-Free***

    Meijer Brand - Frozen

    Spartan Brand - Frozen
    Stop & Shop Brand - Frozen
    Wegmans - Blackberries
Blueberries... *All **Fresh** Fruits & Vegetables Are **Gluten-Free***
    Hy-Vee - Frozen
    Meijer - Regular, Individually Quick Frozen
    Spartan Brand - Frozen
    Stop & Shop Brand
    Wegmans
    Wild Oats - Wild Blueberries
Bok Choy... *All **Fresh** Fruits & Vegetables Are **Gluten-Free***
Bologna
    Applegate Farms - Turkey
    Boar's Head - All Varieties
    Dietz & Watson - Beef, German, Original, Ring
    Eckrich - Beef, Head Cheese, Garlic, Jumbo,
      Old Fashioned Loaf, Regular
    Honeysuckle - White Hickory Smoked Turkey
    Hy-Vee - Beef, Garlic, German Brand, Regular Bologna,
      Thick Sliced, Thin Sliced Beef
    Perdue - Deli Turkey
    Russer - Beef, Light Beef, Wunderbar
    Seltzer's - Lebanon
    Shelton's - Uncured (Chicken, Turkey)
Bouillon/Bouillon Cubes
    Albertsons - All Varieties
    Better Than Bouillon - All Varieties
    Celifibr - Bouillon Cubes (Beef, Chicken, Medley)
    Harvest Sun - Bouillon Cubes
    Herb-Ox - Beef, Chicken, Garlic Chicken, Vegetable
    Hy-Vee - Bouillon Cubes (Beef, Chicken), Instant Bouillon
      (Beef, Chicken)

B

Lee Kum Kee - Chicken Bouillon Powder

Marsh Brand - Bouillon Cubes

Massel -

Advantage Bouillon Mix (Beef, Chicken, Vegetable)

Better Bouillon (Beef, Chicken, Vegetable)

Dietary Bouillon Mix (Beef, Chicken, Vegetable)

Perfect Bouillon Mix (Beef, Chicken, Vegetable)

Ultracubes (Beef, Chicken, Vegetable)

McCormick - Bouillon Cubes

Rapunzel - Vegan Vegetable Bouillon (No Salt Added, w/Herbs, w/ Sea Salt)

Spartan Brand - Soup Beef Bouillon (Cube, Granular), Soup Chicken Bouillon (Cube, Granular)

Stop & Shop Brand - Beef Flavored Bouillon Cubes (Instant, Regular), Chicken Flavored Bouillon Cubes (Instant, Regular)

Winn Dixie - Beef, Chicken

Bourbon... *All **Distilled** Alcohol Is **Gluten-Free**[2]

Bowls

Amy's -

Baked Ziti Bowl

Black-Eyed Peas & Veggies Bowl

Brown Rice Bowl

Light In Sodium Brown Rice & Veggies Bowl

Mexican Casserole Bowl

Santa Fe Enchilada Bowl

Teriyaki

Vegetables Bowl

Instant Gourmet Bowls - BBQ Chicken, Chicken Gumbo, Mountain Chili, Santa Fe Chili, Stroganoff

Thai Kitchen - Noodle Bowls (Hot & Sour, Lemongrass & Chili, Mushroom, Roasted Garlic, Spring Onion, Thai Ginger)

Trader Joe's - Chicken Tandoori Rice Bowl
Bratwurst... see Sausage
Bread

> **Barkat** - Cinnamon Raisin Rice Bread, Flax Seed Rice Bread
>
> **Cybros Inc** - 100% Rice, Mock Rye & Rolls, Rice & Raisin, Rolls & Nuggets, Tapioca Almond
>
> **El Peto** - Bread (Brown Rice, Cheese, Italian, Multi Grain, Raisin, Tapioca, White Rice)
>
> **Ener-G Foods** -
>
>> Brown Rice
>>
>> Cinnamon Rolls
>>
>> Citrus Fiber Free Yeast Free Brown Rice
>>
>> Citrus Free Light Brown Rice Loaf
>>
>> Corn
>>
>> Egg-Free Raisin
>>
>> Four Flour
>>
>> Harvest
>>
>> Hi-Fiber
>>
>> Light White Rice
>>
>> Loaf (Fruit, Light Brown Rice, White Rice Flax (Light, Regular))
>>
>> Papas
>>
>> Raisin Loaf w/Eggs
>>
>> Regular Sliced Tapioca (& Light)
>>
>> Rice Starch
>>
>> Seattle Brown
>>
>> Tapioca Dinner Rolls
>>
>> Tapioca Loaf (Thin Sliced)
>>
>> White Rice
>>
>> Yeast Free (Brown Rice, Sweet, White Rice)
>
> **Enjoy Life** - Bread (Original Sandwich, Rye-less "Rye")

B

Food For Life -

Brown Rice

Raisin Pecan

Rice Almond

Rice Pecan

White Rice

Whole Grain (Bhutanese Red Rice, Brown Rice, China Black Rice, Millet)

Yeast Free (Fruit & Seed Medley, Multi Grain, White Rice, Whole Grain Brown Rice)

Gillian's Foods - All Varieties

Glutino - All Varieties

Good Juju Bakery - All Products

Jo-Sef - All Varieties

Kinnikinnick -

Brown Sandwich

Candida Yeast Free Multigrain Rice

Many Wonder Multigrain Rice

Robins Honey Brown Rice

Sunflower Flax Rice

Tapioca Rice (Cheese, Italian White Rice, Raisin, Regular, Yeast Free)

Tru Fibre Multigrain Rice

White Sandwich Bread

Namaste Foods - All Varieties

Nu-World Foods - All Varieties

Schar - Baguette, Bon Matin, Croissant, Duo, Ertha, Focaccia, Pain Campagnard, Pan Carre, Panini, Rustico, Sunna

Trader Joe's - Gluten-Free French Rolls, Ryeless "Rye"Bread

Whole Foods Market - Gluten-Free Bakehouse (Cinnamon Raisin, Cornbread, Cream Biscuits, Prairie, Sandwich, Sundried Tomato & Roasted Garlic)

B

Bread Mix... (includes Baking, etc)

Arrowhead Mills - All Purpose Baking Mix

Authentic Foods - Bread Mix Home Style, Cinnamon Bread Mix

Bob's Red Mill - Biscuit & Baking Mix, Bread Mix (Cinnamon Raisin, Hearty Whole Grain, Homemade Wonderful)

Breads From Anna - Bread Mix (Banana, Gluten-Free, Pumpkin)

Cause You're Special - Bread Mix Homestyle White, Traditional French

Chebe -

Bread Mix (All Purpose, Cinnamon Roll-Ups, Focaccia, Original)

Frozen Dough (Bread Sticks, Sandwich Bun, Tomato Basil Bread Sticks, Rolls

Garlic Onion Breadsticks Mix

Ener-G - Mix (Corn, Potato, Rice)

Fearn - Baking Mix (Brown Rice, Rice)

Food-Tek Fast & Fresh - Bread Mix (White)

Gillian's Foods - All Varieties

Gluten-Free Pantry - All Varieties

Glutino - All Varieties

Jo-Sef - All Varieties

Kinnikinnick -

Candida Yeast Free Rice

Cornbread & Muffin Mix

Kinni-Kwik Bread & Bun Mix

Kinni-Kwik Sunflower Flax Bread & Bun Mix

Tapioca Rice

White Rice

Miss Roben's - Bread Mix (Dinner, French, Homestyle, Potato, White Sandwich), Gingerbread Mix

B

Namaste Foods - All Varieties

Orgran - Bread Mix (Alternative Grain Wholemeal, Regular)

Pamela's Products - Amazing Bread Mix

Really Good Foods - Bread Mix (Banana, Cinnamon, French, Pumpkin, Rye-Style, White), Chocolate Cupcake Mix, Old Time Biscuit Mix

Sylvan Border Farm - Bread Mix (Classic Dark, Non-Dairy, White)

Whole Foods Market -

Almond Scone

Banana Bread

Gluten-Free Bakehouse (Cinnamon Raisin Bread, Cranberry Orange Scone, Cream Biscuits, Prairie Bread, Sandwich Bread, Sundried Tomato & Roasted Garlic Bread)

Breadcrumbs... see Coating

Breadsticks

Chebe - Garlic & Onion Breadsticks Mix

Glutino - Pizza Breadstick, Sesame Breadstick

Breakfast

Amy's - Tofu Rancheros Breakfast, Tofu Scramble Breakfast

Applegate Farms - Chicken & Apple Breakfast Sausage

Carnation - Instant Breakfast Powder All Varieties *(Except Chocolate Malt & No Sugar Chocolate Malt)*

Dietz & Watson - Breakfast Ham Filets

Gardenburger - Veggie Breakfast Sausage

Honeysuckle - White Turkey Breakfast Sausage

Jennie-O - Turkey Store Fresh Breakfast Sausage (Mild Links, Mild Patties, Maple Links)

Johnsonville - Breakfast Sausage (Heat & Serve Maple Syrup, Heat & Serve Original, Hickory Smoked Flavored, Original, Vermont Maple Syrup)

Price Chopper - Breakfast Sausage

Shelton's - Turkey Breakfast Sausage

Trader Joe's - Chicken Breakfast Sausage

Broccoli... *All Fresh Fruits & Vegetables Are Gluten-Free*

365 Every Day Value - Frozen Florets

365 Organic Every Day Value - Frozen Florets

Albertsons - Canned & Frozen

B&J - Normandy, Spears

Birds Eye - All Frozen Vegetables *(Except With Sauce)*

Freshlike - Frozen Plain Vegetables *(Except Pasta Combos & Seasoned Blends)*

Green Giant

Frozen Alfredo Vegetables (Broccoli Carrots & Peas)

Frozen Broccoli, Cauliflower, Carrots & Cheese Sauce

Frozen Broccoli (Chopped, Cuts, Cuts No Sauce)

Frozen Broccoli & (Carrots w/Garlic & Herbs Seasoned, Cheese Sauce, Three Cheese Sauce, White Cheddar Cheese Flavored Sauce, Zesty Cheese Sauce)

Frozen Broccoli Spears & (Butter Sauce, No Sauce, Zesty Cheese Sauce)

Frozen Select w/No Sauce Florets

Frozen Simply Steam Broccoli Spears

Frozen Simply Steam Seasoned Broccoli & Carrots

Hy-Vee - Chopped, Cuts, Florets

Meijer Brand - Frozen (Chopped, Cuts)

Midwest Country Fare - Frozen (Chopped, Cuts)

Nature's Promise - Organic Broccoli Mini Spears

Pictsweet - All Plain Vegetables (Frozen)

Stop & Shop Brand - Broccoli (Chopped, Cuts, Spears), Broccoli & Cauliflower

Success - Broccoli

Wegmans - Broccoli (Chopped, Cuts), Broccoli Cuts & Cauliflower Florets

Wild Oats - Organic Frozen Florets

B

Broth

365 Organic Every Day Value - Chicken (Low Sodium, Organic), Vegetable

Baxters - Chicken

Bowman & Landes - Chicken, Turkey

College Inn Broth - Garden Vegetable

El Peto - Broth Concentrate (Beef, Chicken)

Ener-G - George Washington Brown

Hains - Fat Free Chicken Broth, Vegetable Broth

Health Valley -

Fat Free (Beef Flavored, Chicken, Vegetable)

Fat Free No Salt Added Beef

No Salt Added Chicken

Hy-Vee - Chicken Broth

Imagine - Organic (Beef, Free Range Chicken (Low Sodium, Regular), No Chicken, Vegetable (Low Sodium, Regular))

Kitchen Basics - All Varieties

Lipton - Cup-A-Soup Chicken Broth

Manischewitz - Chicken Broth

Marsh Brand - Canned (Beef, Chicken)

Meijer Brand - Chicken (First Line)

Nature's Promise - All Natural Beef Broth, Organic Chicken Broth, Organic Vegetable Broth

Pacific Natural Foods -

Beef Broth

Natural Free Range Chicken

Organic (Free Range Chicken, Low Sodium Chicken, Mushroom, Vegetable Broth)

Safeway - Chicken Broth

Shaw's - Chicken Broth (Low Sodium, Regular)

Shelton's -

Chicken (Fat Free Low Sodium, Regular)

Organic (Chicken, Chicken Fat Free Low Sodium, Turkey, Turkey Fat Free Low Sodium)

Steitenbacher - Vegetable Broth & Seasoning

Stop & Shop Brand - Beef, Chicken, Ready To Serve Chicken Broth

Swanson - Beef, Chicken, Lower Sodium Beef, Natural Goodness Chicken, Vegetable

Thrifty Maid - Clear Chicken

Trader Joe's - Chicken (Low Sodium, Regular), Vegetable

Wild Oats Label - Chicken, Organic Vegetable

Brown Sugar... see Sugar

Brownies/Brownie Mix

Arrowhead Mills - Gluten-Free Brownie Mix

Betty Lou's - Chocolate Brownie

Bob's Red Mill - Gluten-Free Brownie Mix

Choices Rice Bakery - Brownies

Crave - Brownies (Dark Chocolate, Toasted Pecan)

Ener-G - Brownies

Foods By George - Brownies

Frankly Natural Bakers - Carob Almondine, Cherry Berry, Java Jive, Misty Mint, Wacky Walnut

Gillian's Foods - All Varieties

Gluten-Free Pantry - Chocolate Brownie Mix, Chocolate Truffle Brownie Mix

Hol Grain - Chocolate Brownie Mix

Namaste - Brownie Mix

Pamela's Products - Chocolate Brownie Mix

Really Good Foods - Aunt Tootsies' Brownie Mix

The Cravings Place - Ooey Gooey Chococolate Brownie Mix

Whole Foods Market - Gluten Free Bakehouse (Walnut Brownies)

Brussel Sprouts... *All **Fresh** Fruits & Vegetables Are **Gluten-Free**

B

   Birds Eye - All Frozen Vegetables *(Except With Sauce)*
   Green Giant - Frozen Baby Brussels Sprouts & Butter Sauce
   Hy-Vee - Frozen Vegetables (Brussel Sprouts)
   Meijer Brand - Brussel Sprouts
   Midwest Country Fare - Frozen Brussels Sprouts
   Pictsweet - All Plain Vegetables (Frozen)
   Stop & Shop Brand - Brussel Sprouts
Buckwheat Bread... see Bread
Buffalo Meat... *All Fresh Meat Is Gluten-Free (Non-Marinated, Unseasoned)*
   Trader Joe's - Flame Grilled Buffalo Patties
Buffalo Wing Sauce... see Wing Sauce
Buffalo Wings... see Wings
Buns
   Ener-G Foods -
      Hamburger Buns (Brown Rice, Seattle Brown, Tapioca, White Rice)
      Hot Dog Buns (Seattle Brown, Tapioca)
   Kinnikinnick -
      Hamburger Tapioca Rice Buns (Hamburger Buns, Hot Cross Buns, Multigrain Seed & Fiber Buns, Tray Buns
      Hot Dog Tapioca Rice Buns
   Quejos - Cheese Buns (Frozen)
Burgers... *All Fresh Ground Meat Is Gluten-Free (Non-Marinated, Unseasoned)*
   Applegate Farms - Organic (Beef, Turkey)
   Honeysuckle White - Fresh Ground Turkey Patties
   Jennie-O - Fresh Lean Turkey Patties, Frozen Turkey
   Johnsonville - Homestyle Patties, Sweet Italian Patties
   Nature's Promise - Veggie (Garlic & Cheese, Soy, Vegan Soy)
   Original Sunshine Burgers - All Varieties

B

    Perdue - Ground Burgers (Chicken, Turkey)
    Ruth's - Omega Burgers (All Flavors)
    Shaw's - Ground Beef Patties
    Shelton's - Turkey
    Sol Cuisine - Veggie (Frozen)
    Trader Joe's - Australian, Salmon, Southwest Style Turkey
    Wegmans - Beef (Fully Cooked)
    Wellshire Farms - All Natural (Beef Hamburgers, Turkey Burgers)

Butter

    365 Every Day Value - Sweet Cream Butter, Unsalted Butter
    365 Organic Every Day Value - Organic (Butter, Unsalted Butter)
    Cabot - Salted, Unsalted
    Earth Balance - All Varieties
    Horizon - Organic Butter
    Hy-Vee -
        Best Thing Since Butter
        Sweet Cream Butter (Quarters & Solid)
        Unsalted Sweet Cream Butter Quarters
        Whipped Sweet Cream Butter
    I Can't Believe It's Not Butter - All Varieties
    Land-O-Lakes - Salted, Unsalted, Whipped *(Light is NOT Gluten-Free)*
    Laura Lynn - Butter
    Lucerne - Butter
    Nature's Promise - Organic Butter
    Price Chopper - Salted, Unsalted
    Shaw's - Butter
    Smart Balance - 37%, 67%, Light Buttery Spread, Light w/Flax Oil

B
C

Stop & Shop Brand - Butter Quarters (Salted, Unsalted)
Soy Garden - All Natural Buttery Spread
Trader Joe's - All Butter
Wegmans -
  Club Pack
  Solid Butter
  Sweet Cream Butter Sticks (Salted, Unsalted)
  Whipped (Salted, Tub, Unsalted)
Wellesly Farms - Unsalted Butter Quarters

Buttermilk
  Friendship Dairy
  Lucerne - Fat Free, Low Fat, Regular
  Shamrock Farms
  Winn Dixie - Nonfat Buttermilk

C

Cabbage... *All **Fresh** Fruits & Vegetables Are **Gluten-Free***
Caesar Salad Dressing... see Salad Dressing
Cake/Cake Mix
  Arrowhead Mills - Vanilla Cake Mix
  Authentic Foods - Cake Mix (Chocolate, Lemon, Vanilla)
  Bob's Red Mill - Chocolate Cake Mix
  Cause You're Special - All Varieties
  Cherrybrook Kitchen - Chocolate Cake Mix
  Choices Rice Bakery - Carrot Cake, Pudding Cakes (Blueberry, Chocolate, Chocolate Marble, Lemon Poppy Seed)
  Crave - Mama Z's Chocolate Cake
  Dowd & Rogers - Cake Mix (Dark Vanilla, Dutch Chocolate, Golden Lemon)
  Dr. Schar -
    Fantasia

Magdalenas

Margherita

Meranetti

Mix (B, C)

Panettone

Panettone Al Cioccolato

El Peto - Cake Mix (Chocolate, Lemon)

Ener-G - Pound Cake

Food-Tek - Fast & Fresh Cake Mix (Dairy Free Chocolate, Chocolate, Double Chocolate, White, Yellow)

Foods By George - Cake (Crumb, Pound)

Glutino - Sans Gluten-Free Cake Mix (Chocolate, White)

Jo-Sef - All Varieties

Kinnikinnick - Angel Food Cake Mix, Chocolate, Sponge Cake Mix, White

Miss Roben's - Cake Mix (Chocolate, One-Step Angelfood, Pound, White, Yellow)

Namaste Foods - All Varieties

Orgran - Cake Mix (Chocolate, Vanilla)

Pamela's Products - Luscious Chocolate Cake Mix

Really Good Foods - Cake Mix (Brownie, Coffee Crumb, Devils Food, Golden, Lemon Poppy, Orange, Pineapple, Pound, Yellow)

Sylvan Border Farm - Cake Mix (Chocolate, Lemon)

The Cravings Place - Cinnamon Crumble Coffeecake Mix

Trader Joe's - Flourless Chocolate Cake

Whole Foods Market - Gluten-Free Bakehouse (Carrot Cake)

Candy/Candy Bars

Andes - Thins (Cherry Jubilee, Crème de Menthe, Mint Parfait, Toffee Crunch), Crème de Menthe Changemaker

B&J - Gourmet Mini Jelly Bean Jar, Sugar Free Assorted Hard Candy

C

Candy Tree - Licorice Vines (Black, Strawberry)

Cella's - Dark, Milk

Charleston Chew - Chocolate, Mini Vanilla, Strawberry, Vanilla

Charms -

Blow Pops (Junior, Regular, Super)

Charm's Sour Balls

Charm's Squares

Flat Pop (Junior, Regular)

Fluffy Stuff

Zip-A-Dee-Doo-Da Pop

Christopher's - Assorted Fruit Jellies

Cry Baby Sour

Dots - Crows, Hot Dots, Regular, Tropical Dots, Wild Berry Dots

Goelitz - Candy Corn

Haribo -

Alphabet Letters

Build-A-Burger

Centipedes

Clown Fish

Colossal Crocs

Fizzy Cola

Frogs

Fruit Salad

Gold-Bears

Grapefruit

Gummi Apples

Happy-Cola

Haribo Brixx

Mini Rainbow Frogs

Peaches

Pink Grapefruit
Raspberries
Rattle-Snakes
Sour Cherries
Strawberries (& Cream, Regular)
Super Cola
Techno Bears
Twin Cherries

Hershey's -
Almond Joy
Classic Caramels
Heath Bar
Jolly Ranchers
Kisses
Milk Chocolate Bar (Original, w/Almonds)
Mounds
Payday
Reese's Peanut Butter Cups
Tastetations

Hy-Vee -
Assorted Gum Balls
Butterscotch Buttons
Chocolate (Caramel Clusters, Covered Raisins,
    Peanut Clusters, Stars)
Cinnamon Imperials
Circus Peanuts
Double Dipped Chocolate Covered Peanuts
Dubble Bubble Gum
Dum Dum Suckers
Gum Drops
Gummi (Bears, Peach Rings, Sour Squiggles, Squiggles)

C

Lemon Drops
Milk Chocolate Peanut Butter Cups
Milk Kraft Caramels
Orange Slices
Smarties
Spice Drops
Starlight Kisses
Tootsie Flavored Rolls
Tootsie Pops
Wax Bottles

Jelly Belly - Jelly Beans

Junior Mints - Junior (Caramels, Mints), Inside Out

Let's Do...Organic -

Fruity Gummi Feet
Ginger Gummi Guys
Gummi Bears (Black Licorice, Classic, Jelly, Super Sour)

Maple Grove Farms of Vermont - Blended Maple, Pure Maple

Mars -

3 Musketeers
Dove Products (All Varieties) *(Except Chocolate Covered Almonds)*
M&M's (Plain, Peanut, *(Except Crispy)*)
Mars Almond Bar
Midnight Milky Way
Milky Way Eggs
Skittles
Snickers *(Except Crispy)*
Snickers Munch Bar
Starburst Fruit Chews & Jelly Beans

Necco -

Banana Split & Mint Julep Chews

candy/candy bars

C

Canada Mint & Wintergreen Lozenges
Haviland Peppermint & Wintergreen Patties
Haviland Thin Mints & Candy Stix
Mary Janes (Peanut Butter Kisses, Regular)
Necco Candy Eggs (Easter)
Necco Wafers
Squirel Nut Caramels & Squirrel Nut Zippers
Sweethearts Conversation Hearts *(Valentines Only)*
Talking Pumpkins (Halloween)
Ultramints

Nestle -

Baby Ruth
Bit-o-Honey
Bottlecaps
Butterfinger
Chunky
Gobstoppers
Laffy Taffy
Milk Chocolate Goobers
Mix Ups
Nerds
Nips
Oh Henry!
Pixy Stix
Raisinets
Runts
Shocktarts
Sno-caps
Spree
Sweetarts

C

Tangy Taffy
Tart-n-Tiny
Treasures *(Except Crispy)*
Turtles
Wonderball Fun Dip

Newman's Own Organics -
Butter Toffee Crunch
Milk Chocolate
Sweet Dark Chocolate
Sweet Dark Chocolate Espresso
Sweet Dark Chocolate Orange

Nik-L-Nip - Wax Bottles

Orgran - Molasses Licorice

Peeps - All Marshmallow Peeps

Razzles

Shufra - Halvah

Spangler - Candy Canes

St. Claire's Organics - All Varieties

Steitenbacher -
Cherry Dolphins
Fruity Sunhats (Black Currant, Cherry, Passion fruit, Strawberry)
Roses For You
Smooch Lions
Strawberry Alligators
Vampires Lunch

Stop & Shop Brand -
Assorted (Fruit Filled Candy, Star Drops, Starlights)
Blue Gummi Sharks
Butter Toffee
Butterscotch Disks

Canada Wintergreen
Candy Corn
Candy Necklaces
Cinnamon Starlights
Fish
Gum Balls
Gum Drops
Gummi Bears
Jelly Beans
Kiddie Mix
Lemon Drops
Neon Sour Crawlers
Orange Slices
Pastel Mints
Peach Rings
Pina Colada Coated Cashews
Red Jug Coins-Coins
Root Beer Barrels
Royal Mix
Silver Mints
Smarties
Soft Peppermints
Sour Balls
Sour Gummi Worms
Spearmint Leaves
Spearmint Starlights
Spice Drops
Starlight Mints
Strawberry Buds
Watermelon Hard Candy

Sugar Babies - Chocolate Sugar Babies.

C

Sugar Daddy, Sugar Mama
The Ginger People - Ginger Chews
Timothy's Confections - Sugar Free Chocolate (Milk & Dark)
Tongue Splashes
Tootsie Roll -

Candy Cane Pops

Caramel Apple Pops

Forties Tootsie Pops

Fruit Smoothie Pops

Tootsie (Fruit Rolls, Miniature Pops, Miniature Pops Sugar Free)

Tootsie Pops Tropical Stormz

Tootsie Roll

Tootsie Roll Mini Chews

Trader Joe's -

Almond Clusters

Black Licorice Scottie Dogs

Candy Coated Peanuts

Cocoa Almonds

English Toffee

Figments

Fruit Leathers

Milk Chocolate (Clouds, Covered Banana Chips, Covered Peanuts, Covered Raisins, Cranberries, Peanut Butter Cups, Pistachios)

Milk & Dark Chocolate Covered (Almonds, Cashews)

Mini Fruit Slices

Mini Milk Chocolate Peanut Butter Cups

Peanut Butter Cups

Pecans Praline

Soft Peanut Toffee

UFO's Mint Chocolate Wafers

Yogurt Covered Raisins

Tropical Source - All Chocolate Bars

Canned Chicken... see also Chicken

B&J - Chunk Chicken Breast Meat

Meijer Brand - Chicken Chunk White

Swanson - Premium Chunk White Chicken

Sweet Sue - Premium Chicken Breast

Canned Ham... see also Ham

Black Label - Canned Hams

Hormel - Chunk Meats (Ham)

SPAM - Classic, Less Sodium, Lite

Canned Salmon... see Fish

Canned Tuna... see Tuna

Canned Turkey... see also Turkey

Hormel - Chunk Meats (Turkey)

SPAM - Smoked & Oven Roasted Turkey

Canola Oil... see Oil

Capers

B&J - Moroccan Nonpariel Capers

Safeway Select - Capers

Caramel... see Candy

Carrots... *All Fresh Fruits & Vegetables Are **Gluten-Free***

365 Every Day Value - Sliced Carrots

365 Organic Every Day Value - Organic Peas & Carrots

Albertsons - Canned, Frozen

Birds Eye - All Frozen Vegetables *(Except With Sauce)*

Del Monte - All Varieties

Freshlike - Frozen Plain Vegetables *(Except Pasta Combos and Seasoned Blends)*

Grand Selections - Frozen Petite Whole Carrots

Haggen - Carrots Sliced

C

    Hy-Vee -
      California Carrots
      Classic Cut & Peeled Baby Carrots
      Frozen Crinkle Cut Carrots
      Shredded Sliced Carrots
    Laura Lynn - Sliced Carrots, Whole Baby Carrots
    Marsh Brand - Sliced Carrots
    Meijer Brand - Frozen Carrots (Crinkle Cut, Whole Baby)
    Pictsweet - All Plain Vegetables (Frozen)
    S&W - All Varieties
    Safeway - Carrots (Baby Peeled)
    Spartan Brand - Frozen Peas & Carrots
    Stop & Shop Brand - Carrots
    Wegmans - Slice Carrots (No Salt Added, Regular), Whole Style
    Wild Oats Label - Organic (Baby Carrots, Table Carrots)

Cashews... see Nuts

Cauliflower... *All **Fresh** Fruits & Vegetables Are **Gluten-Free***
    Albertsons - Canned & Frozen
    Birds Eye - All Frozen Vegetables *(Except With Sauce)*
    Freshlike - Frozen Plain Vegetables *(Except Pasta Combos & Seasoned Blends)*
    Green Giant - Cauliflower & (Cheese Sauce, Three Cheese Sauce)
    Hy-Vee - Cauliflower
    Meijer Brand - Frozen Cauliflower Florets
    Midwest Country Fare - Frozen Cauliflower
    Pictsweet - All Plain Vegetables (Frozen)

Celery... *All **Fresh** Fruits & Vegetables Are **Gluten-Free***

Celery Salt... see Seasoning

Cereal
    Amaranth - Cereal Snap, Cinnamon Snaps Cereal, Puffed Cereal

C

Alti Plano Gold - Chai Almond, Oaxacan Chocolate, Spiced Apple Raisin, Variety

Arrowhead Mills - Corn Grits White and Yellow, Maple Buckwheat Flakes, Rice and Shine

Baker On Main - Apple Raisin Walnut, Extreme Fruit & Nut, Nutty Maple Cranberry

Barbara's Bakery - Brown Rice Crisps, Corn Flakes, Honey Rice Puffins

Bob's Red Mill - Creamy Rice Hot, Mighty Tasty Hot, Organic Creamy Buckwheat

Eat Natural - Breakfast

Ener-G - Crumbles, Rice Bran

Enjoy Life - Cinnamon Crunch, Cranapple Crunch, Granola, Very Berry Crunch

Erewhon -

Aztec (Crunchy Corn & Amaranth Cereal)

Corn Flakes

Crispy Brown Rice (Regular, w/Mixed Berries)

Rice Twice

Food Club - Instant Grits

General Mills - Dora The Explorer, Neopets Island Berry Crunch

Gerber -

Boxed Cereal Rice w/(Applesauce, Bananas, Mixed Fruit)

Rice Single Grain Cereal

Glutino - All Varieties

Healthy Valley - Blue Corn Flakes, Corn Crunch-ems, Rice Crunch-ems

Heartland's Finest - Flavored Ceros Cereal (Cinnamon, Original)

Kashi - Cranberry Sunshine

C

Kinnikinnick - KinniKrisp Rice Cereal

Lundberg - Hot 'n Creamy Purely Rice

Malt-O-Meal - Corn Burst, Crispy Rice, Fruity Dyno-Bites, Puffed Rice

Markal - Buckwheat Flakes, Millet Flakes, Quinoa Flakes

Meijer Brand - Grits (Buttered Flavored Intant, Quick)

Nabisco - Cream Of Rice Hot Cereal

Nature's Path Envirokidz -

Corn Flakes (Honey'd, Regular)

Crispy Rice

Eco Pac (Cornflakes, Mesa Sunrise)

Mesa Sunrise

Organic (Amazon Forested Flakes, Gorilla Munch, Koala Crisps, Puff Cereal)

Panda Puffs

New Morning - Cocoa Crispy Rice

Nu World Foods -

Amaranth Berry

Amaranth O's (Original, Peach, Strawberry)

Cereal Snaps (Cinnamon, Cocoa, Original)

Delicious Hot Cereal

Puffed Amaranth Cereal

Orgran - Muesli w/Fruit & Almonds, Rice Porridge w/Apricots

Pacific Grain - Nutty Rice Cereal

Perky's - Apple Cinnamon O's, Frosted O's, Nutty Flax, Nutty Rice, Original O's

Pocono - Cream of Buckwheat

Safeway - Cocoa Nuggets, Fruity Nuggets, Golden Corn Nuggets, Puffed Corn

Shaw's - Puffed Rice Cereal

Seitenbacher - Maize Flakes, Musli, Soy Flakes

C

Wegmans - Fruity Rice Crisps, Organic Strawberry Corn Flakes
Winn Dixie - Corn Puffs, Fruity Nuggets Cereal

Chamomile Tea... see Tea

Champagne... *All* Champagne made in *USA* is *Gluten-Free*[2]

Cheddar Cheese... see Cheese

Cheese

    365 Every Day Value -

        Colby Jack

        Medium Cheddar

        Mild Cheddar (Bar, Shredded)

        Monterey Jack (Bar, Shredded)

        Mozzarella (Bar, Shreds)

        Sharp Cheddar

        Swiss Cheese

        Two Cheese Shredded Blend

    Albertsons - Ricotta Cheese

    Alpine Lace -

        American Yellow

        Brie 60%

        Danish Havarti Dill

        Havarti Lite

        Mozzarella

        Provolone

        Reduced Sodium Muenster

        Reduced Fat (Hot Pepper, Medium Cheddar, Muenster, Provolone, Swiss)

    Andrew & Everett -

        American

        Colby Jack

        Harvarti

        Mild Cheddar

C

    Mozzarella

    Muenster

    Pepper Jack

    Provolone

    Swiss

Applegate Farms - All Varieties *(Except Muenster Kase Cheese)*

Athenos - All Varieties

B&J - 100% Parmesan Cheese

Belgioso - Provolone Ball

Boar's Head -

    American (White, Yellow)

    Baby Swiss

    Blue Cheese

    Cheddar (White, Yellow)

    Edam

    Gold Import Swiss

    Gold Label Swiss

    Gouda

    Havarti (Dill, w/Jalapeño)

    Lacy Swiss

    Monterey Jack (Regular, w/Jalapeños)

    Mozzarella

    No Salt Swiss

    Provolone

    Smoked Swiss Gruyere

    Vermont (Cheddar, White, Yellow)

Borden - All Varieties

Boursin - Garlic & Fine Herbs, Light, Pepper, Shallot & Chives

Cabot - All Varieties *(Except Horseradish Cheddar, Harpoon IPA Beer)*

Cracker Barrel - Cheddar

Crowley - Mozzarella Cheese (Block)

Dofino - Danish Havarti

Finlandia - All Varieties

Food Club - Ricotta Cheese (Part Skim, Whole Milk)

Frigo -

  Feta

  Grated Parmesan

  Grated Romano

  Mozzarella Chunks

  Provolone Slices

  Ricotta (All Types)

  Shredded (Mozzarella, Pizza, Provolone, Romano, Taco)

  String

  Wedges (Parmesan, Romano)

Galaxy Nutritional Foods - All Varieties

H&H - Domestic Swiss

Heluva Good - All Varieties

Hoffman's - American Cheese, American Yellow, Pepper Cheese, Super Sharp

Horizon - Organic Hard Cheese All Varieties *(Except American Singles)*

Hy-Vee -

  American (Cheese Food, Deluxe Sliced Singles, Fat Free Singles, Party Cheese, Singles, Singles 2% Milk)

  Cheddar (Extra Sharp, Fancy Shredded Jack, Fancy Shredded Mild 2%, Finely Shredded Mild, Medium, Medium Longhorn, Mild, Mild Cubes, Mild Hunk, Mild Shredded, Mild Slices, Sharp, Sharp Hunk, Sharp Longhorn, Sharp Party, Sharp Shredded)

  Colby (Half Moon Jack Longhorn, Half Moon Longhorn, Fancy Shredded Jack, Finely Shredded Jack, Hunk, Jack,

C

    Jack Cubes, Jack Hunk, Jack Slices, Longhorn, Shredded Cheese Jack)

Hot Pepper

Monterey Jack (Hunk)

Mozzarella (Hunk, Fancy Shredded Mozzarella, Fancy Shredded Mozzarella 2% Milk, Shredded Cheese, Sliced Low-Moisture Part-Skim)

Muenster (Slices)

Parmesan (Grated, Shredded)

Pepper Jack Cheese (Cubes, Hunk, Singles, Slices)

Provolone Cheese (Slices)

Ricotta Cheese (Low Fat, Part Skim)

Shredded Blends (Fancy 4 Italian Cheese, Mexican Blend, Pizza, Taco)

Swiss (Fat Free Slices, Singles, Slices)

Jarlsberg - Lite Cheese, Norwegian

Kraft -

100% Grated Parmesan *(Except Parmesan Plus)*

Blue

Brick

Cheddar

Colby

Feta

Kraft Singles Processed Slices

Monterey Jack

Mozzarella

Ricotta

Romano

Swiss

Velveeta (All)

Kronenost Farmers - Cheese

Land-O-Lakes -

American/Swiss

Cheddarella

Colby (Longhorn, Regular)

Onion American

Monterey Jack

Mozzarella

Muenster

White American

Laughing Cow - All Varieties

Laura Lynn - Parmesan, Parmesan & Romano, Cheese Chunks, Ricotta

Lifetime - Cheese Bars All Varieties (Fat Free, Lactose Free, Low Fat, Rice Cheese)

Lifeway - All Products

Lisanatti -

Almond Cheese (Cheddar, Jalapeño Jack, Mozzarella)

Premium Soy-Sation (Mozzarella, Pepper Jack)

Lorraine - Reduced Fat Swiss

Lucerne - Cheese (All Varieties), String Cheese

Marsh Brand -

American Slices

Cheese Bar (Cheddar Mozzarella)

Grated Parmesan

Shredded (Mozzarella, Cheddar)

Marsh Brand - String Cheese

Meijer Brand -

Aerosol Cheese (American, Cheddar, Sharp Cheddar)

American Processed (Slices)

Cheddar (Bar Mild, Bar Sharp, Bar X-Sharp, Fancy Mild Shredded, Fancy Sharp Shredded, Midget Horn,

C

Mild Chunk, Sharp Chunk, Sharp Shredded,
Shred Zip Pouch, Shredded, Sliced Longhorn
Half Moon)

Cheddar Marble (C&W Cheddar)

Cheddar/Monterey Jack (Bar, Fancy Shred Zip Pouch)

Cheese Food Individually Wrapped (2%, Fat Free Sharp,
Sliced Sharp, Swiss)

Cheezy Does It (Jalapeño, Spread Loaf)

Colby Jack (Bar, Chunk, Fancy Shred, Longhorn
Half Moon Large Cut, Midget Horn, Sliced Shingle)

Colby Longhorn (Full Moon, Half Moon, Sliced)

Fancy Italian Blend (Shred)

Hot Pepper Jack (Chunk)

Mexican Blend (Fancy Shredded, Shredded)

Monterey Jack (Chunk)

Mozzarella (Fancy Shredded, Shredded, Slice Shingle)

Mozzarella Low Moisture Part Skim (Bar, Shred Zip Pouch,
Square, String Cheese)

Muenster (Slice Single)

Parmesan & Romano (Grated)

Parmesan (1/3 Less Fat, Grated)

Pepperjack (Sliced Stack Pack)

Pizza Blend (Mozzarella/ Cheddar) Shredded

Provolone (Stacked Slice)

Ricotta (Part Skim, Whole Milk)

String Cheese

Swiss (Chunk, Slice Single, Sliced Sandwich/Cut)

Midwest Country Fare -

American Sandwich Slices

Shredded Cheese (Cheddar, Mozzarella)

Mini Babybel - All Varieties

C

Penn Maid - Mozzarella Cheese Block *(Except Shredded Mozzarella)*

Price Chopper -

All Parmesan *(Except Fat Free)*

Cheese Singles

Shredded Mozzarella

Rice Shreds (Galaxy Nutritional Foods) - Rice (Shreds, Slices, Topping)

Safeway - Aerosol (American, Cheddar, Sharp), Cheese Spread, Grated Parmesan Cheese

Sargento -

Chef Style Shredded Cheese (Double Cheddar, Mild Cheddar, Sharp Cheddar)

Deli Style Sliced Cheese (American Burger Cheese, Colby, Medium Cheddar, Monterey Jack, Mozzarella, Muenster, Reduced Fat Swiss, Swiss)

Fancy Shredded (Colby Jack, Monterey Jack, Sharp Cheddar, Swiss)

Grated (Parmesan, Parmesan & Romano)

Reduced Fat Shredded (Four Cheese Italian, Four Cheese Mexican)

Shaw's - All Dairy Cheese, American (Fat Free, Regular), Grated Parmesan, Mozzarella, Provolone

Singleton's - White Stilton w/Apricots

Smart Balance - Cheese Shreds, Creamy Cheddar Flavor Slices

Sorrento - Provolone, Ricotta Cheese (Part Skim, Whole Milk)

Soymage - Vegan Cheese Chunks, Vegan Cheese Singles, Vegan Parmesan

Spartan Brand -

Cheddar Chunk Cheese (Medium, Mild, Sharp, X-sharp)

Colby Cheese (Chunk, Shredded, Sliced Singles)

Colby Jack Cheese (Chunk, Shredded, Sliced Singles)

C

Fancy Shredded Cheese (Colby Jack, Italian Blend, Mexican Blend, Mild Cheddar, Mozzarella, Parmesan, Pizza Blend, Sharp Cheddar, Taco)

Mild Cheddar Cheese (Slices)

Monterey Jack Cheese (Chunk, Shredded)

Mozzarella Cheese (Chunk, Round, Shredded, Sliced Singles)

NY Sharp Cheddar Cheese (Chunk)

Parmesan (Grated, Grated Tray Pack)

Parmesan Romano Grated (Shaker)

Pepper Jack Cheese (Chunk, Slices)

Processed American

Provolone Cheese (Sliced Singles)

Shredded Cheddar Cheese (Mild, Sharp)

String Cheese

Swiss Cheese (Chunk, Sliced Single)

Stop & Shop Brand -

Cheddar Cheese (Horseradish, Port Wine, Vermont White)

Colby (Half Moon Single Slices)

Colby & Monterey Blend (All Varieties)

Fat Free White Cheese Single

Feta (All Varieties)

Havarti (All Varieties)

Mexican Cheese Blend

Mild Cheddar (All Varieties)

Mild Longhorn Style Cheddar (All Varieties)

Monterey Jack (All Varieties)

Mozzarella (All Varieties)

Muenster (All Varieties)

NY Extra Sharp Cheddar (All Varieties)

NY Sharp Cheddar (All Varieties)

Parmesan Cheese (All Varieties)
Provolone (All Varieties)
Ricotta (All Varieties)
Sharp Cheddar (All Varieties)
String Cheese
Swiss Cheese (All Varieties)
Taco Cheese Blend
Vermont Sharp Cheddar (All Varieties)
Wisconsin Sharp (All Varieties)

Silver Goat - Chevre

Trader Joe's -
All (Blocks, Shredded, Wedges)
Parmesan & Romano Cheese Blend
Reduced Fat Cheese Crunchies
Soy Cheese Slices

Ukrop's - Provolone Loaf, Swiss Loaf, White American, Yellow American

Veggie (Galaxy Nutritional Foods) - All Veggie (Shreds, Slices, Super Stix, Topping)

Wegmans -
Colby Jack Shredded
Colby Sliced
Extra Sharp Cheddar (White, Yellow)
Fancy Shredded (Mexican, Mild Cheddar, Taco Cheese)
Gruyere
Havarti
Longhorn Style Colby
Mediterranean Cheddar
Mild Cheddar (Shredded, White, White Shredded, Yellow)
Monterey Jack
Mozzarella Cheese Shredded (Low Moisture-Part Skim, Whole Milk)

C

Muenster

Parmesan Cheese (Finely Shredded, Grated, Grated w/Romano)

Pepper Jack

Provolone (Balls, Wedge)

Romano (Grated, Wedge)

Sharp Cheddar (Shredded, Vermont, White, Yellow)

Swiss (Chunk, Sliced)

Wellesly Farms - Cheddar Cheese (Premium White, White Sharp, White Extra Sharp, Yellow Sharp, Yellow Extra Sharp)

Wensleydale - Cheese

Whole Kids Organic - String Cheese

Winn Dixie -

Cheddar (Extra Sharp, Fancy Shredded, Medium, Mild, Sharp)

Monterey Jack

Mozzarella

Cheese Fondue

Safeway Select - Cheese Fondue

Cheese Puffs... see Snacks

Cheese Spread... see Cheese and/or Spread

Cherries... *All **Fresh** Fruits & Vegetables Are **Gluten-Free***

B&J - Colossal Maraschino Cherries w/Stems

Cella's - Chocolate Covered Cherries (Dark, Milk)

Haribo's - Cherries (Sour, Twin)

Hy-Vee -

Cherry Berry Blend

Dried Cherries

Green Maraschino Cherries

Maraschino (Green, Red)

Red Maraschino Cherries (Regular, w/Stems)

Lucky Leaf - Red Tart Pitted Cherries
Meijer Brand -
Dark Sweet
Dark Sweet Individually Quick Frozen
Maraschino Cherry (Red, Red w/ Stems)
Tart
Tart Pitted Unsweetened
Midwest Country Fare - Maraschino Cherries
Musselman's - Red Tart Pitted Cherries
Safeway - Maraschino Cherries, Red Tart Pitted
Shaw's - Maraschino Cherries
Spartan Brand - Cherries Dark Sweet, Maraschino Cherries
(Green, Red, Red w/Stems, Salad)
Stop & Shop Brand - Dark Sweet Cherries
Trader Joe's - Dark Chocolate Covered Cherries
Wegmans - Dark Sweet Cherries, Maraschino (Jumbo,
w/Stems, w/out Stems)

Chestnuts
Hy-Vee - Shredded Sliced (Water Chestnuts)

Chewing Gum
Adam's - Black Jack Gum
Beeman's - Gum
Charms - Blow Pops (Junior, Regular, Super)
Dentyne Ice - All Varieties
Dubble Bubble
El Bubble Cigar
Hubba Bubba - Bubble Gum
Hy-Vee - Assorted Gum Balls, Dubble Bubble Gum
Stride - All Varieties
Trident - All Varieties
Wegmans - Sugar Free Peppermint Gum

C

Wrigley's -
- Big Red
- Doublemint
- Eclipse
- Extra
- Freedent
- Juicy Fruit
- Orbit
- Orbit White
- Spearmint
- Winterfresh

Chick Peas (Garbanzo Beans)... see Beans

Chicken... *All Fresh Chicken Is Gluten-Free (Non-Marinated, Unseasoned)*

Always Tender - Flavored Fresh Chicken (Italian, Lemon-Pepper, Roast)

Applegate Farms - Organic (Roasted Chicken Breast, Smoked Chicken Breast)

B&J - Canned Chunk Chicken Breast Meat

Boar's Head - Hickory Smoked Chicken Breast Deli Meat

Butcher's Cut - Boneless Skinless Chicken Breast

Carl Buddig - Original Deli Pouch (Chicken), Oven Roasted Cured Chicken Breast Deli Cuts

Dietz & Watson - Chicken Breast (BBQ, Buffalo, Oven Roasted)

Dinty Moore - Microwave Meal (Rice w/Chicken)

Eagle Valley - Oven Roasted Teriyaki Chicken Breast

Homestyle Meals - Bulk Chicken BBQ Cooked, Shredded Chicken In BBQ Sauce

Honeysuckle - Oil Browned Chicken Breast, White Buffalo Style Chicken Breast Deli Meat

Hy-Vee - 98% Fat Free Breast Of Chicken, Thin Sliced Chicken

C

Ian's - Chicken Nuggets

Jennie-O - Deli Chicken Breast (Buffalo Style, Oven Roasted, Mesquite Smoked)

Land-O-Lakes -

Premium Deli Style Sliced Meats (Oven Roasted Chicken Breast)

Shaved Deli Meat (Chicken)

Thin Sliced Meat (Chicken, Honey Chicken)

Laura Lynn - Boneless Skinless Chicken Breast

Manor House - All Varieties In 4lb Resealable Bags Frozen

Meijer Brand - Canned Chicken Chunk White

Perdue -

Buffalo Chicken Wings (Hot n Spicy)

Carving Chicken Breast (Oven Roasted)

Ground Chicken (Burgers, Regular)

Individually Frozen Chicken (Breasts, Tenderloins, Wings)

Oil Fried Sliced Chicken Breast

Rotisserie (Barbeque Chicken, Lemon Pepper Chicken, Oven Stuffer Roaster (Oven Roasted Chicken, Tuscany Herb Roasted Chicken), Toasted Garlic Chicken

Short Cuts (Carved Chicken (Grilled Italian, Grilled Lemon Pepper, Grilled Southwestern, Honey Roasted, Original Roasted)

S'Better Farms - Chicken (Ballontine, Fingers, Siciliano, Szechwan), Party Wings

Shaw's - Chicken Hot Dogs, Sweet Chicken Sausage

Shelton's - Free Range (Chicken Thighs, Whole Chicken)

Spartan Brand - Canned Meat Chicken Breast Chunk

Stop & Shop Brand -

Premium Chunk Chicken Breast In Water

Simply Enjoy (Butter Chicken, Pad Thai w/Chicken)

Swanson - Premium Chunk White Chicken (Canned)

C

Sweet Sue - Premium Chicken Breast (Canned)
Taj Ethnic Gourmet - Chicken Tandoori w/Spinach
Tops - Skinless/Boneless Chicken Breasts
Trader Joe's -
  BBQ Shredded Chicken
  Biryani
  Chicken Chile Verde
  Chicken Enchiladas In Salsa Verde
  Chicken Taquitos
  Chicken Wings
  Fully Cooked & Seasoned Roasted
  Grilled Chicken Breast (Balsamic & Rosemary, Lemon
    Pepper)
  Grilled Chicken Strips
  Just Grilled Chicken Strips
  Pollo En Chipotle Salsa
  Thai Style Lemongrass Chicken & Seasoned Rice
Tyson Simply Perfect
  100% All Natural Fresh Chicken
  Boneless
    Skinless Chicken Breasts
    Thin & Fancy Chicken Breasts
    Chicken Breast Tenders
    Skinless Split Chicken Breasts
Wellesly Farms - Grilled Chicken Breast Fillets
Wellshire Farms - Chicken Nuggets, Sliced Oven Roasted
  Chicken Breast
Wellshire Kids - Dino Shaped Chicken Bities (Frozen,
  Refrigerated)
Whole Kitchen - Butter Chicken Entrée
Winn Dixie - Fresh Chicken (All Varieties)

Chicken Broth... see Broth
Chicken Noodle Soup... see Soup
Chicken Wings... see Wings
Chiles
>**Old El Paso** - Green Chiles (Chopped, Whole)

Chili
>**Amy's** - Organic Chili (Black Bean, Medium, Medium Light In Sodium, Medium w/Vegetables, Spicy, Spicy Light In Sodium)
>
>**Dr. McDougall's** - Crowd Pleasing Chili Mix
>
>**Fantastic Foods** - Cha Cha
>
>**Health Valley** -
>>Fat Free (Burrito Flavored, Mild 3 Bean, Mild Black Bean, Spicy Black Bean)
>>
>>Mild Vegetarian, No Salt Added (Mild Vegetarian, Spicy Vegetarian)
>>
>>Spicy Vegetarian
>>
>>Vegetable Lentil
>
>**Healthy Advantage** - Vegetarian
>
>**Hormel** - Chili w/Beans (Chunky, Hot, Regular)
>
>**Meijer Brand** - Chili (No Beans Regular, w/Beans Regular)
>
>**Mimi's Gourmet** - Black Bean & Corn, Spicy White Bean & Jalapeno, Three Bean w/Rice
>
>**Price Chopper** - Chili
>
>**Shelton's** - Free Range (Mild Chicken, Mild Turkey, Spicy Chicken, Spicy Turkey)
>
>**Spartan Brand** - Chili (w/Beans, w/out Beans)
>
>**Stagg** -
>>Chunkero Chili
>>
>>Classic Chili
>>
>>Dynamite Hot Chili
>>
>>Ranch House Chicken Chili

C

       Rio Blanco Chicken Chili
       Silverado Beef Chili
       Steak House Chili
       Turkey Ranchero Chili
       Vegetable Garden Chili
    Trader Joe's -
       3 Bean Beef & Chili
       Beef Chili w/Beans
       Chicken Chili w/Beans
       Vegetarian 3 Bean Chili
       Vegetarian Chili
       Veracruz (Turkey Chili w/Beans, Vegetable & Chili w/Beans)
    Wegmans - Spicy Red Lentil Chili

Chili Powder

    365 Every Day Value - Valle del Sol Chile Powder
    Albertsons
    Bali - Chili & Garlic Seasoning
    Chugwater Chili
    Dr. McDougall's - Crowd Pleasing Chili Mix
    Durkee
    El Paso - Chili Spices & Fixin's
    Hy-Vee
    Marcum Spices
    McCormick
    Meijer Brand
    Midwest Country Fare
    Shaw's
    Spartan Brand
    Spice Islands
    Tone's

Chili Sauce

    A Taste of Thai - Sweet Red

    Food Club

    Frank's - RedHot (Chile 'N Lime)

    Hy-Vee

    Las Palmas - Red

    Laura Lynn

    Lee Kum Kee - Sriracha Chili

    Meijer Brand - Hot Dog Chili

    Shaw's

    Spartan Brand

    Stop & Shop Brand

    Thai Kitchen - Roasted Red, Spicy Thai, Sweet Red

    Wegmans

Chips

    365 Every Day Value -

        Homestyle Potato (Barbecue, Garlic Ranch, Lightly Salted, Salt & Vinegar)

        Restaurant Style Tortilla (No Salt, Regular, Salted)

        Tortilla Blue Salted

        Tortilla White (No Salt, Regular, Salted)

        Veggie

    Baked! Doritos - Cooler Ranch

    Baked! Lay's - Cheddar & Sour Cream, Original, Sour Cream & Onion

    Baked! Ruffles - Cheddar & Sour Cream Flavored, Original

    Baked! Tostitos - Bite Size Tortilla Chips

    Baken-Ets -

        Pork Cracklins (Fried, Hot 'N Spicy)

        Pork Skins (Chile Limon Fried, Fried, Hot 'N Spicy, Salt & Vinegar, Sweet & Tangy BBQ)

C

Barbara's Bakery - Potato (No Salt, Regular, Ripple Yogurt & Green Onion)

Boulder Potato Company - Potato

Cape Cod - All Potato Chips *(Except Barbeque)*

Crackin' Good - Corn, Tortilla

Doritos -

Black Pepper Jack Cheese

Cool Ranch

Cooler Ranch

Fiery Habanero

Four Cheese

Guacamole!

Natural Cool Ranch

Natural White Nacho

Ranchero

Salsa Verde

Spicier Nacho

Taco

Toasted Corn

WOW Nacho Cheesier

Eden - Brown Rice

Ener-G - Cheecha Krackles

Food Club -

Corn

Potato

Ripple (Cheddar, Classic, Sour Cream)

Tortilla

Wavy Original

Fritos -

King Size Corn

Original Corn

Sabrositas Flavored Corn (Lime 'N Chile)

Scoops Corn

Fritos Flavor Twists - Cheddar Ranch Flavored Corn, Honey
BBQ Flavored Corn

Full Circle -

Nacho Tortilla

Potato (Kettle Cooked, Lightly Salted Plain, Ripple)

White Corn Tortilla

Glenny's - Sea Salt, Sour Cream & Onion

Good Health - Sweet Olive Oil Potato

Green Mountain Gringo - Tortilla Strips

Hardbite - Potato

Health Market Organic - Tortilla Corn (Blue, White, Yellow)

Herr's -

Potato Chips

Cheddar & Sour Cream

Crisp N' Tasty

Honey BBQ

Jalapeno Kettle

Jalapeno Ripple

Ketchup

Lightly Salted

Mesquite BBQ Kettle

No Salt

Old Bay

Old Fashioned

Original Kettle

Red Hot

Ripple

Russet Kettle

Salt & Pepper

C

Salt & Vinegar
Tortilla/Corn Chips (All Varieties)
J. Higgs - Regular Potato
Laura Lynn -
Mini Corn Tortilla
Nacho Tortilla
Ranch Tortilla
Regular Corn
Regular Potato
Ripple Potato
Sour Cream & Onion Potato
Wavy Potato
White Corn Tortilla
Lay's -
Potato Chips
Cheddar & Sour Cream
Chile Limon
Classic
Deli Style Original
Dill Pickle
Extra Crunchy
Kettle Cooked (Jalapeno, Mequite BBQ, Regular)
Light Original
Lightly Salted
Limon Tangy Lime
Maui Style Regular
Natural (Country BBQ Thick Cut, Sea Salt Thick Cut)
Salt & Vinegar
Sensations Kettle Cooked (Four Cheese Gourmet,
  Lime & Black Pepper, Sweet Chili & Sour Cream)
Sour Cream & Onion

Wavy (Au Gratin, Hickory BBQ, Regular)
Lay's Stax -
  Cheddar
  Hidden Valley Ranch
  Jalapeno Cheddar
  KC Masterpiece BBQ
  Monterey Pepper Jack
  Original
  Pizza
  Salt & Vinegar
  Sour Cream & Onion
Lundberg -
  Rice Chips
    Fiesta Lime
    Honey Dijon
    Pico de Gallo
    Santa Fe Barbecue
    Sea Salt
    Sesame & Seaweed
    Wasabi
Manischewitz - Potato Chips (All Varieties)
Maui Style - Salt & Vinegar Flavored Potato Chips
Miss Vickie's - Potato Chips
  Jalapeno Flavored
  Lime & Black Pepper
  Mesquite BBQ Flavored
  Original
Munchos - Regular Potato Crisps
O'Keely's - Cheddar & Bacon Potato Skins Flavored
  Potato Crisps
Old Dutch -

C

    All Dressed
    BBQ
    Cheddar & Sour Cream
    Dill Pickle
    Ketchup
    Plain Tortilla Chips
    Salt & Vinegar
    Sour Cream & Onion

Pinnacle - Gold Herb Olive Oil

Price Chopper - Potato Chips

Robert's American Gourmet - Antique Potato Chips

Ruffles -

    Potato Chips
        Cheddar & Sour Cream
        KC Masterpiece BBQ
        Light Cheddar & Sour Cream
        Light Original
        Mesquite BBQ
        Natural Reduced Fat
        Reduced Fat
        Regular
        Regular Sea Salted
        Sour Cream & Onion
        The Works! Flavor

Sabritas -

    Potato (Adobadas Tomato & Chile Flavored)
    Tortilla (Botaneros Salsa Roja, Botaneros Salsa Verde, White Corn Restaurant Style, Yellow Corn)

Safeway - Dipper, Ripple

Seasons - Potato (Lite Salt, Sour Cream Onion)

Snyder's of Hanover - Potato Chips (Original, Ripple)

Spartan Brand -
Potato (Original, Ripple, Sour Cream & Onion)

Tortilla (Authentic, Round Bite Size, White Round)

Stop & Shop Brand -
Potato (Kettle Cooked, Plain, Rippled, Salt & Vinegar, Sour Cream & Onion, Wavy Cut)

Tortilla (Nacho, White Restaurant, White Round, Yellow Round)

Sun Snacks -
Potato (Reduced Fat Ridged, Thick Cut Sea Salted)

White Nacho Tortilla

Tostitos -
Tortilla Chips

    100% White Corn Restaurant Style

    Bite Size Rounds

    Crispy Rounds

    Gold

    Light Restaurant Style

    Natural Blue Corn Restaurant Style

    Natural Yellow Corn Restaurant Style

    Restaurant Style w/Hint Of Jalapeno Flavor

    Restaurant Style w/Hint of Lime Flavor

    Santa Fe Rounds

    Scoops

Trader Joe's -
Chips (BBQ, Buttermilk Garlic Mashed Potato, Inka Roasted Plantain)

Kettle Krisps (Low Fat, Terra Exotic Vegetable, Vegetable Root, Veggie)

Potato Crisps (Garlic & Parmesan, Original)

Tortilla (Baked & Blue Corn, Organic Baked Blue Corn Salted, Organic Rounds, Salsa, Spiced, Soy & Flaxseed

C

Reduced Carb, Soy & Flaxseed Spicy, White Corn (Restaurant Style, Salted))

Yellow Tortilla (Salted, Unsalted White Rounds)

UTZ -

All Natural Kettle Cooked (Dark Russet, Gourmet Medley, Lightly Salted Sea Salt & Vinegar)

Corn Chips (Barbeque, Plain)

Grandma Utz Kettle Cooked (Barbeque, Plain)

Home Style Kettle Cooked Plain

Kettle Classics (Dark Russet, Jalapeno, Plain, Sour Cream & Chive, Smokin' Sweet BBQ, Sweet Potato)

Mystic Kettle Cooked Chips (Dark Russet, Plain, Sea Salt & Vinegar) Regular Chips (Barbeque, Carolina Style BBQ, Cheddar & Sour Cream, No Salt, Plain Flat, Plain Ripple, Plain Wavy Cut, Red Hot, Reduced Fat, Salt & Pepper, Salt & Vinegar, Sour Cream & Onion)

Tortilla Chips (Cheesier Nacho Tortilla Chips, Low Fat Baked Tortilla Chips, Restaurant Style Tortilla Chips, White Corn Tortilla Chips)

Wegmans -

Chips (BBQ, Corn, Dill Pickle Flavored)

Kettle (BBQ, Original, Salt & Pepper)

Krinkle

Organic (Cracked Pepper, Roasted Garlic & Onion, Rosemary & Thyme, Sea Salt)

Regular

Salt & Vinegar

Sour Cream & Onion

Tortilla 100% White Corn (Authentic, Bite Size, Round)

Tortilla Wavy

Wild Oats -

Kettle Potato (Cheddar, Honey Barbeque, Jalapeno, Regular, Ripple, Salt & Vinegar, Salted)

Tortilla Chips (Blue, Salted, Sesame, White)

Winn Dixie - Corn, Tortilla

Wise - Potato Chips (Lightly Salted, Plain, Ridged)

Xochitl - Mexican Style Tortilla (Totopos De Maiz)

Chocolate

365 Organic Every Day Value -

Dark Chocolate Bar (Organic Swiss w/Coconut Flakes, Organic Swiss w/Mint Crisps, Regular, w/Almonds)

Milk Chocolate Bar (Original, w/Almonds, w/Hazelnuts)

Organic Truffles

Baker's - German Chocolate Baking Squares

B&J - Milk Chocolate Covered Raisins

Carb Safe - Sugar Free Chocolate Bars (Dark, Milk)

Cella's - Dark, Milk

Cote d'or - Bouchee (Milk and White), Nougatti

Dagoba - All Chocolate

Dove - All *(Except Chocolate Covered Almonds)*

Ghirardelli - Milk, Mint & Dark Chocolate Squares

Hershey's -

Almond Joy

Classic Caramels

Heath Bar

Kisses

Milk Chocolate Bar (Original, w/Almonds)

Mounds

Payday

Reese's Peanut Butter Cups

Tastetations

Hy-Vee - Chocolate (Caramel Clusters, Covered Raisins, Peanut Clusters, Stars)

Mars -

3 Musketeers

C

All Dove Products *(Except Chocolate Covered Almonds)*

M&M's (Plain, Peanut, *(Except Crispy)*)

Mars Almond Bar

Midnight Milky Way

Milky Way Eggs

Snickers *(Except Crispy)*

Snickers Munch Bar

Maya Chocolates - Chocolate, Chocolate (Coffee, Mint, Orange)

Milka Milk - Chocolate

Necco -

Haviland Peppermint & Wintergreen Patties

Haviland Thin Mints & Candy Stix

Necco Candy Eggs (Easter)

Nestle -

Baby Ruth

Bit-O-Honey

Butterfinger

Choco Bake

Milk Chocolate Goobers

Oh Henry!

Pixy Stix

Raisinets

Turtles

Newman's Own Organics -

Chocolate Bar (Espresso Sweet Dark, Milk, Orange Sweet Dark, Sweet Dark)

Chocolate Cups (Peanut Butter/Dark, Peanut Butter/Milk Peppermint/Dark)

Espresso Sweet Dark

Milk Chocolate & Toffee Crunch

Orgran - Choc-Bar w/Hazelnuts
Stop & Shop Brand -
> Simply Enjoy Dark Chocolate
>> Amaretto Coated Cranberries
>> Cappuccino Crunch Bits
>> Caramel Squares
>> Covered (Cherries, Coffee Beans, Cranberries, Kona Almond Coffee Beans, Strawberries)
>> Raspberry Sticks
> Milk Chocolate
>> Butter Toffee Squares
>> Coated Cashews
>> Cocoa Almonds
>> Covered (Cashews, Cherries, Peanuts, Raisins)
>> Pecan Caramel Patties
> White Chocolate Coated Coffee Nugets
> Whole Chocolate Covered Raspberries

Terry's Twilight - Mints
thinkThin - Chocolate (Fudge, Mudslide), Dark Chocolate, White Chocolate Chip
Toblerone - Dark, Milk, Minis, Pralines, White
Trader Joe's -
> Dark Chocolate (Covered Soy Nuts, Mint Creams, Roasted Pistachio Toffee)
> Dark Chocolate Covered (Caramels, Cherries, Espresso Beans, Ginger, Raisins)
> Gourmet Chocolate Fudge w/Walnuts
> Imported Belgian Chocolate Sea Shells
> Chocolate
>> Almond Clusters
>> Covered Blueberries
>> Espresso Beans

C

Fondue
Orange Sticks
Raspberry Sticks
Seashells
Sunflower Seed Drops
Truffles
Chocolate Bars
  Carb Safe Sugar Free Milk & Dark Chocolate Bars
  Organic Dark Chocolate Bar (73% Super Dark, Truffle)
  Organic Milk Chocolate Bar (Truffle, w/Raisins & Pecans)
  Ounce Plus 3pk Milk & Dark Chocolate Bars
  Pound Plus Bars
Milk Chocolate
  Clouds
  Covered Banana Chips
  Covered Peanuts
  Covered Raisins
  Cranberries
  Peanut Butter Cups
  Pistachios
Milk & Dark Chocolate Covered (Almonds, Cashews)
Tropical Source - Dark Chocolate (Rice Crisps, Rich Dark, Toasted Almond), All Chocolate Bars
Weight Watchers - By Whitman's (English Toffee Squares, English Toffee Squares Bag, Mint Patties Bag, Pecan Crown Bag, Pecan Crown Bar)
Whitman's - Gold Box (Assorted Chocolates, Chocolate Covered Nuts, Pecan Medallions)
Whole Treat - Chococlate w/Almonds
Chocolate Bars... see Candy Bars and/or Chocolate
Chocolate Chips... see Baking Chips

C

Chocolate Dip
> **Lighthouse Foods -** Chocolate Dip
> **Walden Farms** - No Carb Chocolate Dip

Chocolate Milk... see Milk

Chocolate Sauce
> **Wegmans -** Chocolate (Milk, Mint, Raspberry)

Chocolate Syrup... see Syrup

Chole
> **Tamarind Tree -** Alu Chole, Saag Chole

Chutney
> **Baxters -**
>> Albert's Victorian
>> Cranberry & Caramelized Red Onion
>> Crushed Pineapple & Sweet Pepper
>> Mango w/Ginger
>> Spanish Tomato & Black Olive
>> Spiced Fruit
>> Tomato w/Red Pepper
>
> **Trader Joe's -** Apple Cranberry, Mango Ginger

Cider
> **365 Every Day Value** - Apple Cherry Cider
> **Albertson's -** Apple Cider
> **Green Mountain -** Cider Jack (Alcoholic)
> **Hard Pear -** Cider
> **Lucky Leaf** - Apple Cider
> **Magners** - Cider (Alcoholic)
> **Musselman's** - Apple Cider, Sparkling Apple Cider
> **Pinnacle** - Gold Honey Brewed Carbonated Hard Cider
> (Alcoholic)
> **Sonoma Sparkler -** Organic (Apple, Lemonade), Natural
> (Peach, Pear, Raspberry)

C

    White Winter - Winery Hard Apple Cider (Alcoholic)

    Woodchuck - Cider (Amber, Dark & Dry, Granny Smith, Pear, Raspberry) (Alcoholic)

    Woodpecker - Cider (Alcoholic)

Cinnamon

    Albertsons

    Durkee

    Shaw's

    Spice Islands

    Tone's

    Watkins

Clams... *All **Fresh** Seafood Is **Gluten-Free (Non-Marinated, Unseasoned)***

    Bumble Bee - Canned Clams

    Chicken Of The Sea - All Varieties

    Crown Prince - Baby Clams

Club Soda... see Soda Pop

Coating

    A Taste of Thai - Spicy Peanut Bake

    Gillian's Foods - All Varieties

    Hol Grain - Rice Bread Crumbs

    Kinnikinnick - Crispy Chicken Coating Mix

    Miss Roben's - Breading Batter Coating Mix

    Nu World Foods - All Varieties

    Orgran - All Purpose Crumbs

    Schar - Pan Grati

    Southern Homestyle - Corn Flake Crumbs, Tortillas Crumbs

Cocktail Mix

    Holland House - Mixers (Margarita, Strawberry Daiquiri, Sweet 'N Sour, Tom Collins, Whiskey Sour Mix) *(Except Pina Colada)*

Mr. & Mrs. T's -

Cocktail Mixers *(Except Pina Colada)*

Bloody Mary

Bold & Spicy Bloody Mary

Premium Blend Bloody Mary

Mai Tai

Margarita

Sea Breeze

Sweet & Sour

Strawberry Daiquiri-Margarita

Whiskey Sour

Sweet & Sour

Rose's - Cocktail Infusions, Grenadine, Lime Juice, Sweet 'N Sour, Triple Sec,

Stop & Shop Brand - Simply Enjoy Mixer (Cosmopolitan, Lemon Drop Martini, Margarita Cocktail, Mojito Cocktail, Watermelon Martini)

Trader Joe's - Margarita Mix

Cocktail Sauce

Baxters - Seafood

Captain's Choice

Cross & Blackwell - Seafood Cocktail Sauce

Golden Dipt - Extra Hot, Regular

Heinz - Seafood Cocktail Sauce (Regular, Zesty)

Hy-Vee - Cocktail Sauce For Seafood

Laura Lynn

Mayacamas - Seafood

Safeway

Spartan Brand

Stop & Shop Brand - Seafood Cocktail Sauce

Trader Joe's - Seafood Cocktail Sauce

C

Cocoa Powder/Mix

    Ah!Laska - Organic Non-Dairy Cocoa Mix

    Best Friends - Cocoa

    Carnation - Instant Cocoa Mix, Masque

    Coburn Farms - Cocoa Mix

    Dagoba - All Varieties

    Equal Exchange - Organic Hot Cocoa

    Ghirardelli -

        Double Chocolate

        Hazelnut

        Mocha

        Premium Unsweetened Cocoa

        Sweet Ground Chocolate & Cocoa

        White Mocha

    Green & Black - Organic Hot Chocolate

    Hershey's - Cocoa

    Hy-Vee - No Sugar Added, Regular

    Laura Lynn - Cocoa

    Meijer Brand -

        Marshmallow Supreme

        No Sugar Added

        Organic Regular

        Regular

        w/Marshmallows

    Midwest Country Fare - Fare Instant Chocolate Flavored Drink Mix, Hot Cocoa Mix,

    Nestle - Hot Cocoa Mix (Milk Chocolate), Nesquik

    Price Chopper - Hot Cocoa Mix

    Safeway Select -

        Cocoa Mix European

        Drink Mix (Instant Chocolate)

Hot Cocoa Mix (Fat Free, w/ & w/out Marshmallows)

Spartan Brand - Hot Cocoa (No Sugar Added, Regular, w/Marshmallows)

St. Claire's Organics - All Varieties

Stop & Shop Brand - Hot Cocoa (Fat Free No Sugar Added, Light, Mini Marshmallows, Regular)

Swiss Miss - Instant Cocoa

Tops - Hot Chocolate

Trader Joe's - Cocoa (Conacado Organic, Natural Mint, Organic Powder), Sipping Chocolate

Watkins - Cocoa Mix (French Vanilla, Irish Cream)

Whole Kids Organic - Organic Hot Chocolate Drink Mix

Coconut

Baker's - Coconut (Bags, Cans)

Food Club - Sweetened Coconut

Laura Lynn

Let's Do...Organic - Flakes, Lite, Shredded

Safeway - Coconut (Sweetened)

Spartan Brand - Coconut Flakes

Wegmans - Coconut (Regular, Sweetened Flaked)

Coconut Milk

365 Organic Every Day Value - Organic Coconut Milk (Lite, Regular)

A Taste Of Thai - Coconut Milk (Lite, Regular)

Native Forest - Coconut Milk (Light, Regular)

Thai Kitchen -

Indonesia (Premium, Premium-Organic)

Thailand (Lite, Lite Organic, Premium, Premium-Organic)

Trader Joe's - Light

Cod... see Fish

*All **Fresh** Fish Is **Gluten-Free (Non-Marinated, Unseasoned)***

C

Coffee

365 Every Day Value - Colombian Supremo, Ground (Decaf Hazelnut, French Vanilla)

Astor -

All-Purpose (Decaf, Regular)

Creole w/Chicory

Filter Pack

Instant (Decaf, Regular)

Singles (Decaf, Regular)

Rich Roast All-Purpose (Decaf, Lite, Regular)

Whole Bean (100% Colombian, Decaf, Regular)

B&J - 100% Colombian Ground Supreme

Ex. Choice - 100% Colombian (Decaf, Regular) Pouches

Folger's - All Instant & Roasts

General Foods International Coffees - Flavored Instant (Decaf Sugar Free, Decaf Sugar Free & Fat Free, Regular Sugar Free & Fat Free)

Green Mountain - Coffee Roasters (All Varieties)

Hy-Vee -

100% Colombian

Breakfast Blend

Coffee (Instant, Regular)

Decaf (Instant, Regular)

French Roast

Java Soy -

Breakfast Blend (Decaf, Regular)

Caramel Cream

French Vanilla

Vanilla Hazelnut

Laura Lynn - All Varieties

Maxwell House -

Cappuccino Dry Mix (Decaf, Hot, Iced, Reduced

Caffeine/Lite, Regular)
Coffee Bags (Regular, Decaf)
Filter Packs & Singles (Regular, Naturally Decaf)
Instant (Decaf, Regular, Reduced Caffeine/Lite)
Roast & Ground (Regular, Decaf, Reduced Caffeine/Lite)

Nescafe - Taster's Choice

Prestige - All-Purpose 100% Colombian

Price Chopper - Fresh Ground, Instant

Sanka - Instant (Decaf, Reduced Caffeine/Lite, Regular)

Safeway Select -
Espresso Coffee Beans
Swiss Mocha Instant Coffee Beverage
Whole Bean Coffees Flavored

Spartan Brand -
Coffee (Decaf, Instant, Instant Decaf, Regular)
Coffee Ground (Colombian, Decaf, French Roast,
   Light, Regular)

Tecino - Herbal (Almond Amaretto, Hazelnut, Java, Mocha,
Vanilla Nut)

Trader Joe's -
All Coffee
Chai No Sugar Added
Matcha Latte
Spicy Chai Latte
Triple Espresso (Latte, Mocha)

Yuban -
Instant (Decaf, Reduced Caffeine/Lite, Regular)
Roast & Ground (Decaf, Reduced Caffeine/Lite, Regular)

Wegmans -
100% Colombian Whole Bean Ground Coffee Medium
   Roast (Decaf, Regular)

C

    Ground Coffee (Caffeine Lite, Decaf, Espresso Dark Roast, Light Roast, Traditional)

    Coffee

    Traditional Coffee Singles

    Whole Bean Instant Coffee (Dark Espresso Roast, Decaf, French Roast)

Winn Dixie -

    All-Purpose (100% Columbian, Decaf, Regular)

    Creole w/Chicory

    El Cafetal Coffee

    Filter Pack

    Instant (Decaf, Regular)

    Singles (Decaf, Regular)

    Rich Roast All-Purpose (Decaf, Lite, Regular)

    Whole Bean (100% Colombian, Decaf, Regular)

Coffee Beans... see Coffee

Coffee Creamer... see Creamer

Cold Cuts... see Deli Meat

Concentrate... see Drinks/Juice

Cones

    Cerrone Cone - Cerrone Waffle Cones

Cookie Mix

    Arrowhead Mills - Gluten-Free Chocolate Chip

    Bob's Red Mill - Chocolate Chip

    Cause You're Special - Chocolate Chip, Classic Sugar

    Cherrybrook - Chocolate Chip, Sugar

    Gluten-Free Pantry - Chocolate Chip Cookie & Square Mix

    Hol Grain - Chocolate Chip

    Kinnikinnick - All Varieties

    Namaste - All Varieties

    Really Good Foods - Butter Cookie Mix, Crinkle Cookie Mix, Versatile Cookie Mix

The Cravings Place - Chocolate Chunk, Peanut Butter Cookies

    Aproten - Wafers (Chocolate Crème, Vanilla Crème)

    Archway - Coconut Macaroon Cookies

    'Cause You're Special - All Varieties

    Cherrybrook Kitchen - Chocolate Chip, Sugar

    Choices Rice Bakery -

        Bird's Nest

        Brownie White Chocolate Chip

        Chocolate Chip

        Ginger

        Honey Squares

        Mediterranean Macaroons

        Raisin Sunflower Seed

    Crave - Monster Cookie

    Cybros Inc. - Lemon Almond, Peanut Butter

    Dr. Schar -

        Biscotti Con Cioccolato

        Chocolate Wafers

        Cioccolini

        Duetto

        Frollini

        Hazelnut Wafers

        Lebkuchen

        Mini Sorrisi

        Pepitas

        Pepitas Chocolate Chip Cookies

        Quadritos

        Savoiardi

        Solena Biscuits

        Sorrisi

C

Wafers (Al Cacao, Alla Nocciola, Alla Vaniglia)

Vanilla Wafers

El Peto - All Varieties

Ener-G -

Biscotti

Chocolate (Chip Biscotti, Regular, Sandwich, Vanilla Cream)

Cinnamon

Ginger

Lemon Sandwich

Vanilla (Chocolate Sandwich, Cream, Lemon Cream,
Regular)

White Chocolate Chip

Enjoy Life - Soft Baked Cookies (Chewy Chocolate Chip,
Double Chocolate Brownie, Gingerbread Spice, No-Oats
"Oatmeal", Snickerdoodle)

Essensmart - Almond, Ginger w/Flaxseed, Lemon Poppy,
Raspberry

Gillian's Foods - All Varieties

Glutafin - Chocolate Chip & Peanut, Milk Chocolate Digestive

Glutino - All Varieties

Jennies - Macaroons (Carob, Chocolate, Coconut)

Jo-Sef - All Varieties

Kookie Karma - All Varieties

Kinnikinnick -

Almond

Almond Biscotti

Chocolate Covered Almond Biscotti

Ginger Snap

KinniBetik Chunky Chocolate

KinniKritters Animal Cookies

KinniToos Sandwich (Chocolate Vanilla, Vanilla Crème)

C

Montana's Chocolate Chip

Wolfesbread (Double Chocolate Almond, Lemon Cranberry)

Mi-Del - Arrowhead Animal, Chocolate Chip, Ginger Snaps, Mini Pecan

Miss Meringue - Coconut Chocolettes, Vanilla

Namaste Foods - All Varieties

Nana's - No Gluten Cookie (Ginger, Lemon)

Nature's Path Organic - Animal Cookies (Vanilla)

Orgran -

Apricot & Coconut Cookies

Biscotti (Armeretti, Chocolate Chip, Lemon & Poppyseed)

Outback Animals

Sultana & Cinnamon Cookies

Triple Chocolate Chip Cookie

Pamela's Products -

Butter Shortbread

Chocolate Chip (Mini, Walnut)

Chocolate Chunk Pecan Shortbread

Chunky Chocolate Chip

Dark Chocolate/Chocolate Chunk

Espresso Chocolate Chunk

Ginger (Mini Snapz, w/Sliced Almonds)

Lemon Shortbread

Old Fashion Raisin Walnut

Peanut Butter (Chocolate Chip, Regular)

Pecan Shortbread

Shortbread Swirl

Spicy Ginger w/Crystallized Ginger

The Smarter Carb -

Almond Chip Biscotti

C

Chocolate Covered Meringues

Chocolate Fudge Chip Biscotti

Vanilla Meringues

Trader Joe's - Meringues (All Varieties), Mini Coconut Macaroons

Ukrop's -

Amaretti

Brunsli

Chocolate Macaroons

Cinnamon Stars

Coconut Macaroons

Whole Foods Market - Gluten-Free Bakehouse (Chocolate Chip, Molasses Ginger, Peanut Butter, Walnut)

Wild Oats - Gluten-Free Chocolate Chip Mini Cookies

Cooking Spray... see also Oil

B&J - Canola Cooking No Stick Spray

Crisco - Olive Oil Extra Virgin, Original

Manischewitz - All Varieties

Meijer Brand - Butter, Olive Oil Extra Virgin, Vegetable Oil

Pam - Butter Flavor, Olive Oil, Original

Safeway - Butter Flavored

Shaw's - Butter, Canola, Vegetable

Smart Balance - Buttery Burst

Spartan Brand - Butter Flavored, Regular

Stop & Shop Brand - Butter Flavored (Butter Flavored, Canola, Garlic Flavored, Olive Oil, Vegetable), Grill Spray

Trader Joe's - Canola (Spray, Regular)

Tops - All Natural Butter

Wegmans - Canola Oil, Corn Oil, Natural Butter Flavor Canola Oil, Olive Oil

C

Cooking Wine

Holland House - Marsala, Red, Sherry, Vermouth, White, White w/Lemon

Regina - Cabernet Sauvignon, Chardonnay, Marsala, Red, Sherry, White

Corn... *All **Fresh** Fruits & Vegetables Are **Gluten-Free***

365 Every Day Value -

Canned Corn No Salt Added

Canned Corn Whole Kernel Corn

Frozen Cut Corn

365 Organic Every Day Value -

Canned Supersweet White Corn

Frozen Supersweet Corn

Albertsons - Canned (Creamed Style, Regular), Frozen

B&J - Count Mini Cob Corn, Frozen Whole Kernel Cut Corn

Birds Eye - All Frozen Vegetables *(Except With Sauce)*

Del Monte - All Varieties

Freshlike - Frozen Plain Vegetables *(Except Pasta Combos and Seasoned Blends)*

Grand Selections - Crisp & Sweet Whole Kernel Corn, Frozen (Super Sweet Cut, White Shoepeg)

Green Giant -

Canned Cream Style Sweet Corn

Canned Mexicorn

Canned Niblets (Extra Sweet, No Salt Added, Whole Kernel Sweet Corn)

Canned Super Sweet Yellow & White Corn

Canned White Shoepeg Corn

Canned Whole Kernel Sweet Corn (50% Less Sodium, Regular)

Frozen Cream Style Corn

C

Frozen Extra Sweet (12 Ears of Corn-On-The-Cob, Niblets Corn)

Frozen Nibblers 12 Half Ears of Corn-On-The-Cob

Frozen Niblets (Corn, Corn & Butter Sauce)

Frozen Select w/No Sauce Shoepeg White Corn

Frozen Shoepeg White Corn & Butter Sauce

Frozen Simply Steam w/ No Sauce Niblets Corn

Frozen Simply Steam w/ No Sauce Shoepeg White Corn

Haggen - Whole Kernel Corn

Health Market - Organic Whole Kernel

Hy-Vee - Cream Style Corn, Frozen (Cut Golden Corn, Mini Corn on the Cob), Whole Kernel (Corn, White Corn)

Laura Lynn - Corn (Cream Style, Gold 'N White, No Salt Whole Kernel, Vacuum Packed, Whole Kernel)

Marsh Brand - Whole Kernel & Cream Style Corn

Meijer Brand - Frozen Corn (Corn Cob Mini Ear, Corn On Cob, Whole Kernel)

Midwest Country Fare - Cream Style, Frozen Cut, Whole Kernel

Nature's Promise - Organic Corn (Corn On The Cob, Cut)

Pictsweet - All Plain Vegetables (Frozen)

Safeway - Cream Style Corn

Spartan Brand - Frozen Corn

Stop & Shop Brand - Corn (& Butter, & Peas, Cut, Mexican Style, On The Cob, Super-sweet Corn On The Cob, Whole Kernel)

Wegmans - Bread & Butter, Creamed, Whole Kernel (Crisp 'n Sweet, No Salt, Regular)

Wild Oats Label - Organic Frozen Supersweet Yellow Corn

Corn Dog

Ian's - Popcorn Turkey Corn Dogs

S'Better Farms - Beef Corn Dogs

C

Corn Oil... see Oil

Corn Starch

> Argo
> Authentic Foods
> Bob's Red Mill
> Clabber Girl
> Hearth Club
> Hy-Vee
> Kingsford
> Laura Lynn
> Marsh Brand
> Meijer Brand
> Price Chopper
> Rumford
> Safeway Brand
> Spartan Brand

Corn Syrup... see Syrup

Cornbread/Cornbread Mix

> **Chi-Chi's** - Fiesta Corn Cake Mix
> **Bob's Red Mill** - Cornbread Mix
> **El Torito** - Sweet Corn Cake Mix
> **Food-Tek** - Fast & Fresh Dairy Free Minute Cornbread Mix, Bread Mix (Corn)
> **Gluten-Free Pantry** - Yankee Cornbread Muffin Cake
> **Glutino** - All Varieties
> **Kinnikinnick** - Cornbread & Muffin Mix
> **Whole Foods Market** - Cornbread

Corned Beef... see also Beef

> **Albertsons** - Corned Beef Hash
> **Armour** - Corned Beef, Corned Beef Hash
> **Carl Buddig**

C

    Dietz & Watson

    Hormel - Corned Beef, Corned Beef Hash, Deli Sliced Cooked Corned Beef

    Meijer Brand - Corned Beef Hash, Meijer Sliced Chipped Corned Beef Meat

    Safeway - Corned Beef Hash

Cornflake Crumbs... see Coating

Cornmeal

    Arrowhead Mills - Blue, Yellow

Cottage Cheese

    Albertsons

    Breakstone - 2%, Fat Free, Regular

    Cabot

    Creamland Dairies

    Crowley

    Food Club - Low Fat, Regular

    Friendship Dairy

    Haggen - Cottage Cheese, Small Curd

    Hood

    Hy-Vee - 4% Large & Small Curd, Low Fat 1% Small Curd

    Lactaid - 1% Milk Cottage Cheese

    Laura Lynn - Cottage Cheese

    Lucerne - Cottage Cheese *(Except Fruit Added)*

    Marsh Brand

    Midwest Country Fare - 1% Small Curd

    Nancy's - All Products

    Price Chopper - All Varieties

    Spartan Brand - Large Curd 4% Milk Fat, Low Fat 1 %, Small Curd (Nonfat, Regular)

    Stop & Shop Brand - Cottage Cheese (Calcium Added, Lowfat, Nonfat w/Pineapple)

C

Wegmans - 1% Large Curd, Nonfat Small Curd (1%, 4%),

Winn Dixie - 1%, 4%, Fat Free, Low Fat

Crabmeat... *All **Fresh** Seafood Is **Gluten-Free (Non-Marinated, Unseasoned)***

Chicken Of The Sea - All Varieties *(Except Imitation Crab)*

Crown Prince - Crab Meat (Fancy, Regular, White)

Trader Joe's - Crabmeat

Crackers

365 Every Day Value - Rice Crackers (Seaweed, Sesame, Tamari, Wasabi)

Andre's -

Crackerbread

Cheddar Cheese

Country Onion

Old World Rye

Original

Roasted Garlic

Sweet Cinnamon

Tangy Parmesan

Toasted Sesame

Zesty Italian

Artisan - Rice (Crackers, Triangles)

Blue Diamond Natural - Nut Thins (Almond, Cheddar Cheese, Country Ranch, Hazelnut, Pecan)

Eden - Brown Rice, Nori Maki Rice

Edward and Sons -

Brown Rice Snaps

Black Sesame

Buckwheat Tamari

Cheddar

Onion Garlic

C

    Salsa

    Tamari Seaweed

    Tamari Sesame

    Toasted Onion

    Unsalted Plain

    Unsalted Sesame

    Vegetable

Ener-G - Cinnamon, Garlic, Gourmet Crackers, Seattle

Glutino - Gluten-Free Crackers

Healthy Valley - Rice Bran Crackers

Hol Grain - All Crackers

Hot Kid Rice Crisps - Rice Crisps (Baby Mum Mums, Natural, Sesame, Super Slim)

Jo-Sef - All Varieties

Kookie Karma - All Varieties

Mary Gone Crackers - All Varieties

Mr. Krispers - Baked Rice Krisps

Orgran - Crispbreads (Corn, Rice, Rice & Cracked Pepper, Rice & Garden Herb, Salsa Corn)

Plum-m-Good - Rice Cakes

Real Foods - Corn Thins (Cracked Pepper & Lemon, Multigrain, Original, Sesame, Soy & Linseed), Rice Thins (Wholegrain)

Roland - Rice Crackers (Hot Wasabi, Nori Seaweed, Original, Wasabi)

Sakata - Rice Crackers All Varieties *(Except Seaweed)*

San-J - Rice Crackers (Black Sesame, Sesame)

Savory Thins - Original, Teriyaki

Sesmark Foods - Brown Rice Thins

Tiger Garden - Rice Crackers (Barbeque, Salt & Pepper)

The Kitchen Table Bakers - All Varieties

Cranberries... *All **Fresh** Fruits & Vegetables Are **Gluten-Free***

B&J - Dark Chocolate Covered Cranberries (Acrylic Jar)

Ocean Spray - Craisins (Sweetened Dried Cranberries (Cherry, Orange, Original))

Stop & Shop Brand - Yogurt Coated Cranberries

Cranberry Juice... see Juice

Cranberry Sauce

Baxters - Cranberry Sauce

Hy-Vee - Jellied, Whole Berry

Manischewitz - Cranberry Sauce

Ocean Spray - Jellied, Whole Berry

S&W - Jellied, Whole Berry

Safeway - Jellied, Whole

Spartan Brand - Jellied, Whole

Stop & Shop Brand - Jellied, Whole Berry

Wegmans - Jellied, Whole Berry

Wild Oats - Organic (Jellied, Whole Berry)

Cream Cheese

365 Every Day Value - Low Fat Neufchatel, Regular, Soft, Whipped

Albertsons - Regular

Food Club - Plain Block Style (Neufchatel, Regular), Soft Style (Lite, Regular)

Hy-Vee -

1/3 Less Fat Cream Cheese

Blueberry

Garden Vegetable

Onion/Chives

Regular

Soft Light

Strawberry

Laura Lynn -

Cream Cheese Bar (Fat Free, Regular)

C

Neufchatel Bar

Onion & Chive

Soft

Strawberry

Whipped

Lifeway - All Products

Lucerne -

Fat Free

Garden Vegetable

Light, Neufchatel

Onion & Chive

Soft Bars

Strawberry

Whipped Spread

Marsh Brand - Regular

Nancy's - All Products

Nature's Promise - Organic Cream Cheese

Philadelphia Cream Cheese -

Block (Light, Regular)

Light Chili Philly Pourovers (Capsicum, Mango, Sweet Chili)
Mini Tubs (Light, Regular)

Spreadable (Extra Light, Garlic & Herb, Light, Light Chive & Onion, Regular)

Shaw's - Fat Free, Neufchatel, Regular

Spartan Brand -

Bar Tray

Light

Neufchatel Cream Cheese Box (Tray)

Soft Strawberry

Soft Tub

Stop & Shop Brand -

    Fat Free

    Neufchatel Cheese

    Lite (Chive & Onion, Garden Vegetable, Honey Walnut, Plain, Strawberry)

    Regular

    Whipped

Trader Joe's - All Varieties

Wegmans -

    Chive & Onion

    Fat Free Tub

    Light

    Soft (Pineapple, Regular, Strawberry)

    w/Honey Nut Flavor

Whole Soy & Co. - Cream Cheese Style Soy Spread

Winn Dixie - Regular

Creamer

Albertsons - Coffee Creamers (All Flavors Liquid/Dry), Non-Dairy Creamer

Coffee-mate - All Varieties (Liquid, Liquid Concentrate, Powder, Soy Liquid)

Hood - Country Creamer

Hy-Vee -

    Coffee Creamer (Fat Free, French Vanilla, Hazelnut, Original)

    Refrigerated (French Vanilla, Hazelnut)

    Refrigerated Fat Free (French Vanilla, Hazelnut)

International Delight - All Varieties

Laura Lynn - Non-Dairy Creamer

Lucerne - Coffee Creamer, Flavored, Half & Half, Light Non-Dairy Creamer

Meijer Brand - Ultra Pasteurized Non-Dairy Creamer

Silk Creamer - All Varieties

C

> **Spartan Brand** - Coffee Creamer Powdered (Non-Dairy, Non-Dairy French Vanilla, Non-Dairy Hazelnut, Non-Dairy Light)
>
> **Stop & Shop Brand** - Fat Free Non-Dairy Creamer, Instant Nonfat Dry Milk
>
> **Wegmans** - Non-Dairy Creamer

Crispbread

> **Orgran** - Crispbread (Corn, Rice, Rice & Cracked Pepper, Rice & Garden Herb, Salsa Corn)

Crisps

> **365 Every Day Value** - Crispette (Barbecue Soy, Cheddar Soy, Creamy Ranch, Soy Sea Salt)
>
> **Baked Lay's** - Original Potato
>
> **Baked Ruffles** - Cheddar & Sour, Original Potato
>
> **Barbara's Bakery** - Brown Rice
>
> **Genisoy** -
>
> > Potato Soy (Country Style Ranch, Parmesan & Roasted Garlic, Sea Salt & Black Pepper, Texas Roadhouse BBQ)
> >
> > Soy (Apple Cinnamon, BBQ, Cheddar Cheese, Creamy Ranch, Deep Sea Salted, Garlic & Onion, Nacho, Tangy Salt 'N' Vinegar)
>
> **Glenny's** -
>
> > Apple Cinnamon
> >
> > Barbeque
> >
> > Cheddar
> >
> > Creamy Ranch
> >
> > Lightly Salted
> >
> > No Salt Added
> >
> > Onion & Garlic
> >
> > Salt & Pepper
> >
> > Veggie Fries
> >
> > White Cheddar
>
> **Herr's** - Veggie Crisps

C

Lay's Stax -
- Cheddar
- Hidden Valley Ranch
- Jalapeno Cheddar
- KC Masterpiece BBQ
- Monterey Pepper Jack
- Original
- Pizza
- Salt & Vinegar
- Sour Cream & Onion

Nature's Promise - Soy (BBQ, Ranch)
The Kitchen Table Bakers - All Varieties
Trader Joe's -
- Kettle Krisps (Low Fat, Terra Exotic Vegetable, Vegetable Root, Veggie)
- Potato Crisps (Garlic & Parmesan, Original)

Robert's American Gourmet - Potato, Soy (BBQ, Ranch, Rich Cheddar)
Stop & Shop Brand - Rice (BBQ, Caramel, Cheddar, Ranch)
Trader Joe's - BBQ Soy

Cucumbers... *All **Fresh** Fruits & Vegetables Are **Gluten-Free***

Curry Paste
- **A Taste of Thai** - Curry Paste (Green, Panang, Red, Yellow)
- **Thai Kitchen** - Curry Paste (Green, Red)

Curry Powder
- **Astor**
- **Bali Spice** - Coconut Chicken Curry Seasoning
- **Durkee**
- **Spice Island**
- **Tones**
- **Whole Pantry**

C
D

Winn Dixie
Curry Sauce

Mr. Spice - Indian Curry Sauce

Trader Joe's - Curry Simmer, Pasta Sauce (Thai Red Curry, Thai Yellow Curry), Tuna In Curry (Red, Yellow)

Custard

Orgran - Custard Mix

D

Dark Chocolate... see Chocolate
Deli Meat

B & K - Corned Beef
Boar's Head -

Arbruzza

Black Forest Turkey Breast

Deluxe Roast Beef

Hickory Smoked Chicken Breast Deli Meat

Lebanon Bologna

Mesquite Turkey

Seasoned Top Round Of Beef

Sopressata

Carl Buddig - Original Deli Pouch (Chicken), Oven Roasted Cured Chicken Breast Deli Cuts

Dietz & Watson - Corned Beef, Gourmet Lite Turkey, Pepper Garlic Turkey

Esskay Silver Label - Ham

Fiorucci - Genoa Salami, Hard Salami, Sliced Pepperoni

Hebrew National - Cooked Tongue

Honeysuckle - Oil Browned Chicken Breast, White Buffalo Style Chicken Breast Deli Meat

Hormel - Cooked Corned Beef, Seasoned Roast Beef

Hy-Vee - Loaf (Old Fashioned, Pickle, Spiced Luncheon)

Jennie-O - Deli Chicken Breast (Buffalo Style, Mesquite Smoked, Oven Roasted)

Joyner Smithfield - Ham

Land O' Lakes -

Premium Deli Style Sliced Meats (Oven Roasted Chicken Breast)

Shaved Deli Meat (Chicken)

Thin Sliced Meat (Chicken, Honey Chicken)

Marval - Turkey Breast (Regular, Smoked), Turkey Ham

Naturally Good - Chicken Breast

Nature's Promise - All Varieties

Northwestern Deli Turkey - Hickory Smoked, Oven Roasted, Turkey Pastrami

Plainville Farms - Roasted Turkey, Turkey Breast (Honey, Smoked)

Safeway - Primo Paglio Lunch Meats (Beef Strip Loin, Mortadella, Pastrami, Roast Beef, Salami)

Sahlens - Smokehouse Ham

Smithfield - Lean Generation Honey Cured Ham

Todds Country - Ham

Ukrop's - Danish Ham, Deli Turkey

Wellshire Farms - Sliced Oven Roasted Chicken Breast

Dill Pickles... see Pickles

Dinner Meals... see Meals

Dip/Dip Mix

Albertsons - Refrigerated (Avocado, Clam, French Onion, Guacamole, Ranch)

Cabot - Nacho, Ranch, Salsa Grande, Veggie

Cedarlane - 5 Layer Mexican Dip

Fantastic Foods - Soup & Dip Recipe Mix (Garlic Herb, Onion, Onion Mushroom, Vegetable)

D

Frito Lay -
Bean
Chili Cheese
Hot Bean
Jalapeno & Cheddar Flavored Cheese
Mild Cheddar Flavored Cheese

Herr's - Bean, Jalapeno Cheddar, Mild Cheddar, Salsa & Cheese

Hy-Vee -
Bacon & Cheddar
French Onion Snack
Ranch w/Dill
Salsa
Toasted Onion Snack
Vegetable Party

Laura Lynn - Ranch Dip Mix

Lay's -
Creamy Ranch
Flavored Dry Mix (French Onion, Green Onion, Ranch)
French Onion

Litehouse -
Avocado
Chocolate
Chocolate Caramel
Chocolate Yogurt Fruit
Dilly of a Dip
Lowfat Caramel
Onion
Original Caramel
Ranch
Roasted Garlic

    Southwest Ranch

    Strawberry Yogurt Fruit

    Toffee Caramel

    Vanilla Crème

    Vanilla Yogurt Fruit

Lucerne -

    Avocado

    Bacon Onion

    Clam

    French Onion

    Green Onion

    Guacamole

    Ranch

Old El Paso -

    Medium Cheese 'N Salsa Dip (Low Fat, Regular)

    Mild Cheese 'N Salsa Dip

Philadelphia Dips -

    BBQ

    French Onion

    Gherkin

    Light French Onion

    Onion & Bacon

    Prawn & Crab

    Smoked Salmon

Progresso - Ranch Dip Mix

Road's End Organics - Nacho & Cheese (Mild, Spicy)

Ruffles -

    French Onion (Dry Mix, Party Bowl)

    Ranch (Dry Mix, Regular)

Snyder's Of Hanover - Cheddar Cheese, Sweet Salsa, Three Bean

D

    Spartan Brand - French Onion, Ranch

    Stop & Shop Brand - Refrigerated (Artichoke & Cheese, French Onion, Ranch, Spinach, Veggie)

    Tostitos - Zesty Bean & Cheese

    Trader Joe's -

        Blue Cheese w/Roasted Pecan

        Cilantro & Chive Yogurt

        Fat Free Spicy Black Bean Spinach

        Tuscan White Bean

        Vegetable Tray w/Ranch Style

    UTZ - Cheddar & Jalapeno, Mild Cheddar Cheese

    Wegmans - French Onion, Salsa Con Queso (Cheddar Cheese Dip)

Dipping Sauce

    Safeway Select - Gourmet (Cook'n Grill Plum, Honey Mustard)

Doughnut

    Ener-G - Chocolate Iced Doughnuts, Plain (Doughnut Holes, Doughnuts)

Dressing... see Salad Dressing

Dried Fruit

    365 Organic Every Day Value -

        Apricots

        Cherries

        Cranberries

        Cranberries & Apples

        Cranberries & Pecans

        Diced Apples

        Fruit Delight Mix

    B&J -

        3 Variety Dried Fruit

        Mariani (California Pitted Dried Plums, Dried Ultimate Apricots, Mixed Dried Fruit)

D

Sweetened Dried Cranberries

Dole - Dates, Prunes, Raisins

Eden - Cranberries, Montmorency Dried Tart Cherries, Wild Blueberries

Hy-Vee -

Apples

Apricots

Banana Chips

Blueberries

Cherries

Cranberries

Mixed Berries

Mixed Fruit

Pineapple

Safeway - Apples, Apricots, Cherries, Peaches, Prunes, Raisins

Sun-Maid

California Pitted Prunes

Golden & Cherries

Fruit Bits

Raisins (Baking, Golden, Jumbo, Regular)

Mixed Fruit

Washington Apples

Zante Currants

Wegmans - Dried Plums, Pitted Prunes, Raisins

Drink Mix

Albertsons - All Drink Mixes

Hy-Vee - Splash Drink Mix (Cherry, Grape, Lemonade, Orange, Tropical Fruit Punch)

Kool-Aid - Soft Drink Mix

Meijer Brand -

Breakfast Orange

D

Cherry
Chocolate Flavor
Grape
Lemon Sugar Free
Lemonade
Orange
Pink Lemonade (Regular, Sugar Free)
Punch
Raspberry Sugar Free
Strawberry
Safeway Select -
Instant Chocolate
Lemonade
Sugar Free Raspberry
Spartan Brand -
Cherry
Grape
Lemonade Flavor
Pink Lemonade
Sugar Free Lemonade
Sugar Free Pink Lemonade
Sugar Free Raspberry
Tropical Punch
Stop & Shop Brand -
Cherry
Grape
Iced Tea
Lemonade
Orange
Pink Lemonade
Strawberry

Sugar Free (Fruit Punch, Iced Tea, Lemon Lime, Lemonade)

Tropical Punch

Wegmans - Frozen Juice Concentrate - Drink Mix (Lemonade Flavor, Pink Lemonade)

Winn Dixie - Sugar Free Punch Mix

Drinks/Juice

365 Every Day Value -

100% Juice (Cranberry, Tangerine, Valencia Orange)

Juice (Cranberry Cocktail, Cranberry Grape, Grape, Gravenstein Apple, Lemonade, Orange, Orchard Peach, Ruby Red Grapefruit, Vegetable Medley)

Orange Juice (High Pulp, Organic Pulp Free, Organic w/Pulp, w/Calcium)

365 Organic Every Day Value -

Organic Apple Juice

Organic Cranberry Juice Cocktail

Organic Juice (100% Concord Grape, Apple, Apple Cranberry, Berry, Cherry, Fresh Squeezed Orange, Gravenstein Apple, Lemonade, Orange, Red Grape)

Organic Juice Blend (Orange Peach Mango, Orange Strawberry, Pineapple Orange Banana)

Apple & Eve - All Products

B&J - Apple, Cran Raspberry, Juice Cocktail From Concentrate (Cranberry, Cran-Raspberry), Premium Orange

Blue Diamond - Almond Breeze (Chocolate, Original, Vanilla)

Campbell's -

All Diet V8 Splash Juice Blends

All Tomato Juice

All V8 Splash Juice Blends

All V8 V-Fusion Blends

All V8 Vegetable Juices

V8 Splash Smoothies (Orange Crème, Peach Mango, Strawberry Banana)

D

Capri Sun - All Flavors

Coca Cola Company -

All 100% Juices

Minute Maid Light Lemonade

Powerade Mountain Blast

Cott Beverages - All Varieties

Country Time - All Flavors

Del Monte - All 100% Fruit Juice

Dole - All Fruit Juice

Eden - Apple Concentrate, Apple Juice, Montmorency Tart Cherry Juice

Five Alive - Frozen Juice

Gardner Groves - 100% Grapefruit Juice

Hansen's - All Products

Hawaiian Punch - All Varieties

Hi-C Fruit Drinks - All Varieties

Hy-Vee -

100% Juice Blend (Cranberry, Cranberry Apple, Cranberry Raspberry)

Frozen Concentrate (Apple, Fruit Punch, Grape Juice Cocktail, Grapefruit Juice, Lemonade, Orange (Regular, w/Calcium), Pink Lemonade)

Fruit Splash (Fruit Punch, Orange)

Juice (All Natural Tomato, All Natural Vegetable, Apple, Concord Grape, Cranberry Strawberry, Grapefruit, Pineapple, V-8)

Juice Cocktail From Concentrate (Cranberry, Cranberry Apple, Cranberry Grape, Cranberry Raspberry, Ruby Red Grapefruit)

Juice From Concentrate (100% Apple, 100% Unsweetened Prune, 100% White Grape, Apple, Tomato, Vegetable)

Juice Splash (Fruit Punch, Orange Drink)

Just Juice (Apple, Berry, Cherry, Grape, Lemon, Punch, Strawberry)

Non Concentrate (Country Style Orange, Orange Juice, Orange Juice w/Calcium, Ruby Red Grapefruit)

Splash (Cherry, Grape, Lemonade, Orange, Raspberry, Strawberry, Tropical Punch)

Strawberry Nutritional Supplement (Plus, Regular)

Tropical Punch Coolers

Vanilla Nutritional Supplement (Plus, Regular)

Izze - All Varieties

Jammin Nectars -

C-Beta Carrot

Ginger Party

Mambo Mango

Pure Passion

Razz-Ade

Knudsen - Organic Blueberry Pomegranate Juice

Lakewood - All Varieties

Langer Juice Company - Raspberry/ Cranberry

Laura Lynn -

Juices

All Cocktail

All Organic

All Vegetable

Apple

Cranberry

Cranberry Blend

Grape

Grapefruit

Lemon

Light Cranberry Blends

D

Light Fruit Punch

Orange Breakfast Drink, Sports Drink

Peach

Prune

White Cranberry

White Cranberry Blend

White Grape

Lifeway - All Products

Meijer Brand -

100% Juice (Berry, Cherry, Grape, Punch)

Cranberry Juice Drink (Grape, Raspberry, Strawberry)

Frozen Concentrate Juice (Apple, Fruit Punch, Grape, Grapefruit, Lemonade, Limeade, Orange, Pink Lemonade)

Frozen Concentrate Orange Juice (High Pulp, Pulp Free, w/Calcium)

Juice (Apple, Grape, Grapefruit, Lemon, Orange, Peach, Prune, Ruby Red Grapefruit, White Cranberry, White Grape, White Grapefruit)

Juice Cocktail (Cranapple, Cranberry, White Cranberry)

Juice Refrigerated Orange Premium (Original, w/Calcium)

Juice Refrigerated Orange Reconstituted (Original, Pulp, w/Calcium)

Lemon Juice Squeeze Bottle

Midwest Country Fare -

Apple Cider

Concentrate (Apple Cider, Apple Juice, Grape Juice, Orange Juice)

Cranberry Raspberry Juice

Juice Cocktail (Cranberry, Cranberry Apple, Ruby Red)

Minute Maid - All Varieties

Motts Apple Juice - Clear & Natural

Nantucket Nectars - All Varieties

D

Nestle - Juicy Juice

Newman's Own -

Juice Cocktail (Grape, Orange Mango, Raspberry Kiwi)

Lemonade (Pink, Regular)

Lemonade Iced Tea

Limeade

Ocean Spray -

100% Cranberry Juice (Regular, w/Concord Grape, White, w/Mixed Berry, w/Pacific Raspberry)

100% Grapefruit Juice (Pink, Ruby Red, White)

Cranberry Blends (Cran-Apple, Cran-Cherry, Cran-Grape, Cran-Mango, Cran-Raspberry, Cran-Strawberry, Cran-Tangerine)

Diet (Cranberry Spray, Orange Citrus Spray)

Juice Cocktail (Cranberry Regular, Cranberry w/Calcium)

Grapefruit Juice Drinks (Light Ruby, Ruby Red, Ruby Tangerine)

Light (Cranberry, Cran-Grape, Cran-Raspberry, Ruby, White Cranberry)

Organic 100% Cranberry Juice (Blend, Blueberry Blend, Pure)

White Cranberry (Regular, Peach, Strawberry, Wildberry)

Odwalla - All Drinks *(Except Super Protein Vanilla Al Mondo & Superfood)*

Orangina

Parisia - Sparkling Pink Lemonade

Real Lime - 100% Lime Juice

Reed's - Extra Ginger Brew

Safeway Select -

Juice

Apple

Apricot Nectar

D

    Cranberry (Apple, Grape, Raspberry, White)
    Grape
    Lemon
    Lemonade
    Orange
    Pineapple
    Prune
    Ruby Red
    Splash (Berry, Strawberry/Kiwi, Tropical)
    Tomato
    White Pink Grapefruit

Samantha Fresh - Tangerine Juice

Shelby's Grove - Apple Juice (100% Juice)

SoBe -
  Black & Blue Berry Brew
  Courage
  Cranberry Grapefruit Elixir
  Dragon
  Fuerte
  Grape Grog
  Lean (Cranberry Grapefruit, Energy, Mango Melon)
  Liz Blizz
  Lizard (Fuel, Lava, Lightning)
  MacLizard's Lemonade
  Nirvana
  Orange Carrot Elixir
  Pomegranate Cranberry Elixir
  Power
  Tsunami

Snapple - All Varieties

Spartan Brand -

Apple Juice (Natural, Regular)

Cranberry Drink (Apple, Grape, Raspberry, Strawberry)

Cranberry Juice Cocktail (Low Calorie, Regular)

Dr. Quencher Drink

Frozen Concentrate (Apple Juice, Grape Juice Cocktail, Fruit Punch, Grapefruit Juice, Orange Juice (Countrystyle, w/Calcium, Pulp Free, Regular), Pink Lemonade)

Grape Juice (Regular, White)

Grapefruit Juice

Juice Refrigerated Orange Premium (Country Style-Pulp, Regular, w/Calcium)

Juice Refrigerated Orange Reconstituted (Country Style-Pulp, Regular, w/Calcium)

Juice Refrigerated Premium Ruby Red Grapefruit

Lemon Juice

Pineapple Juice

Prune Juice

Ruby Red Grapefruit Juice

Tomato Juice

Vegetable Juice Cocktail

Stop & Shop Brand -

100% Juice (Apple From Concentrate (Added Vitamin C, Regular), Berry Drink, Cherry, Cranberry Blend, Grape (Blend, Cranberry), Grapefruit (Unsweetened, White), Natural Sparkling Apple, Raspberry Cranberry Blend, White Grape)

Chilled Pasteurized Juices (Grapefruit, Orange (Cranberry, Strawberry), Sunrise Valley Orange (Calcium Added, Regular))

Concentrate (Apple From Concentrate (Added Vitamin C, Regular), Apple Juice Cocktail, Artificially Flavored Fruit Drink, Juice Cocktail (Cranberry Lime, Light Cranberry),

D

Organic Cranberry Juice, Vegetable Juice)

Cooler (Berry Berry, Big Apple, Cosmic Orange, Fruity Punch, Goofy Grape)

Cranberry Juice Cocktail (Apple, Grape, Raspberry, Lite Raspberry, White)

Drink (Fruit Punch Juice, Grape, Lemon Lime, Orange, Tropical Juice, White Cranberry (Peach Juice, Strawberry Juice), Wild Cherry Juice, Wildberry)

Frozen Concentrate (100% Grape Juice, Apple Juice, Cranberry Cocktail, Fruit Punch, Grape Cocktail, Lemonade, Limeade, Orange Juice, Pink Lemonade, White Grape Cocktail, Wildberry Punch)

Fruit Punch

Juice (Natural Apple Juice (Added Calcium, Unsweetened), Prune Juice w/Pulp, Ruby Red Grapefruit Tangerine, Strawberry Kiwi, Tomato, Unsweetened Apple Juice w/Added Vitamin C)

Lemon Juice Reconstituted

Lite Grape Juice Cocktail

Pink Lemonade

Tropical Carrot/ Strawberry/ Kiwi Blend

Sun Drop - All Varieties

Sunny Delight - All Flavors

Tang

Thrifty Maid - Cranberry Juice Cocktail, Cranraspberry Juice

Trader Joe's -

Concentrates (Lemonade, Orange)

Fresh

100% Juices

Apricot Peach Medley

Blackberry Crush

Carrot Juice

Dixie Peach

Dynamo w/Calcium
French Market Lemonade (French Berry, Pink, Regular)
Grape Juice
Grapefruit Juice
Gravenstein Apple Juice
Just for Kids Juice Boxes
Lemonade French Market (French Berry, Pink, Regular)
Lemonade Organic Mango
Macintosh Apple
Mango & Antioxidants
Matcha Latte
Orange Juice (All Varieties)
Organic (Cranberry Apple Juice, Grapefruit Sunset, Italian Volcano Orange Juice, Mango Lemonade, Mango Nectar, Morello Cherry Reserve)
Protein w/Pzazz
Sir Strawberry Juice
Spicy Chai Latte
Strawberry Smoothie
Super Cee

Tropicana - All Varieties

V8 - All Varieties

Vruit - Apple/Carrot, Berry/Veggie, Orange/Veggie, Tropical

Wegmans -

Frozen Juice Concentrate
Drink Mix (Lemonade Flavor, Pink Lemonade)
Grapefruit
Juice Cocktail (Cranberry, Cranberry Raspberry)
Lemonade
Limeade
Orange Juice (Country Style, Pulp Free, w/Calcium)

D

Juice

> 100% Juice (Cranberry Blend, Cranberry Raspberry, Fruit Punch, Ruby Red Grapefruit Blend
>
> Apple (Natural, Regular, w/Calcium)
>
> Apple Blend (Berry Flavor, Grape, Raspberry)
>
> Apple Natural
>
> Apple w/Calcium
>
> Frizzante (Blood Orange, Blueberry Lemon, Sicilian Lemon, Sour Cherry Lemon)
>
> Grape
>
> Grapefruit
>
> Juice Blends (Berry, Cherry, Concord Grape Cranberry, Cranberry (Apple, Peach, Raspberry, Regular), Ruby Red Grapefruit, White Grape Cranberry)
>
> Lemon Juice Reconstituted
>
> Orange Juice
>
> Prune Juice
>
> White Grape (Peach Blend, Raspberry Blend, Regular)

Juice From Concentrate

> 100% Juice (Orange, Tomato, Vegetable (& No Salt Added)
>
> Blueberry Flavor Juice Blend
>
> Lemon
>
> Lemonade/Limeade
>
> Orange Juice (& w/Calcium)
>
> Pomegranate Flavor Juice Blend
>
> Punch (Berry, Citrus, Fruit)

Organic Juice From Concentrate

> Apple
>
> Apricot Nectar
>
> Cranberry
>
> Mango Nectar
>
> Orange

Premium 100% Juice

Orange (Extra Pulp, No Pulp, Some Pulp, w/Calcium, w/Calcium & Vitamins)

Ruby Red Grapefruit

Premium Orange Juice (No Pulp, Some Pulp)

Welch's - All Welch's Products

Whole Kids Organic - Organic (Concord Grape Juice, Fruit Punch)

Wild Oats Label -

Juices

Black Cherry

Black Raspberry

Cranberry Lemonade

Cranberry Raspberry

Kiwi Carrot Mango

Mango Papaya Blend

NFC Orange (w/Calcium, w/Pulp)

NFC Ruby Red Grapefruit

Natural Apple

Natural Pomegranate

Pure (Blueberry, Concord Grape, Cranberry)

Ruby Red Grapefruit

Natural Italian

Orange Passion Mango

Orange Tangerine

Raspberry

Organic Juices

Apple

Apple Cranberry

Berry Blend

Blueberry

D
E

Cranberry

NFC Orange (Regular, w/Calcium)

Organic Lemonade

Winn Dixie - Cranberry Juice Cocktail, Cran-Raspberry Juice, Orange Juice (Regular, w/Calcium)

Zola Acai - Antioxidant Power Juice

Duck... *All Fresh Meat Is Gluten-Free (Non-Marinated, Unseasoned)*

Shelton's - Duckling

E

Edamame... *All Fresh Fruits & Vegetables Are Gluten-Free*

365 Every Day Value - Blanched, Pods, Shelled Beans

365 Organic Every Day Value - Pods

Meijer - In The Shell

Melissa's - In Shell

Stop & Shop Brand - In Pod

Sunrich Naturals - In The Shell

Trader Joe's - Dry Roasted, Regular

Wild Oats Label - Organic Frozen (In Shell Edamame, Shelled Edamame)

Egg Replacer/Substitute

Albertsons - Egg Substitute

All Whites - White Cheddar

Amy's - Tofu Rancheros, Tofu Scramble

Better'n Eggs - Ham & Cheese, Three Cheese

Deb El - Just Whites

Eggbeaters - Original

Ener-G - Egg Replacer

Laura Lynn - Egg Starts

Lucerne - Best Of The Egg

MorningStar Farms - Scramblers (Egg Substitute)
NuLaid - Egg Substitute
Orgran - No Egg Natural Egg Replacer
Stop & Shop Brand - 100% Egg Whites, Eggs Made Simple
Wegmans - Egg Busters

Eggnog
Hood - Golden, Light
Lucerne - Light, Regular
Stop & Shop Brand - Light, Regular
Vitasoy - Holly Nog

Eggplant... *All Fresh* Fruits & Vegetables Are **Gluten-Free**
Tasty Bite - Punjab Eggplant
Trader Joe's - Eggplant Parmesan (Grilled Not Fried)

Eggs... *All Fresh* Eggs Are **Gluten-Free**

Enchilada Sauce
Casa Fiesta - Mild
Hy-Vee - Mild
Las Palmas - Red
McCormick - Enchilada Sauce Mix
Pace - All Varieties

Enchiladas
365 Every Day Value - Cheese
Amy's -
  Black Bean (Light In Sodium, Vegetable)
  Cheese (Regular, Whole Meal)
  Family Size Black Bean Vegetable
Trader Joe's - Chicken In Salsa Verde, Organic Black Bean & Corn
Whole Kitchen - Chicken

Energy Bars... see Bars

E

Energy Drinks
> **Hansen's** - All Varieties
> **Red Bull**
> **SoBe** - Energy
> **Syzmo**

English Muffins
> **Ener-G** - Brown Rice English Muffins w/(Sweet Potato, Tofu)
> **Foods By George** -
>> English Muffins (Cinnamon Currant, No-Rye Rye, Original)
>> Muffins (Blueberry, Corn)
> **Kinnikinnick** - Tapioca Rice English Muffins

Espresso
> **Trader Joe's** - Triple Espresso (Latte, Mocha)

Extract
> **365 Organic Every Day Value** - Vanilla Extract
> **Albertsons** - Pure Vanilla Extract
> **B&J** - Pure Vanilla Extract
> **Durkee** - Liquid Flavoring Extracts
> **Flavorganics** - All Extract Varieties
> **Hy-Vee** - Imitation Vanilla
> **Marcin** - Imitation Vanilla
> **Marsh Brand** - Imitation Vanilla Extract
> **McCormick** - Pure Vanilla Extract
> **Meijer Brand** - Imitation Vanilla, Vanilla Extract
> **Midwest Country Fare** - Imitation Vanilla Flavor
> **Nielsen-Massey** -
>> 100% Certified Organic Vanilla
>> Pure (Almond, Chocolate, Coffee, Lemon, Madagascar Bourbon, Mexican, Orange, Tahitian, Vanilla)
> **Price Chopper** - Vanilla
> **Spartan Brand** - Imitation Vanilla, Vanilla Extract

Spice Island - Liquid Flavoring Extracts

Tones - Liquid Flavorings/Extracts

Trader Joe's - Bourbon Vanilla Extract, Pure Vanilla (Alcohol Free)

Wegmans - Vanilla Extract

F

Fajita Seasoning Mix... see also Seasoning

Safeway

The Gluten-Free Pantry

Falafel Mix

Authentic Foods

Orgran

Feta Cheese... see Cheese

Fettuccini... see Pasta

Fish... *All Fresh Fish Is Gluten-Free (Non-Marinated, Unseasoned)*

Captain's Choice - Cod Fillets

Chicken Of The Sea - All Varieties *(Except Ahi Tuna in (Grilled Herb Marinade, Teriyaki Sauce), Salmon Steak In A Mandarin Orange Glaze, Mandarin Orange Salmon Cups, Teriyaki Tuna Cups, Crab-tastic!, Tuna Salad Kits)*

Crown Prince - Canned Pink Salmon

Hy-Vee - Canned Alaska Pink Salmon

Meijer Brand - Canned Salmon (Pink, Sock Eye Red)

Member's Mark - Canned Atlantic Salmon Fillet (Skinless/Boneless)

Omega Foods - Salmon, Tuna

Trader Joe's -

Apple Smoked Salmon Roulade

Marinated Wild White King Salmon Fillets

Pink Salmon (Skinless/Boneless)

F

Premium Salmon Patties
Seasoned Mahi Mahi Fillets
Smoked Salmon
Sockeye Salmon Fillets
Tilapia Fillets
Wegmans -
Alaskan Halibut
Atlantic Salmon Fillets (Farm Raised)
Orange Roughy
Sea Bass
Sockeye Salmon
Swordfish (Sashimi Grade)
Tilapia Fillets (Farm Raised)
Yellowfin Tuna (Sashimi Grade)

Fish Sauce
A Taste Of Thai - Regular
Thai Kitchen - Regular, Less Sodium

Fish Sticks
Ian's - Fish Sticks

Flan
Kozy Shack
Royal

Flax Seed
Arrowhead Mills - Golden, Regular
Bob's Red Mill - Organic Flax Seed Meal (Brown, Golden)
Hodgson Mill's - Milled Flax Seeds
Spectrum - Organic Ground Essential Flax Seed
Trader Joe's - Flax Seed w/Blueberries, Whole Flax Seed

Flax Seed Oil... see Oil

Flour
Arrowhead Mills -

All-Purpose Baking Mix

Amaranth

Millet

Organic (Brown Rice, Buckwheat, White Rice, Whole Soy)

Wheat-Free

Authentic Foods -

Almond Meal

Arrowroot

Bette's Featherlight Rice Flour Blend

Bette's Four Flour Blend

Brown Rice Flour Superfine

Garbanzo

Garfava

Gluten-Free Classical Blend

Multi-Blend Gluten-Free

Potato

Potato Starch

Sorghum

Sweet Rice Flour Superfine

Tapioca

White Corn

White Rice Flour Superfine

Bob's Red Mill -

Almond Meal/Flour

Amaranth

Black Bean

Brown Rice

Cooking w/Coconut

Fava Bean

Garbanzo Bean

Gluten-Free All Purpose Baking

F

Gluten-Free Garbanzo & Fava
Gluten-Free Sweet White Sorghum
Green Pea
Hazelnut Meal/Flour
Millet
Organic (Amaranth, Buckwheat, Coconut, Quinoa)
Potato
Sweet White Rice
Tapioca
Teff
White Bean
White Rice

Dowd & Rogers - Italian Chestnut

Ener-G -
Brown Rice
GF Gourmet Blend
Potato (Fine)
Sweet Rice
Tapioca
White Rice

Gillian's Foods - All Varieties
Glutino - All Varieties
Heartland's Finest - All Varieties
Hodgson Mill - Soy Flour
Kinnikinnick - All-Purpose Mix
Lotus Foods - Bhutanese Red Rice Flour
Montina - Baking Blend
Nu-World Foods - All Varieties
Orgran - Pasta, Plain, Self Rising
Papadini - Lentil
Pocono - Buckwheat

Really Good Foods - All Purpose Rice
Sylvan Border Farm - All Varieties

Food Coloring

Durkee

Hy-Vee - Assorted Food Coloring

Safeway

Spice Islands

Tones

Frankfurters... see Sausage

French Fries

Chester's - Flamin' Hot Flavored Fries

Funster - Potato Letter Fries

Meijer Brand - Frozen French Fries (Crinkle Cut, Original, Quickie Crinkles, Shoestring, Steak Cut)

Ore-Ida -

Cottage Fries

Crunch Time Classics (Crinkle Cut, Straight Cut)

Deep Fries Crinkle Cuts

Extra Crispy Fast Food Fries

French Fries

Golden Crinkles

Golden Fries

Pixie Crinkles

Potatoes O'Brien

Potato Wedges w/Skins

Shoestrings

Snackin' Fries T

Steak Fries

Spartan Brand - Frozen French Fries (Shoestring)

Frosting... see Baking Decorations

F

Frozen Desserts... see also Ice Cream

   365 Every Day Value - Soy Cream (Chocolate, Vanilla)

   365 Organic Every Day Value - Frozen Fruit Bar (Caribbean, Coconut, Lime, Mango, Strawberry)

   Rice Dream - Non-Dairy Frozen Desserts

   Carob Almond

   Cocoa Marble Fudge

   Neapolitan

   Orange Vanilla Swirl

   Strawberry

   Vanilla

   Soy Dream - Non-Dairy Frozen Desserts

   Butter Pecan

   Chocolate

   French Vanilla

   Green Tea

   Mint Chocolate Chip

   Strawberry Swirl

   Mocha Fudge Swirl

   Vanilla

   Vanilla Fudge Swirl

Frozen Fruit... see Fruit

Frozen Yogurt... see Yogurt

Fruit Bars... see Bars

Fruit Cocktail... *All **Fresh** Fruits & Vegetables Are **Gluten-Free***

   Del Monte -

   Canned Fruit (All Varieties)

   Fruit Snack Cups (All Metal & Plastic Containers)

   Hy-Vee

   Meijer Brand - Heavy Syrup, In Juice

Midwest Country Fare

Laura Lynn - Canned

Spartan Brand - Heavy Syrup, Light Juice

Stop & Shop Brand - Heavy Syrup, Pear Juice, Splenda

Wegmans - In Heavy Syrup, In Pear Juice, Regular

Fruit Drinks... see Drinks/Juice

Fruit Leather

Stretch Island Fruit Co. - All Varieties

Trader Joe's - All Varieties

Fruit Salad

Dole - All Canned, Cups, Cups In Gel, Jar in Light Syrup *(Except Parfaits)*

Native Forest - Organic

Wegmans - Tropical In Light Syrup

Fruit Snacks... see also Snacks

Fruit Gushers

Rockin' Blue Raspberry

Triple Berry Shock/Passion Berry Punch

Fruitomic Punch

Force Berry Radical

Force Tropical Rage

Variety Pack (Strawberry Splash, Watermelon Blast, Tropical Flavors)

Watermelon Blast

Fruit Roll-Ups

Blastin' Berry Hot Colors

Electric Blue Raspberry

Flavor Wave

Strawberry

Strawberry Kiwi

Sunberry Burst

F
G

Tropical Tie-Dye
Variety Pack

G

Gai Lan... *All **Fresh** Fruits & Vegetables Are **Gluten-Free***
Garbanzo Beans... see Beans
Garlic... *All **Fresh** Fruits & Vegetables Are **Gluten-Free***
    Trader Joe's - Crushed
Garlic Powder... see Seasoning
Garlic Salt... see Seasoning
Gazpacho
    Trader Joe's - Garden Fresh, Regular
Gelatin Mix
    Albertsons - Gelatin Fruit Cups
    Hy-Vee -
        Gelatin (Cherry, Cranberry, Lemon, Lime, Orange, Raspberry, Strawberry)
        Sugar Free (Cherry, Cranberry, Orange, Raspberry, Strawberry)
    Kraft - Jello Brand (All Varieties)
    Laura Lynn - Gelatins RTE Dairy (All Items)
    Marsh Brand - Gelatins
    Meijer Brand -
      Gelatin Dessert
        Berry Blue
        Cherry
        Cranberry
        Grape
        Lime
        Orange
        Raspberry

    Strawberry

    Unflavored

    Wild Strawberry

  Sugar Free Gelatin Dessert

    Cherry

    Cranberry

    Lime

    Orange

    Raspberry

    Strawberry

Price Chopper - All Varieties

Royal - All Varieties

Safeway - All Flavors Instant Gelatins (Regular, Sugar Free)

Spartan Brand -

  Gelatin Dessert

    Berry Blue

    Cherry

    Cherry Sugar Free

    Lemon

    Lime

    Lime Sugar Free

    Orange (Regular, Sugar Free)

    Raspberry (Regular, Sugar Free)

    Strawberry (Regular, Sugar Free)

    Unflavored

Stop & Shop Brand -

  Gelatin (Cherry, Cranberry, Orange, Raspberry)

  Refrigerated (Gelatin Fun Pack, Rainbow Fruit Gelatin)

  Refrigerated Sugar Free Gelatin Fun Pack

Wegmans -

  Orange & Raspberry Variety Pack

G

Strawberry

Sugar Free (Cherry & Black Cherry, Orange & Raspberry, Strawberry)

Gin... *All **Distilled** Alcohol Is **Gluten-Free**[2]

Ginger

Trader Joe's - Crystallized Ginger

Wel-Pak - Sushi Ginger

Ginger Ale... see Soda Pop/Carbonated Beverages

Ginger Sauce

Troy's

Glaze

Daddy Sam's - Salmon Glaze

Litehouse - Dessert Glaze (Blueberry, Peach, Strawberry, Sugar Free Strawberry)

Grains

Arrowhead Mills - Amaranth, Hulled Millet, Quinoa

Bob's Red Mill -

Amaranth (Organic Amaranth, Regular) Grain

Quinoa Organic Grain

Teff Whole Grain

Grapefruit... *All **Fresh** Fruits & Vegetables Are **Gluten-Free**

Del Monte -

Canned Fruit (All Varieties)

Fruit Snack Cups (All Metal & Plastic Containers)

Grapes... *All **Fresh** Fruits & Vegetables Are **Gluten-Free**

Gravy/Gravy Mix

Maam - Miso Gravy

Massel - Gravy Mix (Brown Rich, Gravy)

Mayacamas - Brown, Chicken, Savory Herb, Turkey

Orgran - Gravy Mix

G

Pacific Natural Foods - Natural (Beef Flavored, Chicken, Mushroom Gravy, Turkey)

Road's End Organics - Gravy Mix (Golden, Savory Herb, Shiitake Mushroom)

Roux - Gravy Mix

Green Beans... see Beans

Green Olives... see Olives

Green Peppers... *All Fresh Fruits & Vegetables Are Gluten-Free*

Green Tea... see Tea

Greens... *All Fresh Fruits & Vegetables Are Gluten-Free*

Albertsons - Canned & Frozen Turnip Greens

Birds Eye - All Frozen Vegetables *(Except With Sauce)*

Bush's Best - Chopped Turnip Greens (Canned)

Laura Lynn - Canned (Chopped Collard Greens, Turnip Greens, Turnip Greens w/Diced Turnips), Chopped Mustard Greens

Meijer Brand - Chopped (Kale Greens, Turnip Greens), Mustard Greens

Pictsweet - All Plain Vegetables (Frozen)

Stop & Shop Brand - Collard Greens, Mustard Greens

Groats

Arrowhead Mills - Buckwheat

Pocono - Whole Buckwheat

Ground Beef...see Beef

All Fresh Meat Is Gluten-Free (Non-Marinated, Unseasoned)

Ground Turkey...see Turkey

All Fresh Meat Is Gluten-Free (Non-Marinated, Unseasoned)

Guacamole...see also Dip/Dip Mix

Trader Joe's - Avocados Number, E=Guaca Salsa, Fire Roasted, Regular

Gum... see Chewing Gum

H H

Ham

Applegate Farms - Uncured Ham (Black Forest, Organic, Regular)

Bar S - Chopped, Cooked

Black Label - Canned Hams

Boar's Head - All Varieties

Butcher's Cut - Shank Cut, Spiral Sliced *(Glaze Packet is NOT Gluten-Free)*

Carando - Spiral Ham (w/Rack, w/o Rack)

Carl Buddig - Baked Honey, Honey, Regular, Smoked

Cure81 - Ham (Bone-In, Boneless, Old Fashioned Spiral)

D&W Vac Pack Meats - Black Forest Smoked, Cooked, Gourmet Lite Virginia

Dietz & Watson -

Baked Champagne Honey

Black Forest (Cooked, Pear, Regular, Smoked)

Gourmet Lite Virginia

Maple Honey, Peppered

Eagle Valley -

Baked Honey Crust

Bavarian Ham Off The Bone (Brown Sugar & Cinnamon, Regular)

Honey

Light & Tasty

Maple

Premium Baked Pear Shaped

Premium Hot

Spiral Sliced

Virginia

Ejay's - Black Forest Ham Steak, Honey Ham Steak

Five Star Brand - Spiced Ham Roll
Giant Deli - Honey Ham
Girgenti - Hot Ham Capicola
Healthy Choice - Honey Maple, Virginia
Heavenly Ham - Without Glaze
Hormel -
   Black Label (Canned, Chopped, Ham Patties)
   Canned Ham Chunk Meats
   Deli Sliced (Black Forest, Cooked, Double Smoked, Honey, Prosciuto)
   Fully-Cooked Entrées (Glazed Ham w/Maple & Brown Sugar)
   Natural Choice (Cooked Deli, Honey Deli, Smoked Deli)
   Spiced
Hy-Vee -
   96% Sliced Cooked
   Brown Sugar Spiral Sliced
   Chopped
   Cooked
   Deli Thin Slices (Honey, Smoked)
   Ham & Cheese Loaf
   Honey & Spice Spiral Sliced
   Thin Sliced (Ham, Honey Ham)
Isaly's - Chipped Chopped Ham, Honey, Old Fashioned Deli
Jennie-O - Turkey Ham
Krakus - Imported Polish Ham
Meijer Brand -
   97% Fat Free (Sliced Cooked Ham, Honey Ham)
   Double Smoked
   Honey Roasted
   Sliced Chipped
   Ham Meat

H

Russer - Light Cooked, Virginia
Safeway - Primo Taglio Ham (All Varieties), Shank Cut Ham
Smithfield -
　Chopped
　Cooked
　Lean Generation (Honey Cure, Maple)
　Spiral Ham (w/Rack, w/o Rack)
SPAM - Classic, Less Sodium, Lite
Stop & Shop Brand -
　Cooked Ham (97% Fat Free, w/Natural Juices 98% Fat Free)
　Danish Brand Ham w/Natural Juices 97% Fat Free
Trader Joe's - Healthy, Spiral w/Glaze Pack
Underwood Spreads - Deviled
Wegmans - w/Natural Juices Thin Sliced (Ham, Smoked, Smoked Honey)
Wellesley Farms - Spiral Ham (w/Rack, w/o Rack)
Wellshire Farms -
　Black Forest (Boneless Nugget, Deli, Sliced)
　Buffet Half
　Old Fashioned Boneless (Half, Whole)
　Salt Cured Cafe Slices
　Semi-Boneless Half
　Sliced (Capicola, Mortadella, Tavern, Turkey)
　Sunday Breakfast
　Turkey
　Turkey Steak
　Virginia Brand (Boneless Steak, Buffet, Sliced)
Hamburgers... *All **Fresh** Meat Is **Gluten-Free (Non-Marinated, Unseasoned)***
　Butcher's Cut - Beef Burgers
　Jennie-O - Frozen Turkey Burgers

Wellshire Farms - All Natural Beef Hamburgers

Hash Browns... see Potatoes

Hearts Of Palm... *All **Fresh** Fruits & Vegetables Are **Gluten-Free***

  Del Monte -

    Canned Fruit (All Varieties)

    Fruit Snack Cups (All Metal & Plastic Containers)

  Native Forest - Organic Hearts Of Palm

Herbal Tea... see Tea

Hoisin Sauce

  Premier Japan - Wheat Free

Hollandaise Sauce

  Mayacamas

  Winn Dixie

Hominy

  Bush's Best - Golden, White

  Hy-Vee - Golden, White

  Safeway - White

Honey

  Albertsons - Honey

  B&J - US Premium Clover Honey

  Hy-Vee - Honey, Honey Squeeze Bear

  Meijer Brand - Honey, Honey Squeeze Bear

  Safeway - Creamed, Pure

  Spartan Brand - Honey Squeeze Bear, Pure Clover

  Trader Joe's - Honey

  Wegmans - Clover, Honey Orange Blossom, Squeezable
    Bear Clover Honey

Honey Mustard Sauce

  Mr. Spice

  Safeway Select

Horseradish Sauce
>   Baxters
>   Di Lusso
>   **Wegmans** - Horseradish Cream

Hot Chocolate Mix... see Cocoa Mix

Hot Dogs... see Sausage

Hot Sauce
>   **365 Organic Every Day Value** - Hot Pepper Sauce
>   **Bayou** - Hot Sauce
>   **Frank's RedHot** - Buffalo Wing, Chile 'N Lime, Original, Xtra Hot
>   **Hy-Vee** - Hot Picante Sauce (Hot, Medium, Mild)
>   **Mr. Spice** - Tangy Bang! Hot
>   **The Wizard's** - Hot Stuff
>   **UB The Everything Sauce** - Not So Spicy, Spicy

Hotdog Buns... see Buns

Hummus
>   **Athenos** - All Varieties
>   Azars
>   Casbah
>   **Fantastic World Foods** - Garbanzo, Original
>   **Trader Joe's** - All Varieties
>   **Tribe Mediterranean Foods** - All Natural Hummus (All Varieties)
>   **Wildwood Harvest** - All Varieties *(Except Roasted Pepper)*

Ice Cream... includes Sherbet, Sorbet
>   **365 Every Day Value** -
>   French Vanilla

I

    Mint Chocolate Chip

    Peppermint

    Soy Cream (Chocolate, Vanilla)

    Vanilla

Alpine Ice - Sorbet (Bolder Berry, Hibiscus Rose, Mango Passion, Plum Lucky)

Breyer's -

    Chocolate

    Maple Walnut

    Smart Scoop (Black Cherry, Strawberry)

    Strawberry

    Vanilla

Chapman's -

    Canadian Vanilla

    Frozen Yogurt (Cappuccino, Mixed Berry, Vanilla)

    Mint Chip

    No Sugar (Butterscotch Ripple, Dutch Chocolate)

    Strawberry & Vanilla

    Vanilla

Edy's -

    Grand

        Almond Praline

        Andes Cool Mint

        Butter Pecan

        Caramel Delight

        Cherry (Chocolate Chip, Vanilla)

        Chocolate (Caramel Swirl, Chip, Fudge Chunk, Fudge Sundae, Regular)

        Coffee

        Double Vanilla

        Dulce de Leche

Espresso Chip
French (Canilla, Vanilla)
Fudge (Swirl, Tracks)
Mint Chocolate Chip
Neapolitan
Nestle Turtle Sundae
Peanut Butter Cup
Real Strawberry
Rocky Road
Spumoni
Toffee Bar Crunch
Ultimate Caramel Cup
Vanilla (Bean, Chocolate, Regular)
Slow Churned
Almond Praline
Chips
Mocha Almond Fudge
Neapolitan
Peanut Butter Cup
Raspberry Chip Royale
Rocky Road
Strawberry
Vanilla (Bean, Chocolate, Regular)
Gaga's - Sherbetter (Chocolate, Lemon, Orange, Raspberry)
Haagen-Dazs -
Frozen Yogurt
Coffee
Dulce de Leche
Strawberry
Strawberry Banana Swirl
Vanilla (Raspberry Swirl, Regular)

I

Ice Cream
  Almond Hazelnut Swirl
  Banana Split
  Black (Raspberry Chip, Walnut)
  Butter Pecan
  Cherry Vanilla
  Chocolate (Chocolate Chip, Peanut Butter, Regular)
  Coffee
  Crème Brulée
  Dulce de Leche
  English Toffee
  Limited Edition Eggnog
  Macadamia Brittle
  Mango
  Mayan Chocolate
  Mint Chip
  Mocha Almond Fudge
  Peaches & Cream
  Pineapple Coconut
  Pistachio
  Rocky Road
  Rum Raisin
  Strawberry
  Swiss Almond
  Vanilla (Bean, Chocolate Chip, Fudge)
  White Chocolate Raspberry
Ice Cream Bars
  Chocolate & Dark Chocolate
  Coffee & Almond Crunch
  Dulce de Leche
  Mint & Dark Chocolate

Raspberry & Vanilla
Vanilla (& Almonds, & Dark Chocolate, & Milk Chocolate)
Light
  Cherry Fudge Truffle
  Coffee
  Dulce de Leche
  Dutch Chocolate Chip
  Mint Chip
  Vanilla Bean
Sorbet
  Chocolate
  Mango
  Orchard Peach
  Raspberry
  Strawberry
  Tropical
  Zesty Lemon
Hy-Vee -
  Ice Cream Bars
    Assorted Twin Pops
    Chocolate & Strawberry Sundae Cups
    Freedom Pops
    Fudge Bars (Fat Free No Sugar Added, Regular)
    Galaxy Reduced Fat
    Grape
    Orange
    Pops-Cherry
  Regular
    Butter Crunch
    Cherry Nut (Light, Regular)
    Chocolate

I

Chocolate Chip (Light, Regular)
Chocolate Marshmallow
Flavored (Chocolate, Vanilla)
Dutch Chocolate Light
Fudge Marble
Mint Chip
Neapolitan (Light, Regular)
New York Vanilla
Orange Blossom Ice Cream & Sherbet
Peanut Butter Fudge
Peppermint
Sherbet (Lime, Orange, Pineapple, Rainbow, Raspberry)
Strawberry
Vanilla Light

It's Soy Delicious -
Almond Pecan
Awesome Chocolate
Black Leopard
Carob Peppermint
Chocolate (Almond, Peanut Butter)
Espresso
Green Tea
Mango Raspberry
Pistachio Almond
Raspberry
Tiger Chai
Vanilla (Fudge, Regular)

Lucerne -
Ice Cream Bars
Fudge
Orange

Root Beer Float

Toffee Brittle

Vanilla (Sherbet, Sundae)

Mapleton's Organic -

Cappuccino

Chocolate

French Vanilla

Frozen Yogurt (Lemon, Raspberry, Strawberry, Vanilla)

Vanilla Chocolate Chip

Marsh Brand - Vanilla, Fudge Swirl, Rainbow Sherbet, Strawberry Swirl

Meijer Brand -

Awesome Strawberry

Brr Bar

Black Cherry

Butter Pecan (Lite No Sugar Added w/Splenda, Meijer Gold Georgian Bay, Original)

Candy Bar Swirl

Caramel Pecan (Fat Free No Sugar Added)

Chocolate (Bordeaux Cherry, Carb Conquest, Chocolate Chip, Chocolate Peanut Butter Fudge, Chocolate Thunder, Meijer Gold Double Nut Chocolate, Mint, Original)

Combo Cream

Cotton Candy

Dream Bars

Dulce De Delche

Fudge Bars (No Sugar Added, Original)

Fudge Swirl

Heavenly Hash

Ice Cream Bars

Juice Stix

■

Mackinaw Fudge

Meijer Gold (Caramel Toffee Swirl, Peanut Butter Fudge Swirl, Peanut Butter Fudge Tracks, Thunder Bay Cherry)

Neapolitan (Lite, Original)

Novelties (Gold Bar, Toffee Bar)

Orange Glider

Party Pops (No Sugar Added Assorted, Orange/Cherry/Grape, RB/B/BR)

Peppermint

Praline Pecan

Red

Scooperman

Sherbet (Cherry, Lemonberry Twist, Lime, Orange, Pineapple, Rainbow)

Tin Roof

Twin Pops

Vanilla (Carb Conquest, Fat Free No Sugar Added w/Splenda Golden, Lite No Sugar Added w/Splenda, Meijer Gold Victorian, Original)

White & Blue Pops

Midwest Country Fare - Chocolate (Chip, Regular), Neapolitan, Vanilla (Light, Regular)

Mountain Pride - Butter Pecan, Chocolate Chip Mint, French Vanilla (Regular, Light)

Natural Choice - Full of Fruit Bars, Sorbets

Organic So Delicious -

Creamy Bars (Fudge, Orange, Raspberry, Vanilla)

Quarts (Chocolate (Peanut Butter, Velvet), Creamy Vanilla, Dulce De Leche, Mint Marble Fudge, Mocha Fudge, Neapolitan, Peanut Butter, Strawberry, Twisted Vanilla Orange)

Vanilla & Almond Bars

Purely Decadent -
Dairy Free Pints
Cherry Nirvana
Chocolate Obsession
Mint Chocolate Chip
Mocha Almond Fudge
Peanut Butter Zig Zag
Praline Pecan
Purely Vanilla
Rocky Road
Swinging Anna Banana
Turtle Tracks
Vanilla Swiss Almond
Bars
Purely Vanilla Bar
Vanilla Almond Bar
Safeway Select -
Fat Free Ice Cream (Caramel Swirl, No Sugar Added Vanilla)
Fruit Bars (All Flavors)
Caramel Caribou
Chocolate Chunk
Dutch Chocolate
Light Peppermint
Mother Load
Sherbet
Sorbet (Chocolate, Raspberry)
Shamrock Farms -
Carmelback Mountain
Grand Butter Pecanyon
Peppermint Stick Forest
Rocky Route 66

Showlow Carb Butter Pecan

Snowbowl Vanilla

Skondra's - Caramel Pecan Lite

Spartan Brand -

Black Cherry

Butter Pecan

Chocolate

French Vanilla

Golden Vanilla

Mackinac Island Fudge

Mint Chocolate Chip

Moose Tracks

Neapolitan

Peanut Butter Cup

Vanilla (Low Fat, Regular)

Stoney Creek Diary - Naturelle Plus (Dutch Chocolate, French Vanilla)

Stoneyfield Farms -

After Dark Chocolate

Javalanche

Mint Chocolate Chip

Vanilla (Fudge Swirl Frozen Yogurt, Regular)

Stop & Shop Brand -

GV Ice Cream

Chocolate (& Marshmallow)

Fudge Royal

Neapolitan

Rainbow Sherbet

Vanilla (Orange, Regular)

Ice Cream

Butterscotch Ripple

I

      Chocolate Chip
      Coffee
      Country Club
      Heavenly Hash
      Neapolitan
      Peppermint Stick
      Strawberry
      Vanilla (Fudge Swirl, Regular)
   Natural Ice Cream
      Butter Pecan
      Chocolate (Chip, Reugalr)
      Coffee
      French Vanilla
      Mint Chocolate Chip
      Mocha Almond
      Strawberry
      Refrigerated Rainbow Parfait
      Vanilla (Bean, Fudge Ripple)

The Skinny Cow -

   Fudge Bar (Fat Free, No Sugar Added Fat Free)
   Philly Swirl (Fudge Swirl Stix, Sorbet Philly Swirl Stix, Sugar Free Swirl Popperz, Swirl Stix, The Original Italian Ice Swirl)

Wegmans -

   Assorted Fruity Pops (Regular (Cherry, Grape Flavors, Orange), Sugar Free (Cherry, Grape, Orange))
   All Natural (Chocolate, Coffee Explosion, French Vanilla, Mint Chocolate Chip, Neapolitan, Vanilla (& Fudge)
   Black Raspberry
   Café Latte w/Whipped Cream Flavored Ripple Coffee
   Chocolate (Chip, Marshmallow, Regular, Vanilla)

I

Crème De Menthe

Egg Nog Flavored

French Roast Coffee

French Vanilla

Hazelnut Chip Coffee

Heavenly Hash

Ice Cream Bars (Cherry w/Dark Chocolate, Fudge (& No Sugar Added), Vanilla & Dark Chocolate Premium)

Ice Cream Cups (Ice, Peanut Butter Candy Sundae Cups)

Low Fat (Cappuccino Chip, Chocolate Indulgence, Mint Chip, Praline Pecan, Raspberry Truffle, Vanilla)

Maple Walnut

Neopolitan

Peak Of Perfection (Black Cherry, Blueberry, Mango, Peach, Raspberry, Strawberry)

Peanut Butter (Cup, Sundae, Swirl)

Pistachio Vanilla Swirl

Premium (Chocolate Caramel, Peanut Butter Cup, Vanilla)

Raspberry Cashew Swirl

Strawberry

Super Premium (Butter Pecan, Cherry Armagnac, Chocolate, Coconut Mango, Creamy Caramel, Crème Brulée, French Roast, Hazelnut Chip, Jamocha Almond Fudge, Rum Raisin, Peanut Butter & Jelly)

Tin Roof

Vanilla

Vanilla Raspberry Sorbet

Vanilla w/Orange Sherbet

Venetian Cappuccino-ITC

Winn Dixie -

2 Assorted Pops

Butter Pecan

I
J

Chocolate

Classic Chocolate Low Fat

Classic Vanilla Low Fat

Cream Bars

Prestige (Cherry Vanilla, Chocolate Almond, French Vanilla)

Rainbow Sherbet

Strawberry

Vanilla

Ice Cream Toppings... see also Syrup

Smucker's - All Milk & Chocolate Ice Cream Toppings *(Except Sundae Syrup Toppings & Sundae Toppings)*

Hershey's - Chocolate Syrup

Iced Tea/Iced Tea Mix... see Tea

Icing... see Baking Decorations

Instant Coffee... see Coffee

Italian Dressing... see Salad Dressing

J

Jalfrazi

Tamarind Tree - Vegetable Jalfrazi

Jam/Jelly

365 Every Day Value -

Fruit Spread

Apricot

Black Cherry

Blackberry

Forest

Raspberry

Strawberry

Wild Blueberry

Albertsons - All Jelly, Jams & Preserves

Baxters -

Jelly (Beetroot in Red Currant, Cranberry, Mint, Red Currant)

Marmalade (Orange/Lemon & Grapefruit, Thick Cut Seville Orange)

Preserves (Blackcurrant, Raspberry, Rhubarb & Ginger, Strawberry)

Bionaturae - Fruit Spread (All Varieties)

Deep South - Jellies, Preserves (All Varieties)

Dorothy Lane Market - All Jams & Preserves

Eden - Apple Cherry Sauce

Food Club - Apricot, Grape (Jam, Jelly), Peach, Strawberry

Full Circle - Fruit Spread (Raspberry, Strawberry)

Laura Lynn -

Grape Jam

Jelly (Apple, Grape)

Orange Marmalade

Peanut Butter & Grape Jelly Spread

Peanut Butter & Strawberry Jelly Spread

Preserves (Apricot, Peach, Red Raspberry, Strawberry)

Marsh Brand - All Varieties

Nature's Promise - Organic (Grape Jelly, Raspberry Fruit Spread, Strawberry Fruit Spread)

Polaner - All Fruit, Jams, Jellies, Preserves

Safeway Select - Jams/Jellies

Smucker's - All Jams, Jellies, Preserves, Marmalades

Stop & Shop Brand -

Concord Grape Jelly (Spreadable, Squeezable)

Jelly (Apple, Currant, Mint)

Preserves (Apricot, Grape, Peach, Pineapple, Red Raspberry, Seedless Blackberry, Strawberry)

J

Orange Marmalade

Simply Enjoy (Red Pepper Jelly, Roasted Garlic & Onion Jam)

Simply Enjoy Preserves (Balsamic Sweet Onion, Blueberry, Raspberry Champagne Peach, Spiced Apple, Strawberry)

Spread (Apricot, Blueberry, Strawberry)

Squeezable Grape Jelly

Sugar Free Preserves (Apricot, Blackberry, Red Raspberry, Strawberry)

Trader Joe's - James Keiller & Son Dundee Orange Marmalade, Preserves (Fresh Fruit, Organic Reduced Sugar)

Wegmans -

Fruit Spread

Apricot/Peach/Passion Fruit

Blueberry Cherry/Raspberry

Raspberry/Strawberry/Blackberry

Raspberry/Wild Blueberry/Blackberry

Strawberry/Plum/Raspberry

Gourmet Preserves

California Peach

Northwest Strawberry

Oregon Red Raspberry

Jelly

Apple

Blackberry

Cherry

Grape

Mint Apple

Red Currant

Red Raspberry

Strawberry

Just Fruit Spread
  Apricot
  Blueberry
  Red Raspberry
  Strawberry
Preserves
  Apricot
  Blackberry-Seedless
  Cherry
  Grape
  Orange Marmalade Peach
  Pineapple
  Red Raspberry
  Strawberry
Sugar Free Fruit Spread
  Apricot/Peach/Passion Fruit
  Raspberry/Wild Blueberry/Blackberry
  Strawberry/Plum/Raspberry
Welch's - All Jams & Jellies
Winn Dixie - All Jellies & Preserves

Jerky

Applegate Farms - Pork Joy Stick
Double B - Beef Jerky (Smoked Applewood, Spicy Pecan)
Golden Valley - Natural Beef Jerky (Jerky Sweet, Original, Peppered, Spicy)
Hormel - Dried Beef
Hy-Vee - Original
Old Wisconsin - All Varieties
Rustler's - Beef Jerky, Spicy Flavor Beef Stick
Safeway - Original, Peppered

J
K

  Shelton's - Free Range Turkey Jerky (Hot Turkey, Regular), Turkey Stick Pepperoni

  Wellshire Farms - Snack Sticks (Hot n' Spicy, Matt's Beef Pepperoni, Turkey Tom Tom)

Juice... see Drinks/Juice

Juice Mix... see Drinks/Juice

K

Kale... *All Fresh Fruits & Vegetables Are Gluten-Free*

  Pictsweet - All Plain Vegetables (Frozen)

  Stop & Shop Brand

Kasha

  Pocono

  Shiloh Farms - Organic

Kefir

  Lifeway - All Varieties

Kernels

  Bob's Red Mill - Organic Buckwheat Kernels

Ketchup

  365 Every Day Value - Ketchup, Organic Ketchup

  Annie's Naturals - Organic Ketchup

  Food Club

  Full Circle

  Heinz Ketchup - Hot & Spicy Kick'rs, No Sodium Added, One Carb, Organic, Regular

  Hy-Vee - Regular, Squeezable

  Kurtz

  Manischewitz

  Midwest Country Fare

  Price Chopper

  Safeway

    Shaw's
    Spartan Brand - Ketchup (Regular, Squeeze)
    Thrifty Maid
    Tops
    Trader Joe's - Organic Ketchup
    Walden Farms
    Wild Oats - Organic Ketchup
    Winn Dixie
    Woodstock Farms

Kielbasa... see Sausage
Kiwi... *All *Fresh* Fruits & Vegetables Are *Gluten-Free*
Kohlrabi.... *All *Fresh* Fruits & Vegetables Are *Gluten-Free*
Korma
    Amy's - Indian Vegetable
    Taj Ethnic Gourmet - Vegetable
    Tamarind Tree - Navratan

L

Lamb... *All *Fresh* Meat Is *Gluten-Free (Non-Marinated, Unseasoned)*
    Trader Joe's - Australian Lamb Chops, Seasoned Rack of Lamb
Lasagna/Lasagne
    Amy's - Garden Vegetable
Lasagna/Lasagne Noodles... see Pasta
Lemonade... see Drinks
Lemons... *All *Fresh* Fruits & Vegetables Are *Gluten-Free*
    Sunkist
Lentils
    365 Organic Every Day Value - Organic
    Tasty Bite - Bengal, Bombay Potatoes & Madras Lentil,
       Jodphur, Madras

Lettuce... *All **Fresh** Fruits & Vegetables Are **Gluten-Free***

Licorice... see Candy

Limeade... see Drinks

Limes... *All **Fresh** Fruits & Vegetables Are **Gluten-Free***

>   Sunkist

Liquid Aminos

>   **Bragg -** Liquid Aminos

Liver... *All **Fresh** Meat Is **Gluten-Free (Non-Marinated, Unseasoned)***

Liverwurst

>   **Dietz & Watson**

>   **Old Wisconsin -** All Varieties

>   **Wellshire Farms -** Liverwurst (Pork, Turkey)

Lunch Meat... see Deli Meat

M

Macaroni & Cheese

>   **Amy's -** Rice Mac & Cheese

>   **Annie's -** Rice Pasta & Cheddar

>   **Heartland's Finest -** Cheddar Macaroni & Cheese

>   **Land's End Organics -** Penne & Cheese

>   **Namaste Foods**

>   **Pastariso -** Macaroni & White Cheese

>   **Road's End Organics -** Penne & Cheese

Macaroons... see Cookies

Mackerel... *All **Fresh** Fish Is **Gluten-Free (Non-Marinated, Unseasoned)***

>   **Chicken Of The Sea -** All Varieties

>   **Crown Prince -** Mackerel

Mahi Mahi... *All **Fresh** Fish Is **Gluten-Free (Non-Marinated, Unseasoned)***

Makhani

> **Tamarind Tree** - Dal Makhani

Mandarin Oranges... *All **Fresh** Fruits & Vegetables Are **Gluten-Free***

> **365 Every Day Value** - In Light Syrup

> **Albertsons**

> **Del Monte -**

>> Canned Fruit (All Varieties)

>> Fruit Snack Cups (All Metal & Plastic Containers)

> **Dole** - All Canned, Cups, Cups In Gel, Jar in Light Syrup *(Except Parfaits)*

> **Hy-Vee** - Fruit Cups

> **Meijer** - Light Syrup

> **Trader Joe's** - In Light Syrup

> **Wegmans**

Mango... *All **Fresh** Fruits & Vegetables Are **Gluten-Free***

> **Del Monte -**

>> Canned Fruit (All Varieties)

>> Fruit Snack Cups (All Metal & Plastic Containers)

> **Meijer Brand** - Slices

> **Native Forest** - Organic Mango Chunks

> **Stop & Shop Brand** - Mango

> **Trader Joe's** - Mango Passion Exotique

Maple Syrup... see Syrup

Maraschino Cherries... see Cherries

Margarine... see Spread and/or Butter

Marinades

> **Annie's Naturals** - Organic Smokey Tomato

> **Consorzio -**

>> Baja Lime

>> Lemon Pepper

>> Roasted Garlic & Balsamic

M

Southwestern w/Smoked Chipotles

Tropical Grill

Emeril's - Basting Sauce & Marinade, Herbed Lemon Pepper

Food Club - 30 Minute Marinades (Herb & Garlic, Lemon Pepper, Mesquite)

Hendrickson's - Unique Dressing Marinade & Seasoning

Hy-Vee - Citrus Grill, Herb & Garlic, Lemon Pepper, Mesquite

Jack Daniel's EZ Marinader - Garlic & Herb Variety, Teriyaki Variety

LaChoy - Teriyaki Marinade & Sauce

McCormick - Grill Mates BBQ Marinade

Meijer Brand - Garlic & Herb, Lemon, Pepper Mesquite

Tops - Mesquite

Wegmans -

Chicken BBQ

Citrus Dill

Fajita

Greek

Honey Mustard

Lemon & Garlic

Rosemary Balsamic

Steakhouse Peppercorn

Zesty Savory

Zesty Thai

Wild Oats -

Organic

Lime Cilantro

Madras Curry

Smokey Chipotle

Wild Wasabi

Marmalade... see Jam/Jelly

Marsala
>**Taj Ethnic Gourmet** - Bean Marsala
>**Wegmans** - Mushroom Marsala Sauce

Marshmallow Dip
>**Walden Farms** - No Carb Marshmallow Dip

Marshmallows
>**Albertsons**
>**Hy-Vee** - Colored Miniatures, Miniature, Regular
>**Laura Lynn**
>**Lunar Mallows -** Marshmallows (Mini, Regular)
>**Manischewitz**
>**Marsh Brand**
>**Marshmallow Fluff -** All Varieties
>**Meijer Brand** - Mini, Mini Flavored, Regular
>**Safeway**
>**Shaw's**
>**Spartan Brand -** Mini, Miniature Color, Regular

Masala
>**A Taste of India** - Rice Masala
>**Green Guru** - Paneer Tikka
>**Stop & Shop Brand -** Tikka Masala
>**Taj Ethnic Gourmet** - Chicken
>**Tamarind Tree** - Channa Dal Masala
>**Tasty Bite** - Beans Masala & Basmati Rice
>**Trader Joe's** - Chicken, Simmer, Tandoori
>**Whole Kitchen** - Chicken Tikka Masala Entrée

Mashed Potatoes
>**Alexia** - Red Potatoes w/Garlic & Parmesan, Yukon Gold
>   Potatoes & Sea Salt
>**Barbara's Bakery**

Fantastic Foods - Broccoli & Cheddar, Garlic & Herb, Sour Cream & Chives, White Cheddar Cheese

Hy-Vee - Four Cheese, Instant, Roasted Garlic, Sour Cream & Chives

Laura Lynn - Herb & Garlic, Regular, Roasted Garlic, Sour Cream & Chives

Manischewitz - Chicken Flavor Instant

Meijer - Instant Mashed Potatoes

O'Day's

Safeway - Instant Mashed Potatoes (Herb/Butter, Roasted Garlic)

Spartan Brand - Butter & Herb, Instant, Roasted Garlic

Trader Joe's - Garlic Mashed Potatoes

Mayonnaise

Albertsons

B&J - Real Mayonnaise, Squeeze Real Mayonnaise

Best Foods - All Mayonnaise

Cain's - All Natural Mayonnaise

Di Lusso - Mayo, Sandwich Spread

Enlighten

Ex. Choice

Follow Your Heart - Vegenaise (All Varieties)

French's GourMayo - Sundried Tomato, Wasabi Horseradish

Hellmann's - Canola, Light, Real, Reduced Fat

Hy-Vee - Mayonnaise (Regular, Squeezable), Sandwich Spread

Laura Lynn - Fat Free, Regular

Manischewitz

Miracle Whip

Nasoya - Nayonaise

Safeway Select - Fat Free Distilled w/Wood, Reduced Fat, Regular

M

Spectrum -

Canola Mayo

Eggless-Vegan Light

Eggless Light Canola Mayo

Omega-3 Mayo w/Flax Oil

Organic (Dijon Mayo, Mayo, Olive Oil Mayo, Roasted Garlic Mayo, Wasabi Mayo)

Squeeze Bottle (Canola, Eggless Light Canola, Organic)

Trader Joe's - Real, Reduced Fat, Wasabi Mayo

Wegmans - Classic, Light, Original

Whole Pantry - Canola Mayonnaise

Winn Dixie - Lite, Regular

Meals

A Taste of Thai - Quick Meal (Coconut Ginger Noodles, Peanut Noodles, Red Curry Noodles)

Dinty Moore - Microwave Meals (Scalloped Potatoes & Ham, Rice w/Chicken)

Gluten-Free Pantry -

Pasta Fagioli Skillet Meal

Stroganoff Skillet Meal

Sweet N Sour Noodle Skillet Meal

Szechwan Noodle Skillet Meal

Tex Mex Skillet Meal

Homestyle Meals - Frozen Fully Cooked Baby Back Ribs, Pork Baby Back w/BBQ Sauce

Kid's Kitchen - Beans & Weiners

Mrs. Leepers -

Beef Lasagna Dinner

Beef Stroganoff Dinner

Cheeseburger Mac Dinner

Chicken Alfredo

M

Creamy Tuna Dinner

Old El Paso -

Complete Skillet Meal (Crunchy Enchilada Style Rice & Chicken)

Dinner Kit (Southwestern Style Taco, Stand 'N Stuff Taco, Taco)

Tasty Bite -

Beans Masala & Basmati Rice

Bombay Potatoes

Jaipur Vegetables

Kashmir Spinach

Madras Lentils

Peas Paneer & Basmati Rice

Punjab Eggplant

Spinach Dal & Basmati Rice

Sprouts Curry & Basmati Rice

Thai Kitchen -

Original Pad Thai

Stir-Fry Rice Noodle Meal Kit (Lemongrass & Chili, Original Pad Thai, Pad Thai w/Chili, Thai Peanut)

Meatballs

Aidells - Chipotle Meatballs, Sun-Dried Tomato Meatballs, Teriyaki & Pineapple Meatballs

Melon... *All **Fresh** Fruits & Vegetables Are **Gluten-Free***

Milk

365 Organic Every Day Value - Organic Milk (Fat Free Skim, Low Fat 1%)

Borden Eagle Brand - Sweetened Condensed Milk

Carnation - Sweetened Condensed Milk

Coburn Farms - Evaporated Milk

Garelick - Naturals Colossal Coffee Lowfat Milk, Ultimate Chocolate Lowfat Milk

Health Market Organic - 1% Low Fat Milk, 2% Milk, Skim Milk, Whole Milk

Hood - All Hood Brand Fluid Milk (All Fat Levels), Chocolate (Full Fat, Low Fat)

Hy-Vee -
  1/2%
  1%, 1% Low Fat
  2%, 2% Reduced Fat
  Evaporated Milk
  Fat Free Evaporated
  Fat Free Skim
  Half & Half
  Instant Nonfat Dry Milk
  Skim Milk
  Sweetened Condensed
  Vitamin D

Kemp's - Chocolate Milk

Lactaid - All Varieties

Laura Lynn -
  Evaporated
  Half & Half
  Instant Dry
  Lactose Reduced
  Sweetened Condensed

Lifeway - All Products

Lucerne - Chocolate, Half & Half

Meijer Brand -
  1/2% Lowfat
  1% Lowfat
  2% Reduced Fat
  Chocolate (1%)

Evaporated (Lite Skimmed, Small, Tall)

Fat Free

Instant

Lactose Free Milk (2% w/Calcium, Fat Free w/Calcium)

Milk Sweetened Condensed

Strawberry Milk

Ultra Pasteurized Heavy Half & Half

Vitamin D

Nature's Promise -

Chocolate Soymilk

Organic (1%, 2%, Chocolate Soymilk, Fat Free, Soymilk, Vanilla Soymilk, Whole)

Ricemilk

Vanilla Ricemilk

Pet - Evaporated Milk

Price Chopper - Evaporated, Soy Milk

Safeway -

Milk Drinks

Chillin Chocolate

Marvelous

Mocha Cappuccino

Sweetened Condensed

Vanilla Shake

Very Berry Strawberry

Simply Smart - Fat Free, Half & Half, Low Fat

Spartan Brand -

.5%

1% Low Fat

2% Reduced Fat

Chocolate 1%

Evaporated (Skim Tall, Tall)

M

Ex-light

Homogenized

Powdered Instant

Skim

Sweetened Condensed

Stop & Shop Brand -

Half & Half (Fat Free, Pasteurized, Ultra Pasteurized)

Lactose Free (Calcium Fortified Fat Free, Whole)

Low Fat

Skim

Ultra Pasteurized Cream (Heavy Whipping, Light, Sweetened Whipped Light, Whipping)

Whole

Trader Joe's - Shelf Stable Organic 2% Reduced Fat Chocolate

Wegmans -

1%

2%

Chocolate

Evaporated Milk (Fat Free, Regular)

Fat Free Skim (Regular, Rich-Calcium Fortified)

Half & Half (Fresh, Ultra)

Homogenized

Low Fat Chocolate

Skim Rich

Sweetened Condensed

Winn Dixie - 1%, 2%, Chocolate, Cultured Nonfat Buttermilk, Fat Free, Homogenized

Yoo-Hoo - All Varieties

Mints

Safeway - Dessert, Star Light

Vermints - Café Express, Chai, Gingermint, Peppermint, Wintermint

M

Miso

    South River - Sweet Brown Rice, Sweet White

    Westbrae - Organic Unpasteurized (Brown Rice, White)

Mixed Fruit... *All **Fresh** Fruits & Vegetables Are **Gluten-Free***

    Del Monte -

        Canned Fruit (All Varieties)

        Fruit Snack Cups (All Metal & Plastic Containers)

    Dole - All Canned, Cups, Cups In Gel, Jar in Light Syrup *(Except Parfaits)*

    Hy-Vee - Lite (Chunk Mixed Fruit, Fruit Cocktail), Mixed Fruit Cups

    Meijer Brand - Fruit Mix (Chunky Juice, In Juice), Mixed Fruit (Individually Quick Frozen, Regular)

    Stop & Shop Brand - Fruit Mix In Heavy Syrup, Mixed Fruit, Very Cherry Fruit Mix In Light Syrup

    Spartan Brand - Frozen Fruit Mixed Bowls Heavy Syrup

    Wegmans

Mixed Vegetables... *All **Fresh** Fruits & Vegetables Are **Gluten-Free***

    365 Every Day Value - Frozen (California Blend, Mixed Vegetables)

    365 Organic Every Day Value - Frozen (Mixed Vegetables)

    B&J - Frozen (California Blend Vegetables, Mixed Vegetables)

    Birds Eye - All Frozen Vegetables **(Except With Sauce)**

    Del Monte - All Varieties

    Freshlike - Frozen Plain Vegetables *(Except Pasta Combos and Seasoned Blends)*

    Grand Selections -

        Frozen

            Caribbean Blend Vegetables

            Normandy Blend Vegetables

            Riviera Blend Vegetables

Green Giant -
  Frozen
    Baby Vegetable Medley Seasoned
    Garden Vegetable Medley Seasoned
    Mixed Vegetables
    Simply Steam Seasoned Garden Vegetable Medley
    Southwestern Style
Haggen - Mixed Vegetables
Hy-Vee -
  Canned Mixed Vegetables
  Frozen
    California Blend
    California Mix
    Italian Blend
    Mixed Vegetables
    Oriental Vegetables
    Winter Mix
Laura Lynn - Mixed Vegetables (No Salt, Regular)
Marsh Brand - Mixed Vegetables
Meijer Brand -
  Frozen
    California Style
    Chilies Diced Mild Mexican Style
    Fiesta
    Florentine
    Italian
    Mexican
    Mixed Vegetables
    Oriental
    Parisian Style
    Stew Mix

M

Midwest Country Fare - Frozen (California Blend, Mixed Vegetables)

Pictsweet - All Plain Vegetables (Frozen)

S&W - All Varieties

Spartan Brand - Mixed Vegetables

Stop & Shop Brand -

Country Blend

Latino Blend

Mixed Vegetables (No Added Salt, Regular)

Stew Vegetables

Wegmans - Mixed Vegetables, Promise Organic Mixed Vegetables, Ranchero Blend

Wild Oats Label - Organic Frozen Mixed Vegetable

Mochi

Grainaissance - All Varieties

Molasses

Brer Rabbit - Blackstrap Molasses, Full Flavor, Mild

Mousse

Orgran - Chocolate Mousse Mix

Muffin/Muffin Mix

Authentic Foods - Blueberry Muffin Mix, Chocolate Chip Muffin Mix

Cause You're Special - Classic Muffin & Quickbread Mix

Ener-G - Brown Rice English Muffins w/(Sweet Potato, Tofu)

Foods By George - Biscotti, Muffins (Blueberry, Corn)

Gluten-Free Pantry - Bran Muffin Mix, Muffin & Scone Mix, Yankee Cornbread & Muffin Mix

Hodgson - Apple Cinnamon Muffin Mix

Kinnikinnick - Cornbread & Muffin Mix, Muffin Mix

Orgran - Muffin Mix (Chocolate, Lemon & Poppyseed)

Really Good Foods - Muffin Mix (Apple Spice, Cornbread, Maple Raisin, Vanilla)

Whole Foods Market - Gluten-Free Bakehouse (Blueberry Muffins, Cherry Almond Streusel Muffins, Morning Glory Muffin)

Mushrooms... *All Fresh Fruits & Vegetables Are Gluten-Free*

B&J - Marinated Imported, Pieces & Stems, Sliced (Glass Jar)

Birds Eye - All Frozen Vegetables *(Except With Sauce)*

Green Giant - Canned Mushrooms (Pieces & Stems, Sliced, Whole)

Hy-Vee - Shredded Sliced, Stems & Pieces

Laura Lynn - All Mushrooms

Meijer Brand - Canned Stems & Pieces (No Salt, Regular), Canned Whole, Sliced)

Midwest Country Fare - Mushrooms & Stems (No Salt Added, Regular)

Pennsylvania Dutchman - Sliced, Stems & Pieces

Safeway - Button Sliced

Trader Joe's - Marinated w/Garlic

Wegmans - Button, Pieces & Stems, Sliced

Mustard

365 Organic Every Day Value - Dijon, Mustard

Annie's Naturals - Organic (Dijon, Honey, Horseradish, Yellow)

Bone Suckin' - Mustard

Crystal - Brown, Yellow

Di Lusso - Chipotle, Cranberry Honey, Deli Style, Dijon, Honey, Jalapeno, Yellow

Dorothy Lane Market - Champagne

Eden - Organic (Brown, Yellow)

Food Club - Dijon, Regular (Regular, w/White Wine)

French's Mustard - Classic Yellow, Honey, Honey Dijon, Sweet n Zesty

Grey Poupon - Dijon

Guldens - Regular, Zesty Honey

M

Hellmann's - Deli Brown, Dijonnaise, Honey

Hy-Vee - Dijon, Honey, Regular, Spicy Brown

Laura Lynn - All Varieties

Meijer Brand - Dijon Squeeze, Honey Squeeze, Horseradish Squeeze, Hot & Spicy Squeeze, Salad Squeeze, Spicy Brown

Midwest Country Fare - Regular

Old Cape Cod - Sweet & Tart Cranberry Mustard

Safeway Select - Classic/Country Dijon, Spicy Brown, Stone Ground Horseradish

Shaw's - Dijon

Spartan Brand -

Prepared Mustard

Dijon Squeeze

Honey Squeeze

Horseradish

Spicy Brown Squeeze

Squeeze

Sweet & Hot

Stop & Shop Brand -

Creamy Dijon

Deli

Dijon

Honey

Old Grainy

Raspberry Grainy

Spicy Brown

Tarragon Dijon

Yellow

Trader Joe's - Dijon, Organic Yellow

Wegmans -

Classic Yellow

Dijon
Dijon Traditional
Honey
Horseradish
Spicy Brown
Whole Kids Organic - Organic Yellow, Yellow
Wild Oats Label - Organic (Dijon, Stone Ground, Yellow)
Winn Dixie - Yellow Mustard

Mutter

Tamarind Tree - Dhingri Mutter

N

Nayonaise

Nasoya - All varieties

Nectars

Bionaturae - All Fruit Nectars

Neufchatel...see Cream Cheese

Noodles

A Taste of Thai - Rice Noodles (Regular, Thin, Wild)

Annie Chun's -

Pad Thai Rice Noodles (Original, Thai Basil)
Rice Noodles (Hunan, Original, Thai Basil)

Thai Kitchen -

Noodle Cars (Pad Thai, Roasted Garlic, Thai Peanut,
Toasted Sesame)
Stir-Fry Rice Noodle Meal Kit (Lemongrass & Chili,
Original Pad Thai, Pad Thai w/Chili, Thai Peanut)

Nut Butter... see Peanut Butter

Nutritional Supplements

365 Organic Every Day Value - Whey Vanilla Protein Powder

N

Boost Drink - *(Except for Malt Flavor)*, Boost (High Protein, Plus, Pudding, w/Fiber)

Ensure - Ensure (Fiber, High Protein, Plus)

Glucerna - All Shakes

Hy-Vee - Chocolate (Plus, Regular), Strawberry (Plus, Regular), Vanilla (Plus, Regular)

MLO - Brown Rice Protein, Milk & Egg Protein

Meijer Brand - Diet Quick Extra Thin (Chocolate, Strawberry, Vanilla)

Nature Made - All Supplements

Odwalla - All Drinks *(Except Super Protein Vanilla Al Mondo & Superfood)*

Ruth's - Protein Powders (All Flavors)

Safeway - All Flavors of Nutritional Shakes (Plus, Regular)

Worldwide - Pure Protein Shakes

Nuts

365 Every Day Value -

Almonds (Raw, Roasted & Salted)

Cashews (Raw, Roasted & Salted, Roasted No Salt)

Cranberry Trail Mix

Mixed Nuts-No Peanuts-Roasted & Salted

Pecans (Halves, Wholes)

Pine Nuts (Raw)

Pistachios (Roasted & Salted, Roasted No Salt)

Roasted & Salted (Almonds, Peanuts)

Smoked Almonds

Sunflower Seeds (Raw, Roasted & Salted)

Walnuts (Raw)

365 Organic Every Day Value -

Organic Soynuts (Roasted & Salted, Unsalted)

Walnut (Halves, Pieces)

Whole Almonds

Albertsons - Peanuts (Dry Roasted, Honey Roasted)

B&J -

European Style Blanched Almonds

Milk Chocolate Covered Almonds

Roasted & Salted Almonds

Slivered California Fancy Almonds

US Pistachio Nuts

Eden - Tamari Almonds

Fisher -

Mix (California Style, Pineapple/Banana, Raisin/Cranberry)

Nuts (Almonds, Cashews, Mixed Nuts, Salted In-Shell
Peanuts, Salted In-Shell Sunflower Seeds)

Frito Lay -

Cashews

Deluxe Mixed Nuts

Honey Roasted Peanuts

Hot Peanuts

Salted Peanuts

Smoked Almonds

GeniSoy Roasted Soy Nuts -

Chocolate

Deep Sea Salted

Hickory Smoked

Unsalted

Zesty BBQ

Harrison Select Brand - Dry Roasted Peanuts

Hy-Vee -

Black Walnuts

English Walnut Pieces

Natural Almonds

Natural Sliced Almonds

N

Pecans
Pecan Pieces
Raw Spanish Peanuts
Salted Blanched Peanuts
Salted Spanish Peanuts
Slivered Almonds

Laura Lynn -

Almonds (Roasted, Smoked)
Cashew Halves
Deluxe Mixed Nuts
Dry Roast Nuts
Light Salt (Cashews, Dry Roast Nuts, Mixed Nuts, Peanuts)
Mixed Nuts
Peanuts (Honey Roast, Party, Spanish)
Sunflower Seeds
Unsalted Dry Roast Nuts
Whole Cashews

Meijer Brand -

Almonds (Blanched Sliced, Blanched Slivered, Natural
Sliced, Slivered, Whole)
Blanched (Regular, Slightly Salted)
Butter Toffee
Cashews (Halves w/Pieces, Halves w/Pieces Lightly
Salted, Whole)
Dry Roasted (Lightly Salted, Regular, Unsalted)
Honey Roasted
Hot & Spicy
Nuts Mixed (Deluxe, Lightly Salted)
Pecan (Chips, Halves)
Spanish Pine Nuts
Walnuts (Black, Chips, Halves & Pieces)

Nut Harvest -
Natural
Honey Roasted Peanuts
Lightly Roasted Almonds
Nut & Fruit Mix
Sea Salted Peanuts
Sea Salted Whole Cashews
Sabritas - Picante Peanuts, Salt & Lime Peanuts
Safeway Select -
Baking Nuts (Almonds)
Cashews (Halves, Pieces, Whole)
Dry Roasted
Nuts (Includes Deluxe Mixed)
Peanuts
Roasted/Salted Spanish
Walnut Pieces
Whole Walnuts
Spartan Brand -
Nuts Cashews (Halves w/Pieces, Whole)
Nuts Mixed (Lightly Salted, Nature, w/Macadamias Fancy)
Peanuts (Blanched Roasted, Butter Toffee, Dry Roasted
(Honey), Lightly Salted, No Salt, Salted Jar), Spanish
Bucket)
Tops - Dry Roasted Unsalted Peanuts, Pistachio
Trader Joe's -
All Raw & Roasted Nuts
Almond Nut Meal
Antioxidant Nut & Berry Mix
Candied Pecans
Cinnamon (Almonds, Apple Rings)
Macadamia Nut Clusters

N

Marcona Almonds (Regular, w/Rosemary)

Soy Nuts (Roasted, Salted)

Sweet & Spicy Pecans

Wegmans -

Cashews (Salted, Unsalted)

Dry Roasted (Macadamias, Seasoned Sunflower Kernels, Unsalted Peanuts)

Honey Roasted (Peanuts, Whole Cashews)

Marcona Almonds (Roasted & Salted)

Natural Whole Almonds

Party Peanuts (Roasted/Salted)

Peanuts Dry Roasted (Lightly Salted, Seasoned, Salted-In The Shell)

Peanuts Unsalted-In The Shell

Roasted

Almonds-Salted

Cashew Halves & Pieces-Salted

Deluxe Mixed Nuts w/Macadamias Salted

Jumbo Cashew Mix (w/Almonds, Pecans, & Brazils)

Jumbo Cashews

Mixed Nuts w/Peanuts-Lightly Salted

Party Mixed Nuts w/Peanuts (Salted, Unsalted)

Party Peanuts-Lightly Salted

Spanish Peanuts

Whole Cashews (Salted, Unsalted)

Virginia Peanuts (Chocolate Covered, Salted)

Wild Oats Label -

Almonds (Organic Raw, Sliced, Raw)

Hulled Sesame Seeds

Organic Dry Roasted Unsalted Soynuts

Organic Flax Seed (Golden, Regular)

Organic Raw Pepitas
Organic Walnut Halves & Pieces
Pecan Halves
Pinenuts
Pistachios (Roasted & Salted, Roasted & Unsalted)
Raw Brazil Nuts
Raw Filberts
Raw Shelled Pumpkin Seeds
Raw Whole Cashews
Sesame Seeds
Sunflower Seeds
Walnuts Halves & Pieces (Organic, Raw Hulled)

O

Oil

365 Every Day Value - Expeller Pressed Canola Oil, Extra Virgin Olive Oil (Italian, Regular)

365 Organic Every Day Value - Expeller Pressed Canola Oil, Olive Oil Imported

B&J - 100% Pure (Corn Oil & Vegetable Oil)

Albertsons - Olive Oil

Authentic Food Artisan (AFA) - Lapas Organic Extra Virgin Olive Oil, McEvoy Olive Oil, Nunez de Prado Organic Olive Oil

Bionaturae - Olive Oil

Carapelli - Olive Oil

Consorzio -
Olive Oil
Basil Flavored
Dipping Oil Herb Flavored
Olive Oil Extra Virgin

O

      Organic Meyer Lemon Flavored

      Organic Sicilian Orange Flavored

      Roasted Garlic Flavored

Crisco -

  Oil

    100% Pure Extra Virgin Olive

    Light Olive

    Natural Blend

    Pure (Canola, Corn, Olive, Vegetable)

    Puritan Canola

Di Lusso - Olive Oil

Eden -

  Olive Oil Spanish Extra Virgin

  Organic (Hot Pepper Sesame Oil)

  Safflower Oil

  Sesame Oil

  Soybean Oil

  Toasted Sesame Oil

Ex. Choice - Canola Deep Fry Oil, Peanut Oil, Soybean Vegetable Oil

Grand Selections - 100% Pure & Natural Olive Oil, Extra Virgin Olive Oil

Haggen Brand - Olive Oil, Vegetable Oil

House of Tsang -

  Hot Chili Sesame Oil

  Mongolian Fire Oil

  Sesame Oil

  Wok Oil

Hy-Vee -

  100% Pure (Canola Oil, Corn Oil, Vegetable Oil)

  Natural Blend Oil

O

Laura Lynn - Blended, Canola, Corn, Peanut, Vegetable

Manitoba Harvest - Hemp Seed Oil

Meijer Brand -

Blended Canola/Vegetable

Canola

Corn

Olive

   100% Pure-Italian Classic

   Extra Virgin

   Extra Virgin-Italian Classic

   Italian Select Premium Extra Virgin

   Milder Tasting

Oil Olive Infused

   Garlic & Basil Italian

   Roasted Garlic Italian

   Spicy Red Pepper-Italian

Peanut

Sunflower

Vegetable

Midwest Country Fare - 100% Pure Vegetable Oil, Vegetable Oil

Newman's Own Organics - Balsamic Vinegar, Extra Virgin Olive Oil

Nutiva - Coconut Oil

Ruth's - Hemp Oil

Simply Enjoy -

Apulian Regional Extra Virgin Olive Oil (Apulian, Sicilian, Tuscan, Umbrian)

Flavored Extra Virgin Olive Oil (Basil, Garlic, Lemon, Orange, Pepper)

Spartan Brand - Blended, Canola, Corn, Olive (Extra Virgin, Regular), Vegetable

O

Spectrum Organic Products -

Almond

Canola & Olive

Coconut (Organic, Refined)

Olive (Arebewuina, California, Extra Virgin, Greek Tuscan)

Peanut

Safflower (Organic, Refined, Unrefined)

Sesame (Refined, Toasted Organic, Unrefined (Organic, Regular, Toasted))

Super Canola

Walnut

Stop & Shop Brand - Blended, Canola, Corn, Extra Light Olive, MiCasa (Corn, Vegetable), Pure Olive, Soybean, Vegetable

Tops - Canola

Trader Joe's - Black Truffle, Garlic, Olive, Toasted Sesame

Wegmans -

100% Pure Olive

Basting

Canola

Corn

Extra Virgin

Black Truffle

Campania Style

Novello

Puglia Style

Regular

Sicilian Lemon

Sicilian Style

Tuscany Style

Grapeseed

IC (Campania, Tuscany)

O

    Mild Olive

    Peanut

    Puglia

    Pumpkin Seed

    Pure

    Sandwich (Regular, Submarine)

    Vegetable (100 % Soybean, Regular)

    Walnut Oil Pure

Whole Pantry - Sun Dried Tomato & Herb Oil

Wild Oats Label - Extra Virgin Olive, Natural Expeller Pressed Canola

Winn Dixie - Canola, Olive, Vegetable

Okra... *All **Fresh** Fruits & Vegetables Are **Gluten-Free***

365 Every Day Value - Frozen Cut Okra

Albertsons

Meijer Brand - Chopped, Whole

Pictsweet - All Vegetables (Frozen)

Stop & Shop Brand

Olive Oil... see Oil

Olives

Albertsons

B&G - Black, Green

B&J - Sliced Ripe, Stuffed Manzanilla, XL Pitted Ripe

Calabrese

Delallo - Calamata, Olive Medley, Olive Salad, Pepper Salad, Sicilian

Di Lusso - Green Ionian, Mediterranean Mixed

Hy-Vee -

    Chopped Ripe

    Large Ripe Black

    Manzanilla Olives

O

Medium Ripe Black

Queen

Salad

Sliced

Sliced Ripe Black

Zesty Sweet Chunks

Laura Lynn - All Olives (Green, Ripe)

Midwest Country Fare - Large Ripe Black, Sliced Ripe Black

Peloponnese - Kalamata Olives & Roasted Sweet Peppers

Safeway - Black Olives, Manzanilla

Shaw's - Black, Green

Spartan Brand - Ripe Pitted Olives (Jumbo, Large, Medium, Sliced, Small)

Stop & Shop Brand -

Manzanilla Olives (Sliced, Stuffed)

Pitted Black Ripe Olives Chopped

Stuffed Queen

Whole & Sliced (Jumbo, Large, Medium, Small)

Trader Joe's -

Colossal Olives Stuffed w/(Garlic Cloves, Jalapeño Peppers)

Mingling

Pitted (Kalamata, Moroccan Oil Cured)

Stuffed Queen Sevillano

Wegmans -

Manzanilla w/Pimento

Queen Stuffed

Pitted Ripe Olives (Colossal, Medium)

Ripe Olives (Sliced, X-Large)

Salad

Sliced Spanish Salad

Onions... *All **Fresh** Fruits & Vegetables Are **Gluten-Free***

O
P

Birds Eye - All Frozen Vegetables (Except With Sauce)
Meijer Brand - Chopped
Wegmans - Whole Onions In Brine

Orange Juice... see Juice

Oranges... *All *Fresh* Fruits & Vegetables Are *Gluten-Free**
Sunkist

Oysters... *All *Fresh* Seafood Is *Gluten-Free (Non-Marinated, Unseasoned)**
Bumble Bee - Canned
Chicken Of The Sea - All Varieties
Crown Prince - Whole

P

Pancakes/Pancake Mix & Waffles/Waffle Mix

Arrowhead Mills - Gluten-Free Pancake & Baking Mix, Wild Rice Pancake & Waffle Mix

Bob's Red Mill - Pancake Mix

El Peto - Pancake Mix

Gluten-Free Pantry - Blueberry Muffin/Pancake, Brown Rice Pancake & Waffle Mix, Sugar-Free Mix

Glutino - Sans Gluten-Free Pancake Mix

Hol Grain - Pancake & Waffle Mix

Kingbert Flax Jacks - Pancake & Waffle Mix

Kinnikinnick - Pancake & Waffle Mix

Larrowe's - Instant Buckwheat Pancake Mix

Lifestream - Buckwheat Wildberry Toaster Waffles, Mesa Sunrise Waffles

Manischewitz - Pancake Mix (Potato, Sweet Potato)

Maple Grove Farms - GF Pancake Mix

Miss Roben's - Pancake & Waffle Mix

Namaste - Waffle & Pancake Mix

P

Nature's Path Organic - Buckwheat Wildberry, Mesa Sunrise

Orgran - Apple & Cinnamon Pancake Mix, Buckwheat Pancake Mix, Sorghum Pancake Mix

Pamelas Products - Pancake & Baking Mix

Really Good Foods - Classic Pancake Mix

Sylvan Border Farm - Pancake & Waffle Mix

Trader Joe's - Wheat Free Toaster Waffles

Van's All Natural - Apple Cinnamon, Blueberry, Flax, Mini Waffles, Original

Paneer

Amy's - Indian Mattar Paneer, Indian Palak Paneer

Taj Ethnic Gourmet - Palak, Shashi

Tamarind Tree - Palak Paneer

Tasty Bite - Peas Paneer

Papaya... *All Fresh Fruits & Vegetables Are **Gluten-Free***

Native Forest - Organic Papaya Chunks

Parmesan Cheese... see Cheese

Pasta

Aproten - Anellini, Biscotti, Ditalini, Fettuccini, Fusilli, Penne, Rigatini, Spaghetti, Tagliatelle

Bi-Aglut - Ditalini, Maccheroncini, Penne, Spaghetti

Bionaturae - Elbows, Penne Rigate, Spaghetti, Spirals

DeBoles -

Rice Pasta

Angel Hair

Fettuccini

Lasagna

Penne

Spaghetti

Spirals

Dr. Schar -

Anellini
Conchigliette (Small Shells)
Fusilli
Penne
Pipette
Rigati
Spaghetti
Eden - Bifun, Kuzu, Mung Bean, Quinoa
Ener-G - White Rice (Lasagna, Macaroni, Small Shells, Spaghetti, Vermicelli)
Glutino - All Varieties
Heartland's Finest - All Varieties
Lundberg Organic Brown Rice Pasta - Penne, Rotini, Spaghetti
Mrs. Leepers - 100% Corn Spaghetti, Elbow Pasta
Namaste Foods - Pasta Pisavera
Notta Pasta - Fettuccine, Linguine, Spaghetti
Nutrition Kitchen - Organic Whole Soybean Pasta (Black, Golden, Green)
Orgran -
Rice & Corn Pasta
Herb Pasta
Macaroni
Mini Lasagne Sheets
Penne
Spaghetti Noodles
Spirals
Tortelli
Vegetable Corkscrew
Vegetable Pasta
Papadini - Lentil (Conchigliette, Orzo, Penne, Rotini, Spaghetti), Penne, Rotini

Pastariso -

Brown Rice (Angelhair, Elbows, Fettuccini, Lasagna, Penne, Shells, Spaghetti, Spirals)

Potato Pasta (Elbows, Spaghetti)

Pastato - All Varieties

Quinoa/Ancient Harvest - Elbows, Linguine, Pagoda, Spaghetti, Spirals Veggie Curls

Rizopia -

Brown Rice (Elbows, Fettuccine, Fusilli, Lasagne, Penne, Shells, Spaghetti, Spirals)

Organic Brown Rice (Elbows, Fettuccine, Fusilli, Penne, Spaghetti)

Organic Wild Rice (Elbows, Fusilli, Penne, Radiatore, Shells, Spaghetti)

Spinach Brown Rice Spaghetti

Vegetable Brown Rice Fusilli

White Rice Spaghetti

Schar -

Anellini

Capelli D'Angelo

Conchigliette

Fusilli

Lasagne

Penne

Pipette

Rigati

Rigatoni

Solena Fusilli

Solena Penne

Spaghetti

Tagliatelle

Steitenbacher - Golden Ribbon, Rigatoni

Tinkyada -

Brown Rice (Elbows, Fettucini, Fusilli, Grand Shells, Lasagne, Little Dreams, Penne, Shells, Spaghetti, Spirals)

Organic Brown Rice (Elbows, Lasagne, Penne, Spaghetti, Spirals)

Spinach Brown Rice Spaghetti

Vegetable Brown Rice Spirals

White Rice Spaghetti

Trader Joe's - Organic (Brown Rice Penne Pasta, Fusilli Pasta, Spaghetti Pasta)

Westbrae - Corn Angel Hair Pasta

Pasta Sauce... see Sauce

Pastrami

Boar's Head - Round

D&W Vac Pack Meats

Hormel - Deli Sliced Cooked

Hy-Vee - Thin Sliced

Jennie-O - Refrigerated Dark Turkey

Meijer Brand - Sliced Chipped Meat

Norwestern - Deli Turkey

Perdue - Deli Dark Turkey (& Hickory Smoked)

Pate

Kootenay Kitchen - Vegetarian

Tartex - Vegetarian

Peaches... *All **Fresh** Fruits & Vegetables Are **Gluten-Free***

Albertsons - All Canned Peaches

Del Monte -

Canned Fruit (All Varieties)

Fruit Snack Cups (All Metal & Plastic Containers)

Dole - All Canned, Cups, Cups In Gel, Jar in Light Syrup *(Except Parfaits)*.

P

 Hy-Vee -
  Diced
  Diced Fruit Cups
  Lite (Halves, Slices)
  Natural Lite Diced
  Peaches (Halves, Slices)
  Yellow Cling Lite Sliced
 Laura Lynn - Canned
 Midwest Country Fare - Lite Peaches (Halves, Slices), Slices
 Safeway - Sliced Peaches
 Shaw's - All Canned Peaches
 Wegmans - Halved, Halved Yellow Cling, Sliced In (Heavy Syrup, Juice), Sliced Yellow Cling (In Heavy Syrup, Raspberry Flavor)

Peanut Butter
 365 Every Day Value -
  Nut Butter Almond (Crunchy, Smooth)
  Peanut Butter Creamy
 365 Organic Day Value -
  Nut Butter (Cashew, Creamy, Crunchy, Smooth Almond)
  Organic Crunchy Peanut Butter
 Albertsons - Regular
 Arrowhead Mills -
  Almond Butter (Creamy, Crunchy)
  Cashew Butter (Creamy, Crunchy)
  Honey Sweetened Peanut Butter (Creamy, Crunchy)
  Organic Valencia Peanut Butter (Creamy, Crunchy)
  Valencia Peanut Butter (Creamy, Crunchy)
 B&J - Peanut Butter
 Deep South - Crunchy, Smooth
 Fisher - Almond Butter, Natural (Chunky, Creamy)

Food Club - Creamy, Crunchy

Hy-Vee - Creamy, Crunchy, Reduced Fat

I.M. Healthy - Soy Nut Butter (Chocolate, Original Chunky, Original Creamy, Unsweetened Creamy)

Jiff - Creamy, Extra Chunky

Laura Lynn -
   Peanut Butter & Grape Jelly Spread
   Peanut Butter & Strawberry Jelly Spread

Maranatha - All Products

Marsh Brand - All Varieties

Meijer Brand -
   Creamy
   Crunchy
   Natural Creamy
   Natural Crunchy

Midwest Country Fare - Creamy, Crunchy

Nature's Promise -
   Cashew Butter
   Organic Almond Butter (Smooth)
   Organic Peanut Butter (All Varieties)
   Organic Unsalted

nSpired -
   Almond Butter (Raw, Roasted/Creamy, Roasted/Crunchy)
   Cashew Butter Roasted
   Cashew/Macadamia Butter
   Macadamia Butter Roasted
   Organic Almond Butter (Raw, Roasted/Creamy, Roasted/Crunchy)
   Organic Peanut Butter (Creamy, Crunchy, Crunchy w/Salt)

Panner - Peanut Butter

Price Chopper - All Varieties

P

Safeway - Reduced Fat (Creamy, Crunchy), Regular
Santa Cruz -
   Organic Dark Roasted (Creamy, Crunchy)
   Organic Light Roasted (Creamy, Crunchy)
Shaw's - Crunchy, Regular
Skippy - All Varieties
Smart Balance Omega - Chunky, Creamy
Smucker's - Chunky, Creamy, Honey, No Salt Added
Spartan Brand - Peanut Butter (Creamy, Creamy Reduced Fat, Crunchy, Natural)
Stop & Shop Brand -
   All Natural Smooth Peanut Butter (No Added Salt, Reduced Fat, Regular)
   Peanut Butter (Creamy, Crunchy, Smooth)
Trader Joe's -
   Almond
   Cashew Macadamia
   Cashew
   Peanut
   Pumpkin
   Soybean (Creamy, Crunchy)
   Sunflower Seed
Wegmans -
   Natural Peanut Butter (Creamy, Crunchy)
   Organic Natural Creamy Peanut Butter w/Peanut Skins
   Peanut Butter (Creamy, Crunchy, Reduced Fat)
Whole Kids Organic - Organic Smooth Peanut Butter
Wild Oats Label -
   Almond Butter (Natural Creamy, Organic Raw, Organic Roasted Creamy)
   Natural Cashew Creamy

P

> Peanut Butter (Crunchy, Natural Creamy, Organic Creamy Salted, Organic Crunchy Salted)

Winn Dixie - Crunchy, Smooth

Peanut Sauce

A Taste of Thai - Peanut Satay Sauce, Peanut Sauce Mix

Mr. Spice - Thai Peanut Sauce

Thai Kitchen - Peanut Satay, Spicy Peanut Satay

Troy's - Peanut Sauce

Peanuts... see Nuts

Pears... *All Fresh Fruits & Vegetables Are Gluten-Free*

Del Monte -

> Canned Fruit (All Varieties)
>
> Fruit Snack Cups (All Metal & Plastic Containers)

Dole - All Canned, Cups, Cups In Gel, Jar in Light Syrup *(Except Parfaits)*

Hy-Vee -

> Bartlett Pears (& Halves, & Sliced)
>
> Lite Pears
>
> Natural Lite Diced Pears

Laura Lynn - Canned Pears

Meijer -

> Pears Halves (Heavy Syrup, In Juice (Lite, Regular))
>
> Pear Slices (Heavy Syrup, In Juice Lite)

Midwest Country Fare - Bartlett Pear Halves In Light Syrup

Shaw's - Canned Pears

Spartan Brand -

> Pears Halves (Heavy Syrup, Juice, Lite Syrup)
>
> Pears Slices (Heavy Syrup, Juice)

Stop & Shop Brand - Bartlett Pear Halves (Heavy Syrup, Light Syrup, Pear Juice, Splenda)

Trader Joe's - Pear Halves

P

    Wegmans -
        Heavy syrup (Halved, Sliced)
        Halves (& Lite)
        Sliced (& Lite)

Peas... *All **Fresh** Fruits & Vegetables Are **Gluten-Free***

    365 Every Day Value -
        Black Eyed
        Frozen Green Peas
        Organic (Split Green, Sweet)
        Peas & Diced Carrots
        Sweet (No Salt Added)

    365 Organic Every Day Value -
        Frozen (Green Peas, Petit Peas)
        Sugar Snap Peas

    Albertsons - Canned, Frozen

    B&J - Fancy Garden Peas,

    Birds Eye - All Frozen Vegetables *(Except With Sauce)*

    Bush's Best - Blackeye

    Cascadian Farms - Peas w/Pearl Onion

    Del Monte - All Varieties

    Freshlike - Frozen Plain Vegetables *(Except Pasta Combos and Seasoned Blends)*

    Grand Selections -
        Early June Premium
        Frozen (Petite Green, Sugar Snap)
        Young

    Green Giant -
        Canned Sweet Peas (50% Less Sodium, Regular)
        Frozen Baby Sweet Peas & Butter Sauce
        Frozen Select w/No Sauce (Baby Sweet Peas, Early June Peas, Sugar Snap Peas)

Frozen Simply Steam w/ No Sauce (Baby Sweet Peas, Sugar Snap Peas, Sweet Peas & Pearl Onions)

Frozen Sweet Peas

Health Market Organic - Sweet

Hy-Vee - Black Eyed, Frozen, Green Split, Sweet

Joan of Arc - Black Eyed

Laura Lynn - Canned Black-Eye Peas, Sweet Peas, Tiny June Peas

Marsh Brand - Sweet Garden Peas

Meijer - Canned Blackeye Peas, Frozen Peas (Green, Peas & Carrots, Green Petite)

Midwest Country Fare - Frozen Green, Sweet

Pictsweet - All Plain Vegetables (Frozen)

Safeway Select - Organic

Shop & Stop Brand - Sweet, Vanilla Peas In Light Syrup

Spartan Brand - Frozen Peas & Carrots

Tasty Bite - Agra Peas & Greens

Wegmans - Blackeye, Small Sweet, Sweet (No Salt Added, Regular)

Wild Oats Label - Organic Frozen (Peas, Peas & Sliced Carrots)

Pepper Rings

Spartan Brand - Pepper Rings (Mild, Hot)

Pepper Sauce

365 Organic Every Day Value - Hot Pepper Sauce

A Taste Of Thai - Garlic Chili Pepper Sauce

Pepperoni... see Sausage

Peppers... *All **Fresh** Fruits & Vegetables Are **Gluten-Free***

B&G -

Giardiniera

Hot Cherry Peppers (Red & Green, Regular, w/Oregano & Garlic)

Hot Chopped Roasted Peppers

P

Hot Jalapenos
Hot Pepper Rings
Peperoncini
Roasted (w/Balsamic Vinegar, w/Oregano & Garlic)
Sweet (Fried, Red, Red & Green, Salad w/Oregano & Garlic)
B&J - Red/Green Peppers & Onions,
Birds Eye - All Frozen Vegetables *(Except With Sauce)*
Di Lusso - Roasted Red
Meijer Brand - Frozen Green Peppers (Chopped, Diced)
Stop & Shop Brand - Chopped Green
Trader Joe's -
Fire Roasted (Red, Sweet Red Bell, Yellow & Red)
Marinated Red
Red Pepper Spread w/Garlic & Eggplant
Stuffed Poblano

Picante Sauce

Albertsons - Picante Sauce
Hy-Vee - Hot, Medium, Mild
Laura Lynn - Picante (All Varieties)
Pace - Picante Sauce (All Varieties)

Pickled Beets... see Beets

Pickles

365 Organic Every Day Value -
Kosher Dill
Organic (Baby Dill, Bread & Butter Pickle Chips,
Reduced Sodium Kosher Dills)
B&G -
Bread & Butter
Dill
Hamburger Dill
Kosher Dill (Baby Gherkins, Gherkins, Original)

Midget Gherkins

NY Deli Dill

Pickle In A Pouch

Sour

Sweet (Gherkins, Mixed, Mixed Pickles)

Tiny Treats

Unsalted (Bread & Butter, Kosher Dill)

Zesty Dill

B&J - Sweet Bread & Butter Chips, Midget Kosher Dill, Whole Kosher Dill

Boar's Head - Hans Jurgen

Easton Pickles

Hy-Vee -

Bread & Butter (Sandwich Slices, Sweet Chunk Pickles, Sweet Slices)

Dill (Kosher Sandwich Slices, Relish)

Fresh Pack Kosher Baby Dills

Hamburger Dill Slices

Kosher (Baby Dills, Cocktail Dills, Dill Pickles, Dill Spears)

Polish Dill (Pickles, Spears)

Refrigerated Kosher Dill (Halves, Sandwich Slices, Spears, Whole Pickles)

Special Recipe Baby Dills

Sweet Gherkins

Whole (Dill, Sweet)

Zesty Kosher Dill Spears

Laura Lynn - All Pickles

Midwest Country Fare -

Dill

Hamburger Dill Pickle Slices

Kosher Dill

Whole Sweet

P

Price Chopper - Sweet Whole Midget
Safeway - Pickles, Sweet
Spartan Brand -
   Bread & Butter Pickle
      Sliced Sweet Fresh Pack
      Slices Fresh Pack
      Sweet Sticks Fresh Pack
   Dill Pickle
      Hamburger Slices Processed
      Plain Baby Dills Mild Style Fresh Pack
      Polish & Polish Spears Fresh Pack
   Kosher Pickle
      Baby Dills Fresh Pack
      Length Sliced
      Slices Processed
      Spears Fresh Pack
      Whole Fresh Pack
   Pickle Sweet
      Gherkin
      Slices Processed
      Whole Processed
Trader Joe's -
   Bread & Butter
   Half Sour Kosher Dill
   Sliced Kosher Half Sour Dill
Vlasic - All Varieties
Wegmans -
   Fresh Pack (Kosher Dill Spears, Sweet Sandwich Slices, Whole Polish Dills)
   Hamburger Dill Slices
   Refrigerated Kosher Dill-Halves

Sweet Bread & Butter Chips
Sweet Midgets
Winn Dixie - Dill, Kosher Dill

Pie

Amy's - Mexican Tamale Pie, Shepherd's Pie

Cedarlane - Three Layer Enchilada

El Peto - Apple, Blueberry, Cherry, Peach, Walnut

Foods By George - Pecan Tarts

Gillian's Food - All Varieties

Hy-Vee - 100% Natural Pumpkin

Trader Joe's - Shepherd's Pie (Beef)

Whole Foods Market - Gluten-Free Bakehouse (Apple Pie, Cherry Pie, Southern Pecan Pie)

Pie Crust/Pie Crust Mix

Authentic Foods - Pie Crust Mix

Breads From Anna - Piecrust Mix

Kinnikinnick - Pastry & Pie Crust Mix

Really Good Foods - Pie Crust

Pie Filling

Comstock - All Varieties

Gold Leaf - Apple, Blueberry, Cherry, Peach

Hy-Vee - More Fruit Pie Filling/Topping (Apple, Cherry Pie)

Midwest Country Fare - Apple, Cherry

Price Chopper - All Varieties

Save-A-Lot - Apple, Blueberry, Cherry, Peach

Spartan Brand - Apple, Blueberry, Cherry, Cherry Light

Thrifty Maid - Apple, Blueberry, Cherry

Wilderness - All Varieties

Pilaf

Casbah - Nutted, Spanish

Trader Joe's - Rice, Quinoa Pilaf w/Shrimp & Vegetables,

P

Wild & Basmati Rice

Pineapple... *All **Fresh** Fruits & Vegetables Are **Gluten-Free***

Del Monte -

Canned Fruit (All Varieties)

Fruit Snack Cups (All Metal & Plastic Containers)

Dole -

Cups In Gel *(Except Parfaits)*

In 100% Juice (Chunks, Crushed, Slices, Tidbits)

In Heavy Syrup (Crushed, Chunks, Slices)

In Light Syrup (Chunks)

Hy-Vee - Chunk, Crushed, Sliced, Tidbit Fruit Cup

Laura Lynn - Canned

Meijer Brand - Pineapple (Chunks Heavy Syrup, Chunks In Juice, Crushed Heavy Syrup, Crushed In Juice, Sliced In Juice)

Midwest Country Fare - Chunks, Crushed, Slices, Tidbits

Native Forest - Organic (Chunks, Crushed, Mini Rings, Slices)

Stop & Shop Brand - Frozen Pineapple

Wegmans - Chunk, Crushed, Sliced (In Heavy, Regular), Tidbits

Wild Oats - Unsulphured Pineapple Slices

Pistachio Nuts... see Nuts

Pizza Crust/Mix

Amy's - Rice Crust Cheese Pizza, Rice Crust Spinach Pizza

Arrowhead Mills - Pizza Crust Mix

Authentic Foods - Pie Crust Mix, Pizza Crust Mix

Breads From Anna - Piecrust Mix

Chebe - Pizza Mix

Ener-G Foods - Pizza Shells, Yeast Free (Rice Shells)

Foods By George - Pizza (Crust, Regular)

Kinnikinnick - Pizza Crust Mix

Orgran - Pizza & Pastry Multimix

P

  Nature's Highlights - Pizza Crust (Brown Rice, Soy Rice), Rice Pizza Crust

  Really Good Foods - Pie Crust, Pizza Crust

  Whole Foods Market - Pizza Crust

Pizza Sauce... see also Sauce

  Contadina - All Varieties

  Eden - Pizza Pasta Sauce

  Hy-Vee - Regular

  Meijer - Regular

  Price Chopper - Regular

  Sauces 'N Love - Marinara Fresh Pizza Sauce

  Spartan Brand - Regular w/Basil

  Tops - Regular w/Olive Oil

  Trader Joe's - Fat Free

  Wegmans - Regular Plum Sauce

Plums... *All **Fresh** Fruits & Vegetables Are **Gluten-Free***

  Hy-Vee - Purple Plums

  Stop & Shop Brand - Whole Plums In Heavy Syrup

Polenta

  Alpina (Croix De) Savoie - Instant Italian Polenta

  Food Merchant - Chili Cilantro, Polenta, Pre-Made (Basil Garlic, Sun Dried Tomato, Traditional)

  San Gennaro - Basil Garlic, Sundried Tomato & Garlic, Traditional Italian

  Trader Joe's - Organic Polenta

Pop... see Soda Pop/Carbonated Beverages

Popcorn

  365 Every Day Value - Cheddar, Lightly Salted

  Chester's - Butter Artificially Flavored, Cheese Flavored

  Cracker Jack - Original Caramel Coated & Peanuts

  Crackin' Good - Fat Free Natural Butter Popcorn Cakes,

P

Microwave (No Butter/Natural Flavor), Regular Flavor

Eden - Kernels

Farmer Steve's - Kernels, Organic Microwave

Food Club - Butter Crazy, Light U-Pop All Natural, Popcorn, U-Pop All Natural

Full Circle - Butter Flavor, Natural

Herr's - Light, Original, White Cheddar Ranch

Hy-Vee -

Microwave

94% Fat Free Butter

Butter

Extra Butter

Extra Butter Lite

Kettle

Light Butter

Natural Flavor

Regular

White

Yellow

Jolly Time - Microwave (All Varieties)

Laura Lynn - All Items

Meijer Brand -

Microwave

75% Fat Free

94% Fat Free

Butter

Extra

Extra GP

GP

Hot n' Spicy

Kettle Sweet & Salty

    Lite
    Natural Lite
  Regular
    White
    Yellow

Newman's Own -
  Microwave
    94% Fat Free
    Butter
    Butter Boom
    Light Butter
    Low Sodium Butter
    Natural
    Tender White Kernels Natural
  Regular
    Raw Popcorn

Pop Secret
  Microwave
    1-Step (Cheddar, White Cheddar)
    Butter
    Butter 94% Fat Free
    Extra Butter
    Homestyle
    Jumbo Pop Butter
    Jumbo Pop Movie Theater Butter
    Kettle Corn 94% Fat Free
    Kettle Corn Old Fashioned
    Light Butter
    Movie Theater Butter
  Snack Size Microwave
    100 Calorie Pop Butter

P

100 Calorie Pop Kettle Corn

Butter 94% Fat Free

Homestyle

Kettle Corn 94% Fat Free

Movie Theater Butter

Variety Pack (5 Butter/5 Movie Theater Butter)

Variety Pack 100 Calorie Pop (5 Butter/5 Kettle Corn)

Price Chopper - Butter, Butter Lite, Extra Butter, Lowfat, Natural, Yellow

Robert's American Gourmet - Fra Diavalo, Nude Food, Zen

Safeway - Kettle, Microwave (All Varieties), Yellow

Skeete & Ike's - All Popcorn Varieties

Smartfood - White Cheddar Cheese Flavored (Reduced Fat, Regular)

Snyder's of Hanover - Butter

Spartan Brand -

Microwave

94% Fat Free

Butter

Extra Butter

Extra Butter 6 Pack

Kettle Corn 3 Pack

Light Butter

Natural Light Butter

Popcorn

White

Yellow

Stop & Shop Brand -

Microwave Popcorn

94% Fat Free Butter

Butter Flavored

      Butter Light

      Kettle Corn

      Movie Theatre Butter Flavored

      Natural Light

      Sweet & Buttery

      Yellow Popcorn

Trader Joe's -

    Cranberry Nut Clusters

    Fat Free Caramel

    Gourmet White

    Lite Popcorn 50% Less Salt

    Rosencrunch & Guildenpop

    White Cheddar

UTZ - Popcorn (Butter, Cheese, White Cheddar)

Wegmans -

    Kettle Corn Microwave

    Microwave

      Butter Flavor

      Colossal Butter

      Light

      Light Butter Flavor

      Movie Theater (Butter, Regular)

    Regular

      Natural

      Yellow

Wild Oats Label -

    Organic Caramel Corn Kettle Cooked (& w/Almonds)

    Organic Microwave Popcorn (Butter, Plain)

Winn Dixie - Microwave (No Butter/Natural Flavor), Regular Flavor

P Pork... *All Fresh Meat Is Gluten-Free (Non-Marinated, Unseasoned)*
  Always Tender -
    Flavored Fresh Pork
      Adobo Pork Cubes
      Apple Bourbon
      Citrus
      Fajita Pork Strips
      Honey-Mustard
      Lemon-Garlic
      Mesquite
      Mojo Criollo
      Non-Flavored Fresh Pork
      Onion-Garlic
      Original
      Peppercorn
      Raspberry Chipotle
      Sun-Dried Tomato
    Dietz & Watson - Roast Sirloin Of Pork
    Homestyle Meals - Bulk Pork BBQ Cooked, Shredded Pork In
      BBQ Sauce
    Hormel -
      Pickled Pigs Feet
      Pickled Pork Hocks
      Pork Roast Au Jus
      SW Pork Carnitas
    Lloyd's - Pork or Beef Ribs w/Original BBQ Sauce
    Trader Joe's - BBQ Shredded Pork
  Potato Chips... see Chips
  Potato Crisps... see Crisps
  Potato Puffs... see Snacks

P

Potatoes... *All **Fresh** Fruits & Vegetables Are **Gluten-Free***

365 Every Day Value - Frozen Regular French Fried Potatoes, Frozen Taters, Shredded Hash Browns

365 Organic Every Day Value - Organic (Frozen Shoestring Potatoes, Steak Cut Fries, Tater Tots)

Albertsons - All French Fries *(Except Curly & Seasoned)*

Alexia Foods -

Alexi Julienne Fries (Hanna Gold w/Sea Salt, w/Sea Salt)

Hashed Browns (Regular, Seasoned Salt)

Organic Oven Crinkles (Classic, Onion & Garlic, Salt & Pepper)

Oven Fries (Olive Oil & Rosemary & Garlic, Olive Oil & Sea Salt)

Oven Reds (Olive Oil & Parmesan & Roasted Garlic, Olive Oil Sun-Dried Tomatoes & Pesto)

Haggen - Steak Fries

Hy-Vee - Frozen (Country Style Hash Brown Potatoes, Crinkle Cut Fries, Criss Cut Potatoes, Steak Fries), Hash Brown Potatoes

Laura Lynn - All Frozen Potatoes *(Except Seasoned Fries)*, Cut Sweet Potatoes

Marsh Brand - Canned Potatoes

Meijer Brand -

Frozen Hash Browns

Original

Shredded

Southern Style

Western style

Regular

Hash Browns

Ore-Ida -

Golden Patties

P

Hash Browns (Country Style, Regular, Southern Style)

Shoestrings

Tater Tots (All Varieties)

Price Chopper - Regular Hash Browns

Safeway -

Country Style

Crinkle Cut

Crispy Fries

French Fried

O'Brien

Potato Sticks

Restaurant Style Crinkle Cut

Shoestring

Shredded

Southern Style

Steak Cut

Twice Baked

Stop & Shop Brand -

Cut Sweet Potatoes In Light Syrup

French Fries (Crinkle Cut, Straight Cut)

Fries (Crispy, Extra Crispy Crinkle Cut, Shoestring, Steak)

Frozen Natural Wedges Potatoes

Latkes

Puffs w/Onions

Shredded Hash

Southwestern Style Hash Browns

Twice Baked Potatoes (Butter, Cheddar Cheese, Sour Cream & Chive)

Whole Potatoes (No Added Salt, Regular)

Tasty Bite - Bombay, Bombay Potatoes & Madras Lentils

P

Trader Joe's -
Crinkle Wedge Potatoes
Fries
Chipotle Ranch
Garlic
Organic Frozen French
Sweet Potato French
Potatoes
Pacific Northwest Crinkle Wedge Potatoes
Potato Medley
Wegmans -
Frozen
Crinkle Cut
Shoestring
Straight Cut
Tater Puffs
Frozen Hash Browns
Country Style
Hash Browns O'Brien
Regular
Potatoes
Sliced
Whole
Wild Oats Label -
Organic
French Fries
Frozen Shredded Hashbrowns
Tate Bites
Preserves... see Jam/Jelly
Pretzel Rings
Ener-G - Sesame Pretzel Rings

P

Pretzels

> **Ener-G** - Sesame Pretzel Rings, Wylde (Poppy Seed, Regular, Sesame)
>
> **Glutino** - All Varieties

Protein

> **365 Organic Every Day Value** - Whey Vanilla Protein Powder
>
> **MLO** - Brown Rice Protein, Milk & Egg Protein
>
> **Odwalla** - All Drinks *(Except Super Protein Vanilla Al Mondo & Superfood)*
>
> **Ruth's** - Protein Powders (All Flavors)
>
> **Safeway** - Nutritional Shakes (Plus, Regular) (All Flavors)
>
> **Worldwide** - Pure Protein Shakes

Protein Shakes... see Shakes

Prunes

> **Spartan Brand** - Prunes Pitted

Pudding

> **Boost Drink** - *(Except for Malt Flavor),* Boost Pudding
>
> **Echo Farms** - Butterscotch, Chocolate
>
> **Food Club** - Rice Pudding
>
> **Hunt's** - Snack Pack Pudding (All Flavors)
>
> **Hy-Vee** -
>
>> Cooked Pudding (Chocolate, Vanilla)
>>
>> Instant Pudding
>>
>>> Butterscotch
>>>
>>> Chocolate (Fat Free/Sugar Free, Regular)
>>>
>>> Lemon, Pistachio
>>>
>>> Vanilla (Fat Free/Sugar Free, Regular)
>>
>> Pudding Cups
>>
>>> Butterscotch
>>>
>>> Chocolate (Fat Free, Fudge)
>>>
>>> Tapioca, Vanilla

Jell-O - All Varieties
Kozy Shack -
    Butterscotch
    Cinnamon Raisin Rice
    Coffee
    Creamy Banana
    European Style Rice
    ·Flan (Crème Caramel, Mango Sauce, Restaurant Style)
    Natural Vanilla
    No Sugar Added (Butterscotch, Chocolate, Old Fashioned Tapioca, Original Rice, Real Chocolate, Rice, Tapioca)
Laura Lynn - Pudding RTE Dairy (All Items)
Lifeway - All Products
Lifeway Organics - It's Pudding (Banana, Chocolate, Rice, Tapioca, Vanilla)
Meijer Brand -
    Cook & Serve (Chocolate, Vanilla)
    Instant
        Banana Cream
        Butterscotch Fat Free & Sugar Free
        Vanilla Fat Free & Sugar Free
    Instant Pudding & Instant Pie Filling
        Chocolate
        Coconut Cream
        French Vanilla
        Pistachio
        Vanilla
    Premium
        Chocolate Peanut Butter
        French Vanilla
        Orange Dream

P

Snack
Banana
Butterscotch
Chocolate (Fat Free, Fudge)
Multi-Pack Chocolate & Vanilla
Tapioca
Vanilla
Mori-Nu - Mates Pudding Mix (Chocolate, Lemon Crème, Vanilla)
My T Fine - Lemon, Pumpkin, Tiramisu, Vanilla
Price Chopper - All Flavors
Royal - All Flavors
Safeway - Vanilla Pudding
Shaw's - All Flavors
Spartan Brand -
Cook & Serve (Chocolate, Vanilla)
Instant
Banana Cream
Butterscotch
Chocolate (Regular, Sugar Free)
French Vanilla
Pistachio
Vanilla (Regular, Sugar Free)
Snack
Butterscotch
Chocolate
Tapioca
Vanilla
Stop & Shop Brand -
Butterscotch

    Chocolate (Fudge, Instant Pudding & Pie Filling, Regular, Sugar Free Instant)

    Fat Free (Chocolate, Chocolate/Vanilla)

    Instant Low Calorie Vanilla Pudding & Pie Mix

    Refrigerated (Chocolate, Chocolate/Vanilla)

    Rice

    Tapioca

    Vanilla

Trader Joe's - All Pudding

Wegmans -

    Chocolate (Fat Free, Regular)

    Chocolate Vanilla Swirl (Fat Free, Regular)

    Homestyle (Chocolate, Pudding Snack Cups, Rice, Tapioca)

    Pudding Snacks (Butterscotch, Vanilla)

    Vanilla (Fat Free, Regular)

Zensoy - All Varieties

Pumpkin... *All **Fresh** Fruits & Vegetables Are **Gluten-Free***

    365 Every Day Value - Pure 100% Solid Pack Canned

    Libby's - Canned (100% Pure Pumpkin, Easy Pumpkin Pie Mix)

    Safeway - Canned

    Spartan Brand

    Wegmans - Solid Pack

Puppodums

    Sharwood's - Indian Puppodums

Q

Queso

    Chi-Chi's - Con Queso

    Safeway - Salsa Con Queso

Q

R

Tostitos - Monterey Jack Queso, Salsa Con Queso, Spicy Queso Supreme

Quiche

Wellesley Farms - Spinach & Feta Crustless Quiche

Quinoa

Ancient Harvest - Inca Red

R

Radishes... *All **Fresh** Fruits & Vegetables Are **Gluten-Free***

Ragastani

Green Guru - Dal Ragastani

Raisins

365 Organic Every Day Value - Organic Thompson Raisins

B&J - Milk Chocolate Covered Raisins, Plump & Juicy Raisins

Hy-Vee - California Sun Dried Raisins

Ocean Spray - Craisins (Sweetened Dried Cranberries (Cherry, Orange, Original))

Spartan Brand - Canister, Cello, Seedless

Whole Kids Organics - Raisins

Wild Oats Label - Organic Jumbo (Green Seedless, Red Seedless)

Winn Dixie - Seedless

Raspberries... *All **Fresh** Fruits & Vegetables Are **Gluten-Free***

Hy-Vee - Frozen Red Raspberries

Meijer Brand - Raspberries (Red Individually Quick Frozen, Red Sweetened, Regular)

Spartan Brand - Raspberries, Raspberries Red-Tub (Sliced & Whole)

Stop & Shop Brand - Raspberries, Raspberries In Syrup

Wegmans - Raspberries (Regular, w/Sugar)

Wild Oats - Organic Frozen Raspberries

R

Raspberry Vinaigrette... see Salad Dressing

Refried Beans... see Beans

Relish

> **B&G** - Dill, Emerald, Hamburger, Hot Dog, India, Piccadilli, Sweet, Unsalted
>
> **B&J** - Sweet
>
> **Hy-Vee** - Squeeze Sweet, Sweet
>
> **Midwest Country Fare** - Sweet Pickle
>
> **Price Chopper**
>
> **Shaw's** - Sweet
>
> **Spartan Brand** - Dill, Sweet
>
> **Tops** - Sweet
>
> **Vlasic** - All Varieties
>
> **Wegmans** - Dill, Hamburger, Hot Dog Pickle

Ribs... *All Fresh Meat Is Gluten-Free (Non-Marinated, Unseasoned)*

> **Homestyle Meals** - Frozen Fully Cooked Baby Back, Pork Baby Back w/BBQ Sauce
>
> **Safeway Select** - Signature Ribs St. Louis Style Smoke House
>
> **Trader Joe's** - Baby Back Pork Ribs
>
> **Wegmans** - Barbeque Pork Spare Ribs

Rice

> **A Taste of India** - Spiced, Masala
>
> **A Taste of Thai** - Rice (Coconut Ginger, Garlic Basil Coconut, Jasmine, Yellow Curry)
>
> **Albertsons** - Brown, White (Instant, Regular)
>
> **Arrowhead Mills** - Brown & White Basmati, Long Grain Brown, Short Brown
>
> **Eden** - Rice & (Cajun Small Red, Caribbean Black, Garbanzo, Kidney, Lentils, Pinto)
>
> **Fantastic World Foods** - Arborio, Basmati, Jasmine
>
> **Go Go Rice** - On The Go Cooked Rice (Sweet & Mild Hawaiian)

R

Hormel -
Microwave
Chicken & Rice
Fiesta Rice w/Chicken Cups
Herb Roasted Rice Cups
Southwest Style Rice (& Black Beans, & Rice)
Sweet & Sour Rice

Hy-Vee -
Boil In Bag Rice
Enriched Extra Long Grain (Instant, Regular)
Instant Brown
Natural Long Grain Brown
Spanish

Konriko - Original Brown, White, Wild Pecan

Kraft Minute Rice - Boil In Bag, Brown, Premium, White

Laura Lynn - Boil N' Bag, Flavored Rice (All Varieties), Instant, LL Long Grain White

Lotus Foods - All Varieties

Lundberg -
All Varieties (Flour & Grinds, Rice)
Rice Sensations (Ginger Miso, Moroccan Pilaf, Thai Coconut Ginger, Zesty Southwestern)
RiceXpress (Chicken Herb, Classic Beef, Santa Fe Grill)

Meijer Brand - Brown, Instant (Boil In Bag, Brown, White), White Long Grain, White Medium Grain

Midwest Country Fare - Pre-Cooked Instant Rice

Nishiki - Sushi Rice

Old El Paso - Cheesy Mexican Rice, Spanish Rice

Safeway Select - Basmati, Instant Rice, White Long Grain

Spartan Brand - Instant Box (Boil In Bag, Brown, White), Long Grain 4% Broken

R

Stop & Shop Brand -
Instant Brown
Organic Long Grain (Brown & White)
Simply Enjoy (Butter Chicken, Pad Thai w/Chicken, Tikka Masala)

Success -
Broccoli & Cheese
Jasmine Rice
Natural Long Grain (Brown, Regular)
Ready-To-Serve (Brown, Chicken, Long Grain & Wild, Saffron White, Yellow)

Tasty Bite -
Basmati Rice (& Beans Masala, & Spinach Dal, & Sprouts Curry, & Vegetable Supreme)
Yellow Curry Vegetable & Jasmine Rice

Thai Kitchen -
Jasmine Rice Mixes
    Green Chili & Garlic
    Jasmine Rice
    Lemongrass & Ginger
    Roasted Garlic & Chili
    Sweet Chili & Onion
    Thai Yellow Curry

Trader Joe's -
Arborio
Basmati (Brown, Medley, White)
Chicken Tandoori Rice Bowl
Cooked Organic Brown
Jasmine Rice (Brown, Cooked Organic, Organic, Traditional)
Organic Frozen Rice (All Varieties)
Peruvian Style Chimichurri

R

Spanish Style
Wild
Uncle Bens - Brown, White, Wild
Wegmans -
Boil In Bag
Arborio
Basmati
Enriched Long
Enriched Long Grain White
Instant (Brown, Regular)
Jasmine
Long Grain Brown
Medium Grain
White

Rice Beverage
365 Organic Every Day Value - Rice Beverage (Original, Vanilla)
Grainaissance -
Almond
Amazing Mango
Banana Appeal
Chocolate (Almond, Chimp)
Cool Coconut
Gimme Green
Go Go Green
Go Hazelnuts
Oh So Original
Rice Nog
Tiger Chai
Vanilla (Gorilla, Pecan Pie)
Lundberg - Organic Rice Drink (Original, Vanilla)
Nature's Promise - Ricemilk, Vanilla Ricemilk

Pacific Natural Foods -
Almond Non-Dairy Beverages (Original, Vanilla Hazelnut)
Low Fat Rice (Plain, Vanilla)
Wild Oats - Original, Vanilla
Rice Bread... see Bread
Rice Cakes
Crackin' Good -
Fat Free Natural Butter Popcorn Cakes
Mini Cheddar Cheese
Plain/Unsalted
Earth's Choice - Rice Cakes
Lundberg -
Eco-Farmed
Apple Cinnamon
Brown Rice (Regular, Salt Free)
Buttery Caramel
Honey Nut
Sesame Tamari
Toasted Sesame
Wild Rice
Organic
Brown Rice (Regular, Salt Free)
Caramel Corn
Cinnamon
Koku Seaweed
Mochi Sweet
Popcorn
Sesame Tamari
Tamari Seaweed
Toast
Wild Rice

R

> **Price Chopper** - All Varieties
>
> **Shaw's** - Regular
>
> **Stop & Shop Brand** - Plain Salted Rice Cakes (Multigrain Unsalted, Plain Salted, Plain Unsalted, Sesame Unsalted, Sour Cream & Onion, White Cheddar),
>
> **Winn Dixie** - Mini Cheddar Cheese, Plain/Unsalted

Rice Chips... see Chips

Rice Crackers... see Crackers

Rice Cream

> **Erewhon** - Brown Rice Cream

Rice Noodles... see Noodles

Rice Shakes... see Rice Beverage or Shakes

Rice Snacks... see Snacks

Rice Syrup

> **Lundberg Organic** - Eco-Farmed Sweet Dreams, Organic Sweet Dreams

Rice Thins

> **Sesmark** - Brown, Cheddar, Sesame, Teriyaki

Rice Vinegar...see Vinegar

Risotto

> **Lundberg** -
>
> > Butternut Squash
> >
> > Cheddar Broccoli
> >
> > Creamy Parmesan
> >
> > Garlic Primavera
> >
> > Italian Herb
> >
> > Organic (Alfredo, Florentine, Porcini Mushroom, Tuscan)

Rum... *All **Distilled** Alcohol Is **Gluten-Free**[2]

Rusks

> **Glutino** - Gluten-Free Rusks

Rutabaga... *All **Fresh** Fruits & Vegetables Are **Gluten-Free**

> **Stop & Shop Brand**

S

S

Salad... *All **Fresh** Fruits & Vegetables Are **Gluten-Free***

    Hy-Vee -

        American Blend

        Chopped Romaine

        Cole Slaw

        European Blend

        Garden (Salad, Supreme)

        Italian Blend

        Riviera Blend

        Shredded Lettuce

        Spring Mix

    Trader Joe's -

        Baby Spinach Salad

        Chef

        Chicken Salad (Regular, w/Currants & Almonds)

        Cobb

        Gorgonzola & Walnut Salad

        Greek

        Marinated Bean Salad

Salad Dressing

    A Taste of Thai - Peanut Salad Dressing Mix

    Annie's Naturals -

        Artichoke Parmesan

        Basil & Garlic

        Cilantro & Lime

        Lemon & Chive

        Low Fat (Honey Mustard, Raspberry)

        Organic (Balsamic, Buttermilk, Caesar, Cowgirl Ranch, French, Green Garlic, Green Goddess, No Fat Yogurt w/Dill, Oil & Vinegar, Papaya Poppy Seed, Sesame Ginger w/Chamomile, Red Wine & Olive Oil)

Roasted Red Pepper

Tuscany Italian

B&J -

Balsamic Olive Oil Vinaigrette

Buttermilk Ranch

Extra Chunky Blue Cheese

Garlic Caesar

Thousand Island

Cardini's - Caesar, Lemon Herb

Carole's - Low Fat (Raspberry, Spa)

Consorzio -

Balsamic Vinaigrette

Caesar w/Parmesan & Romano

Fat Free (Mango, Raspberry & Balsamic, Strawberry & Balsamic)

Italian w/Parmesan Cheese

Drew's All Natural -

Buttermilk Ranch

Garlic Italian

Honey Dijon

Kalamata Olive & Caper

Poppy Seed

Raspberry

Roasted Garlic & Peppercorn

Romano Caesar

Rosemary Balsamic

Smoked Tomato

El Torito - Cilantro Pepita, Serrano Ranch

Emeril's - House Herb Vinaigrette, Orange Herb w/Poppy Seed

salad dressing

S

Enlighten -
Balsamic
Garden Italian
Garlic Vinaigrette
Honey Mustard
Red Wine Vinaigrette
Roasted Sweet Pepper

Follow Your Heart -
Organic
Balsamic Vinaigrette
Chipotle-Lime Ranch
Chunky Blue Cheese
Creamy (Caesar, Miso Ginger, Ranch)
Italian Vinaigrette

Glutino - French Herb Balsamic, NA Italian, Peppercorn Garlic

Health Market Organic - Creamy Caesar, Honey Mustard, Raspberry Vinaigrette

Hy-Vee -
Chunky Blue Cheese
Dressing (French, Italian, Lite Salad, Ranch, Salad, Thousand Island, Zesty Italian)
Light Dressing (Italian, Ranch, Thousand Island)
Light Salad Dressing (French, Italian, Ranch)
Squeezable Salad Dressing

Ken's Steak House
Fat Free Dressings
Italian
Raspberry Pecan
Sun Dried Tomato
Lite Dressings
Balsamic & Basil

S

Caesar

Chunky Blue Cheese

Country French w/Vermont Honey

Creamy (Caesar, French, Italian, Parmesan w/Cracked Peppercorn)

Honey Mustard

Italian

Northern Italian

Olive Oil Vinaigrette

Ranch

Raspberry Walnut

Red Wine Vin

Russian, Sweet Vidalia Onion

Regular

Balsamic & Basil

Buttermilk Ranch

Caesar

Christo's Yasou Greek

Chunky Blue Cheese

Country French w/Vermont Honey

Creamy (French, Italian, Parmesan w/Cracked Peppercorn, Tomato Bacon)

Greek

Honey Mustard

Italian (& w/Aged Romano)

New & Improved Ranch

Red Wine Vinegar & Olive Oil

Russian

Thousand Island

Three Cheese Italian

Sweet Vidalia Onion

Zesty Italian

S

Kraft -
Balsamic Vinaigrette
Creamy Cucumber
French
Greek w/Feta
Rancher's Choice
Raspberry Vinaigrette
Zesty Italian

Laura Lynn -
Buttermilk
California (French, Honey French)
Chunky Blue Cheese
Creamy (Cucumber, Italian)
French
Garlic Ranch
Italian (Fat Free, Regular)
Peppercorn Ranch
Poppy Seed
Ranch (Fat Free, Lite, Regular)
Red Wine Vinegar & Oil
Thousand Island, Zesty Italian

Lily's Gourmet Dressings -
Balsamic Vinaigrette
Northern Italian
Poppyseed

Litehouse -
Balsamic Vinaigrette
Big Bleu
Bleu Cheese Vinaigrette
Caesar (Dressing, Sensation)
Chunky (Bleu Cheese, Garlic Caesar)

Coleslaw
Cranberry Vinaigrette
Garlic Caesar
Gourmet Caesar
Greek
Homestyle Ranch
Honey Mustard
Huckleberry Vinaigrette
Idaho Bleu Cheese Crumbles
Jalapeno Ranch
Lite (Bleu Cheese, Honey Dijon, Ranch)
Original Bleu Cheese
Peppercorn Ranch
Pomegranate Blueberry
Ranch
Raspberry Walnut Vinaigrette
Red Wine Olive Oil Vinaigrette
Rustic Ranch
Salsa Ranch
Spinach
Sweet Herb French
Thousand Island
Manzanah - Caesar, Greek
Maple Grove Farms of Vermont -
All Natural
Asiago & Garlic
Blueberry Pomegranate
Champagne Vinaigrette
Ginger Pear
Maple Fig
Strawberry Balsamic

Fat Free
  Cranberry Balsamic
  Greek
  Honey Dijon
  Lime Basil
  Poppyseed
  Vinaigrette (Balsamic, Raspberry)
Organic
  Dijon
  Italian Herb
  Vinaigrette (Balsamic, Raspberry)
Regular & Lite
  Balsamic Maple
  Honey Mustard
  Lite Caesar
  Lite Honey
  Mustard
  Sweet N' Sour
Sugar Free
  Dijon
  Italian Balsamic
  Vinaigrette (Balsamic, Raspberry)
Midwest Country Fare - Ranch
Nasoya - All Varieties
Nature's Promise - Ranch
Newman's Own -
  Light
    Balsamic Vinaigrette
    Caesar
    Honey Mustard
    Italian

S

    Ranch

    Raspberry Walnut

    Red Wine Vinegar & Olive Oil

    Sun Dried Tomato Italian

  Regular

    Balsamic Vinaigrette

    Caesar

    Creamy (Caesar, Italian)

    Olive Oil & Vinegar

    Parisienne Dijon Lime

    Parmesan & Roasted Garlic

    Red Wine Vinegar & Olive Oil

    Two Thousand Island

Olde Cape Cod - All Dressings

Organicville - All Varieties

Ring Bros Markets Dressings - All Varieties *(Except Blue Cheese)*

Ruth's - Honey Mustard

Safeway -

  Italian (Creamy, Light & Zesty)

  Ranch (Lite, Regular)

  Thousand Island

Safeway Select -

  Basil Ranch

  Blue Cheese

  California

  Cranberry/Orange

  Creamy Italian

  Garlic Vinaigrette

  Harvest Vegetable

  Italian Dressing Mix

S

Ranch
Ranch Salad Dressing Mix
Ranch w/Bacon
Raspberry Vinaigrette
Red Wine Balsamic
Roasted Red Pepper
Thousand Island
Tuscan Basil Herb
Zesty Italian

Scargo Café - Balsamic Vinaigrette
Seeds Of Change - All Salad Dressings
Spartan Brand -
  Blue Cheese
  French
  Italian (Light, Regular, Zesty)
  Thousand Island
Stonewall Kitchen - All Salad Dressing
Stop & Shop Brand -
  Balsamic Vinaigrette
  Blue Cheese
  Caesar
  French Dressing (Creamy, Regular)
  Italian Dressing (Creamy, Fat Free, Lite)
  Ranch Dressing (Fat Free, Regular)
  Raspberry Vinaigrette
  Thousand Island
Trader Joe's -
  Balsamic Vinaigrette (Fat Free, Organic, Regular)
  Low Fat Parmesan Ranch
  Pear Champagne Vinaigrette
  Raspberry Lowfat

S

Romano Caesar

Tuscan Italian Dressing w/Balsamic Vinegar

Walden Farms -

Sugar Free No Carb

Blue Cheese

Caesar

Honey Dijon

Oriental Raspberry

Ranch

Thousand Island

Wegmans - Balsamic Delight

Basil Vinaigrette

Caramelized Onion & Bacon

Cracked Pepper Ranch Dressing

Creamy (Caesar, Curry & Roasted Red Pepper, Italian)

Fat Free (Parmesan Italian, Red Wine Vinegar, Roasted Red Pepper)

Honey Mustard

Italian

Light (Garlic Italian, Golden Caesar, Parmesan Peppercorn Ranch, Ranch)

Maple Dijon, Organic (Balsamic Vinaigrette, Raspberry)

Parmesan Italian

Poppyseed Delight

Roasted (Red Bell Pepper & Garlic, Tomato & Cheddar)

Sun-Dried Tomato

Tarragon Vinaigrette

Thousand Island

Three Spice Garden French

Toasted Sesame & Ginger

Traditional Italian

Wild Oats -

Organic

Buttermilk Ranch

Chipotle Ranch

Crumbled Blue Cheese

Garlic Aioli

Homestyle Ranch

Japanese Ginger

Olive Oil & Balsamic

Raspberry Vinaigrette

Sesame Goddess

Tuscany Italian

Regular

Olive Oil & Balsamic

Winn Dixie -

Balsamic Vinaigrette

California French Style

Chunky Blue

Cheese

Creamy (French, Ranch)

Fat Free (Italian, Ranch, Thousand Island)

Garden Ranch

Honey Dijon

Italian (Lite, Regular, Tobust, Zesty)

Ranch (Creamy, Garden, Lite)

Thousand Island

Salami... see Sausage

Salmon... see Fish
    *All **Fresh** Fish Is **Gluten-Free (Non-Marinated, Unseasoned)***

Salsa

Albertsons - Regular

S

Amy's -
Organic
Black Bean & Corn
Fire Roasted Vegetable
Medium
Mild
Spicy Chipotle

Bone Suckin' Salsa - Hot, Regular

Chi-Chi's - Fiesta, Garden, Natural, Original, Picante, Roasted Tomato

Coyote Joe's - All Varieties

Drew's -
Organic
Chipotle Lime
Double Fire Roasted
Fire Roasted
Hot
Medium
Mild

Food Club - Thick & Chunky (Medium, Mild), Santa Fe Style (Medium, Mild)

Full Circle - Hot, Medium, Mild

Grand Selections - Black Bean & Corn, Medium

Green Mountain Gringo - All Varieties

Health Market Organic - Medium, Mild, Pineapple

Herr's - Chunky (Medium, Mild)

Hy-Vee - Hot, Medium, Mild

La Victoria - Salsa Verde, Suprema, Thick 'N Chunky, Traditional

Litehouse

Nature's Promise - Organic (Chipotle, Medium, Mild)

Newman's Own -
  Bandito (Medium, Mild)
  Hot
  Medium
  Mild
  Peach
  Pineapple
  Roasted Garlic
  Tequila
Old El Paso -
  Salsa Thick N' Chunky
    Gotta Have Hot
    Make Mine Medium
    Wild For Mild
Ortega - Homestyle Prima (Medium, Mild), Thick & Chunky
Pace - Chunky (Chipotle, Cilantro, Lime & Garlic, Regular)
Safeway Select - (All Select Varieties), Fiesta Fajita Salsa, Salsa Con Queso
San Carlos - All Varieties
Seeds Of Change - All Varieties
Stop & Shop Brand - Hot, Medium, Mild, Simply Enjoy Salsa (Black Bean & Corn, Peach Mango, Pineapple Chipotle, Tequila Lime)
Tostitos -
  All Natural (Hot, Medium, Mild)
  Medium Organic
  Restaurant Style
  Thick & Chunky (Party Bowl)
Trader Joe's -
  All Fresh Salsa
  Authentica

S

    Black Bean & Roasted Corn

    Chunky

    Corn & Chili

    Double Roasted

    Fresh (Hot, Mild)

    Hot & Smokey Chipotle

    Pineapple

    Spicy/Smokey Peach

    Verde

    UTZ - Mt. Misery Mike's Salsa, Sweet Salsa Dip

    Wegmans - Hot, Medium, Mild, Organic (Hot, Mango, Medium, Mild), Santa Fe Style

    Whole Kids Organic - Caribe, Fire Roasted, Poblano Corn, Salsa Verde, Tepin Black Bean

    Wild Oats - Garlic & Chipotle, Hot, Medium, Mild, Roasted Corn & Bean Salsa

    Winn Dixie - All Varieties

Salt

    Albertsons - Iodized Salt

    Astor

    Lawyr's - Seasoned Salt

    Meijer Brand - Plain, Iodized

    Morton's - Iodized, Kosher Sea Salt, Plain

    Spartan Brand - Plain, Iodized

    Stop & Shop Brand - Iodized Salt, Plain

    Wegmans - Iodized Salt, Plain

    Winn Dixie

Sandwich Meat... see Deli Meat

Sardines

    Bumble Bee - Canned

    Chicken Of The Sea - All Varieties

S

Crown Prince - Brisling In Olive Oil, In Water/No Salt Added, Norway

Underwood Sardines - Mustard Sauce, Olive Oil, Springwater, Soybean Oil

Sauces... (includes Pasta, Marinara, Tomato, Misc.)

365 Every Day Value -

Organic Tomato Sauce

Pesto/Sun Dried Tomato

Roasted Garlic

Roasted Red Pepper

365 Organic Every Day Value -

Organic

Italian Cherry Tomatoes w/Basil

Italian Diced Tomatoes w/Basil

Tomato & Basil

Pasta Sauce

Pasta Sauce Nonfat

Albertsons - Pasta Sauce Regular

Amy's - All Varieties

Aunt Millie's - All Pasta Sauces

Baxters - Sauce (Mint)

Bella Cucina - All Pasta Sauces

Bove's Of Vermont -

All Natural

Basil

Marinara

Mushroom & Wine

Roasted Garlic

Romano Pomodoro Sweet Red Pepper

Vodka

S

    Organic
      Basil
      Marinara
      Roasted Garlic
      Vodka

Capa Di Roma - All Sauces

Classico - All Pasta Sauces

Contadina - All Pasta Sauces

Dave's Gourmet - All Sauces

Del Monte - All Sauces *(Except 4 Cheese Spaghetti Sauce, Spaghetti Sauce Flavored w/Meat)*

Di Lusso - Sweet Onion Sauce

Dorothy Lane Market - All Vera Jane's Varieties

Duso's - Pasta Sauce

Eden - Spaghetti Sauce (No Salt Added, Regular)

Emeril's -
    Pasta Sauce
      Home Style Marinara
      Kicked Up Tomato
      Mushroom & Onion
      Puttanesca
      Roasted Gaahlic
      Roasted Red Pepper
      Sicilian Gravy
      Vodka

Food Club -
    4 Cheese
    All Natural Marinara
    Mushroom & Olive
    Mushroom & w/Meat
    Tomato Basil

S

Traditional Original

Frutti Di Bosco - Marinara, Puttenesca, Truffle-Porcini, Wild Chanterelle

Full Circle - Parmesan Cheese, Portabella Mushroom, Roasted Garlic, Tomato Basil

Gillian's Foods - All Varieties

Glutino - All Varieties

Health Market - Tomato Basil

Hunt's -

Spaghetti Sauce

Cheese & Garlic

Chunky Vegetable

Garlic & Herb

Light, Mushroom

No Added Sugar

Roasted Garlic & Onion

Traditional

Hy-Vee -

Spaghetti Sauce

3 Cheese

Mushroom

Traditional

w/Meat

Tomato Sauce

Italian

Regular

Laura Lynn - Black Pepper, Chili, Elmer Ingle 1922

Manischewitz - Pasta Sauces (All Varieties), Tomato & Mushroom Sauce

Mayacamas -

Chicken Fettuccine

S

    Creamy (Clam, Pesto)

    Mix (Black Olive Pesto, Dried Tomato, Garden Style, Green Olive Pesto, Spicy), Pesto

Meijer Brand -

Extra Chunky Spaghetti Sauce

    3 Cheese

    Mushroom & Green Pepper

    Garden Combo

    Garlic & Cheese

Pasta Sauce

    Four Cheese-Select

    Marinara-Select

    Mushroom & Olive Select

    Onion & Garlic Select

    Original

Regular Spaghetti Sauce

    Plain

    w/Meat

    w/Mushroom

Midwest Country Fare - Tomato Sauce

Muir Glen - Organic Chunky Style Pasta Sauce, Tom Basil Sauce

Nature's Promise - Organic Pasta Sauce (Garden Vegetable Parmesan, Plain)

Newman's Own -

Cabernet Marinara

Diavolo

Five Cheese

Garlic & Peppers

Italian Sausage & Peppers

Marinara

Marinara w/Mushroom

Pasta Sauces

Pesto & Tomato

Sockarooni

Tomato Basil

Tomato & Roasted Garlic

Vodka

Pastapali - Pasta Sauce

Patsy Pasta Sauce - Marinara, Tomato Basil

Pemberton's - All Pasta Sauces

Prego - Mushroom, Three Cheese Sauce, Traditional Sauce

Price Chopper - Tomato Sauce

S&W - Tomato Sauce (Homestyle Recipe)

Safeway - Meat, Mushroom, Traditional

Safeway Select -

All Verdi, Refrigerated Varieties

Classic Pesto

Creamy Parmesan Basil

Garden Vegetable

Herb

Mushroom/Onion

Roasted Garlic

Mushroom

Sauces 'N Love

Pesto

Pink Pesto

Pomodoro & Basilico

Puttanesca

Spicy Arrabbiata

Sugo Rosa

Sazs - Vidalia Onion Cooking Sauce

S

Scarpetta - Arrabbiata, Marinara, Pesto Puttanesca, Tuscan Vodka

Seeds Of Change - All Pasta Sauces

Shaw's - Tomato Sauce

Spartan Brand - Spaghetti Sauce (Meat, Mushroom, Traditional), Tomato Sauce

Stonewall Kitchen Sauce - All Varieties

Stop & Shop Brand -

Simply Enjoy Sauce

Fra Diavolo

Marinara

Roasted Garlic

Sicilian Eggplant

Tomato Basil

Vodka

Tomato Sauce

No Added Salt

Regular

Thai Kitchen - Choice Crop, Lemongrass Splash, Original Pad Thai

Thrifty Maid - Tomato Sauce

Trader Joe's -

Regular Pasta Sauce

Aglio Olio Pesto

Apricot

Bruscetta

Cacciatore Simmer

Creamy (Basil Reduced Fat, Cilantro Dressing Reduced Fat, Prosciutto)

Cuban Mojito

Curry Simmer

Genova Pesto
Italian Sausage
Korma Simmer
Mango
Marinara
Mexican Red
Peach Sauce
Pesto alla Genovese Basil Pesto
Piccata Simmer Sauce
Punjab Spinach
Roasted Garlic Marinara
Rustico
Three Cheese
Tomato Basil (Marinara, Pasta Sauce)
Tuscano Marinara Sauce-Low Fat
Vodka Marinara
Whole Peeled Pear Tomatoes w/Basil (& No Salt Added)

Organic
Marinara Sauce-No Salt Added
Red Wine & Olive Oil Vinaigrette
Spaghetti Sauce
Tomato Basil Marinara
Vodka Sauce

UB The Everything Sauce - Not So Spicy, Spicy

Wegmans -
Bolognese Sauce
Chunky Marinara Pasta Sauce
Clam Sauces
Diavolo Sauce
Four Cheese
Garden Vegetable

S

Grilled Flavor
Lemon & Caper Sauce
Mushroom Marsala Sauce
Mustard
Onion & Mushroom
Organic Pasta Sauce (Marinara, Roasted, Tomato)
Prepared Horseradish
Remoulade
Roasted Garlic Pasta Sauce
Simmer Sauces
Smooth Marinara
Spaghetti Sauce
Sunripened Dried Tomato
Tomato & Basil
Tomato w/IT Sausage
Vodka Sauce
White Clam Sauce

Wild Oats -
Organic
Funghi
Marinara
Norma
Puttanesca
Regular
Natural Vodka Cream
Parmesan Pasta
Red Wine Marinara
Roasted Garlic
Tomato Basil

Winn Dixie -
Classic Style (Marinara Fine, Tomato Basil Fine)

Select Recipe (Double Garlic, Fried Diablo)

Sauerkraut

Albertsons

B&G

Boar's Head

Eden

Haggen

Hy-Vee

Marsh Brand

Safeway

Stop & Shop Brand

Tops

Vlasic

Wegmans

Sausage

365 Every Day Value - Pork Sausage (Classic, Maple, Sage)

Aidells -

Artichoke & Garlic

Bier

Burmese Curry

Cajun Style Andouille (Minis, Regular)

Chicken & Apple (Minis, Regular)

Duck

Habanero & Green Chile

Hot Creole

Mango (Breakfast Links, Regular)

Maple & Smoked Bacon Breakfast Links

New Mexico

Pesto

Portobello Mushroom

Roasted Red Pepper w/Corn

S

    Smoked Chorizo

    Sun-Dried Tomato (Minis, Regular)

    Whiskey Fennel

Applegate Farms - All Varieties

Armour - Vienna

Boar's Head - All Varieties

Butcher's Cut - Italian, Smoked

Casual Gourmet -

    Chicken Sausage

        Cajun Style Andouille

        Jamaican Jerk

        Mild Italian

        Pesto

        Red Pepper & Basil

        Smoked Apple

        Spinach & Asiago

        Sundried Tomato & Herb

Choices Own - Gourmet

Coleman -

    Franks

    Organic Chicken Sausage

        Breakfast Links

        Fresh Spinach & Feta Cheese

        Mild Italian

        Spicy Andouille

        Spicy Italian

        Sun-Dried Tomato & Fresh Basil

Di Lusso - Beef Summer

Dietz & Watson - Braunschweiger, Natural Casing Beef Franks, Pastrami

Eagle Valley - Sandwich Pepperoni

Ejay's - German, Smoked Jalapeno, Smoked Kielbasa
Eppy's - Kosher Wieners
Farmington - Pork (Mild)
Five Star Brand -
   All Meat Weiners
   German Brand Franks
   Slovenian Sausage Garlic Knockwurst
Girgenti - Hot Ham Capicola
Global Gourmet -
   Chicken Sausage
      Andouille
      Apple Oven Roasted
      Chipotle Pepper
      Feta Cheese & Fresh Spinach
      Fontina Cheese & Roasted Garlic
      Sun Dried Tomato
      Spicy Italian
Hargis House - Vienna
Hertel's - Breakfast
Honeysuckle - All Varieties
Hormel -
   Sausage
      Homeland Hard
      Italian Dry
      Pepperoni
      Pickled (Hot, Smoked)
      Smokies
      Summer
      Turkey
      Vienna

S

SPAM

Classic

Less Sodium

Lite

Smoked

Oven Roasted

Turkey

Hormel Pillow Pack - Dried Beef, Hard Salami, Pepperoni, Turkey Pepperoni

Hy-Vee - Bratwurst, Cooked Salami, Grill Pack, Pastrami, Pepperoni, Sausage (Links, Patties)

Jennie-O -

Breakfast Lover's Turkey Sausage

Extra Lean Smoked (Kielbasa Turkey, Turkey)

Fresh Breakfast Sausage (Maple Links, Mild Links, Mild Patties)

Fresh Dinner Sausage (Cheddar Turkey Bratwurst, Hot Italian, Lean Turkey Bratwurst, Sweet Italian)

Premium Dinner Sausage (Apples & Brown Sugar, Bacon & Cheddar, Cajun Style, Garlic & Herb, Sweet Italian)

Johnsonville -

Beddar w/Cheddar

Beef Hot Links

Bratwurst (Cheddar, Heat & Serve, Hot 'n Spicy, Original, Smoked, Smoked Beef, Stadium Style)

Chorizo

Ground Sausage (Hot, Mild)

Heat & Serve Original & Maple Syrup

Irish O'Garlic

Little Smokies

Mild/Hot/Sweet Italian

Natural Casing Wieners

New Orleans Style Smoked Sausage
Original Breakfast
Perri (Hot Italian, Sweet Italian)
Premium Pork Sausage (Hot, Original)
Smoked Hot Links
Smoked Polish Sausage
Stadium Style Beef Franks
Summer Sausage (Beef, Garlic, Old World Summer, Original)
Vermont Maple Syrup

Libby's - Chicken Vienna, Vienna

Little Sizzlers - Links & Patties

Maluma - Bison Sausage

Nature's Promise -
Italian Spicy Pork
Mild Italian Chicken
Red Pepper & Provolone Pork
Spiced Apple Chicken
Spinach & Feta Chicken
Sun Dried Tomato & Basil Chicken

Old Wisconsin - All Varieties

Oscar Mayer - Beef Franks, Bun Length Wieners, Wieners

Price Chopper - Italian Breakfast Sausage

Primo Naturale -
Chorizo (Dried Hot, Sliced Dried, Sliced Hot, Stick Dried)
Chub Salami (w/Black Pepper, w/Herbs, w/Wine)
Pepperoni (Dried, Sliced Dried)
Salami (Chub Hard, Sliced)
Sliced Salami (Coppa, Original w/Wine, Premium Genoa, w/Black Pepper, w/Herbs)
Sopressata (Regular, Sliced)
Sweet Abruzzi Sausage

S

Safeway - Genoa Salami, Hard Salami, Jumbo Franks (Chicken, Pork)

Safeway Select -
Beef (Hot Link, Smoked)
Cajun Style Link
Chicken (Andouille, Apple)
Italian (Pork, Regular)
Polish
Turkey Chicken Parmesan Basil
Turkey Chicken Sun Dried Tomato

Save-A-Lot - Farmington Pork, Hargis House Vienna

Shaw's - Sweet (Chicken, Italian)

Shelton's -
Beef Sticks
Spicy Dogs (Chicken, Smoked Chicken Franks)
Turkey Sausage (Breakfast, Italian, Patties)
Turkey Sticks (Pepperoni, Regular)

Swift - Cooked Salami

Tops - Hot Dogs, Italian Sausage

Trader Joe's -
Best In Show Uncured Beef Hot Dogs
Chicken Breakfast
Gerhards Deli (All Flavors)
Roasted Chicken Sweet Bell Pepper & Onion
Roasted Garlic Chicken
Smoked Chicken Turkey Sweet Basil Pesto
Spicy Jalapeño Chicken
Sun Dried Tomato Chicken
Sweet Italian (Chicken, Pork)
Uncured All Natural Beef Hot Dogs

Villa Roma - All Sausage Flavors

Wegmans - Pepperoni (Italian Style-Sliced)

Wellshire Farms -

Bratwurst (Aged Cheddar, Original, Smoked, Spicy Hot Style)

Bratwurst Hot Links New Orleans Style Smoked

Beef Franks/Hot Dogs (The Old Fashioned, The Premium)

Cheese Franks

Chicken Hot Dogs

Frozen Chicken Apple Sausage (Links, Patties)

Frozen Country Sage Sausage (Links, Patties)

Frozen Original Breakfast Sausage (Links, Patties)

Frozen Sunrise Maple Sausage (Links, Patties)

Frozen Turkey Maple Sausage (Links, Patties)

Morning Maple Turkey Breakfast Link Sausage

NY Style Big Beef Franks

Old Fashioned Deli Style Beef Salami

Original Matt's Select Pepperoni Steaks

Polska Kielbasa

Pork Andouille Sausage

Pork Sausage (Chorizo, Linguica, w/Green Peppers & Onions, w/Jalapeno & Aged Cheddar)

Sausage Patties (Chicken Apple, Country Sage, Original Style Pork, Sunrise Maple, Turkey Maple)

Sliced (Beef Pepperoni, Cooked Salami)

Smoked Pork Kielbasa Links

The Original Deli Franks

Turkey Andouille Sausage

Turkey Dinner Link Sausage (Jalapeno Herb, Mild Italian Style, Roasted Garlic & Parsley)

Turkey Franks

Turkey Kielbasa

S

Turkey Tom Toms (Hot & Spicy, Original)

Wellshire Kids - Uncured Corn Dogs (Beef, Chicken)

Whole Ranch - Franks (Beef, Turkey), Sausage (Bratwurst, Chorizo, Sweet Italian)

Wranglers - Franks

Yorkshire Farms - Linguica, Turkey Kielbasa

Scalloped Potatoes

Dinty Moore - Microwave Meals Scalloped Potatoes & Ham

Scallops

Trader Joe's - Bacon Wrapped Scallops

Seafood Sauce... see Cocktail Sauce

Seasoning

365 Every Day Value - Berber Ground Coriander, Brazilian Arrowroot, Catalina Cream of Tartar, Cayenne Pepper, Coarse Sea Salt, Crushed Red Chili Peppers, Ground Nutmeg, Herbes de Provence, Jamaican Allspice, Sea Salt, Sea Salt-Fine Crystals, Spanish Rosemary, Spanish Wild Thyme, Sweet Paprika, Turkish Bay Leaves, Valle del Sol Chile Powder, Whole Sesame Seeds

365 Organic Every Day Value - Basil, Black Pepper, Black Peppercorns, Cinnamon, Cumin, Garlic Powder, Ginger, Medium Grind, Minced Onion, Oregano, Parsley, Turmeric

A Taste of Thai - Chicken & Rice Seasoning

Accent - Flavor Enhancer

Albertsons - Italian, Onion

Astor - Basil Leaves, Caraway Seed, Cayenne Pepper, Celery (Flakes, Salt, Seed), Chives, Chopped Onion, Cinnamon Sugar, Coarse Grind Black, Cream of Tartar, Crushed Red Pepper, Curry Powder, Dill (Seed, Weed), Fine Grind White Pepper, Garlic (Pepper, Powder, Salt), Garlic & Parsley Salt, Ground (Allspice, Black Pepper, Cinnamon, Cloves, Cumin, Ginger, Mace, Marjoram, Nutmeg, Oregano, Red Pepper, Thyme, White Pepper), Imported Oregano, Instant Minced Garlic, Italian Seasoning, Meat Tenderizer (Gravy Pack),

Minced (Onion, Seed), Onion (Powder, Salt), Oregano, Paprika, Parsley Flakes, Peppermill Black Pepper, Poppy Seed, Rosemary Leaves, Rubbed Sage, Salt & Pepper Twin Pack, Sesame Seed, Thyme Leaves, Turmeric, Whole (Allspice, Bay Leaves, Black Pepper, Cinnamon Sticks, Cloves, Nutmeg, Oregano, Oregano Leaves, Pickling Spice)

Bali Spice - Chili & Garlic Seasoning, Coconut Chicken Curry Seasoning, Shallot & Herb Stir-Fry Seasoning

Dorothy Lane Market - Jack's Grill Rubs (Beef & Burger, Chicken & Poultry, Fish & Seafood, Pork), Jack's Grill Seasoning (Canadian Steak Rub, Chang Ma Fish & Fowl, Citrus Dill Salmon Rub, Lime Pepper Rub, Trout & Salmon Rub)

Durkee - Allspice, Alum, Anise Seed, Apple Pie Spice, Arrowroot, Basil, Bay Leaves, Caraway Seeds, Cardamom, Cayenne Pepper, Celery Flakes, Celery Seed, Chicken Seasoning, Chili Powder, Chives, Cilantro, Cinnamon, Cloves, Coriander, Cream of Tartar, Crushed Red Pepper, Cumin, Curry Powder, Dill Seed/Weed, Fennel, Garlic Minced, Garlic Powder, Garlic Salt, Ginger, Hickory Smoke Salt, Italian Seasoning, Jamaican Jerk Seasoning, Lemon & Herb, Lemon Garlic Seasoning, Lemon Pepper, Lime Pepper, MSG, Mace, Marjoram, Meat Tenderizer, Mint Leaves, Mustard, Nutmeg, Onion Minced, Onion Powder, Onion Salt, Orange Peel, Oregano, Oriental Five Spice, Paprika, Parsley, Pepper (All), Pepper Green Bell, Pickling Spice, Poppyseed, Poultry Seasoning, Pumpkin Pie Spice, Rosemary, Sage, Seasoned Pepper, Sesame Seed, Tarragon, Thyme, Turmeric

Durkee California Style Blends - Garlic Powder, Onion Powder

Emeril's - Asian Essence, Bayou Blast Essence, Baby Bam Essence, Italian Essence, Original Essence, Southwest Essence

Fischer's - Bay Leaves, Celery Salt, Chopped Onion, Cinnamon Sugar, Crushed Red Pepper, Garlic (Pepper, Powder, Salt), Garlic & Parsley Salt, Ground (Black Pepper, Cinnamon, Cumin, Red Pepper, Sage), Minced (Garlic,

Onion), Onion (Powder, Salt), Oregano Leaves, Parsley Flakes

Gayelord Hauser - Herbal Bouquet Italian, Satay Garlic Magic, Spike Salt-Free

Hy-Vee - Basil Leaf, Bay Leaves, Black Pepper, Chicken Grill Seasoning, Chili Powder, Chopped Onion, Dill Weed, Garlic Powder, Garlic Salt, Ground Cinnamon, Ground Cloves, Ground Mustard, Iodized Salt, Italian Seasoning, Lemon Pepper, Meat Tenderizer, Oregano Leaf, Paprika, Parsley Flakes, Plain Salt, Red Crushed Pepper, Rosemary, Salt & Pepper Shaker, Seasoned Salt, Steak Grilling Seasoning, Thyme

Laura Lynn - Black Pepper, Steak Seasoning

Lawry's - Seasoned Salt, Taco Seasoning Mix *(Chicken Only)*

Marcum Spices - Black Pepper, Canadian Steak Seasoning, Chili Powder, Crushed Red Pepper, Crushed Oregano, Coarse Ground Black Pepper, Fried Chicken Seasoning, Garlic Powder, Garlic Salt, Ground Cinnamon, Italian Seasoning, Lemon Pepper, Minced Onion, Onion Powder, Onion Salt, Paprika, Parsley Flakes, Seasoned Meat Tenderizer, Soul Seasoning, Rubbed Sage, Vanilla

McCormick -Alum, Anise Seed, Apple Pie Spice, Basil Leaves, Bay Leaves, Caraway Seed, Celery Flakes, Celery Seed, Chili Powder, Chives, Cilantro Leaves, Cinnamon Sticks, Cinnamon Sugar, Cream of Tartar, Cumin Seed, Curry Powder, Dill Seed, Dill Weed, Fennel Seed, Ground Allspice, Ground Cinnamon, Ground Cloves, Ground Cumin, Ground Ginger, Ground Mace, Ground Marjoram, Ground Mustard, Ground Nutmeg, Ground Oregano, Ground Sage, Ground Thyme, Ground Turmeric, Hot Mexican-Style, Chili Powder, Italian Seasoning, Marjoram Leaves, Mixed Pickling Spice, Mustard Seed, Oregano Leaves, Paprika, Parsley Flakes, Poppy Seed, Poultry Seasoning, Pumpkin Pie Spice, Rosemary Leaves, Rubbed Sage, Sage Leaves, Sesame Seed, Tarragon Leaves, Texas Style Chili Powder, Whole Allspice, Whole Cloves, Whole Mexican, Oregano (Orégano Entero)

Grill Mates Seasoning (Garlic & Onion, Lemon Pepper w/Herbs)

Seasoning Blends (Basil & Garlic , Parmesan Herb , Roasted Garlic & Bell Pepper)

Meijer Brand - Black Pepper, Chili Powder, Cinnamon, Garlic Powder, Garlic Salt, Minced Onion, Onion Salt, Oregano Leaves, Paprika, Parsley Flakes, Seasoned Salt, Spaghetti Mix

Midwest Country Fare - Chili Powder, Chopped Onion, Cinnamon, Garlic Powder, Garlic Salt, Ground Black Pepper, Imitation Vanilla Flavor, Italian Seasoning, Onion Powder, Parsley Flakes, Pure Ground Black Pepper, Season Salt

Mrs. Dash

Nantucket Off-Shore - Rub (Bayou, Dragon, Holiday Turkey, Mt. Olympus, Nantucket, Prairie, Pueblo, Rasta, Renaissance, St. Remy), Summer Shellfish Boil

Nielsen-Massey - Madagascar Bourbon Pure Vanilla Powder

Old Bay - Seasoning

Safeway - Fajita Seasoning Mix

Spartan Brand - Chili Powder, Cinnamon, Garlic Powder, Garlic Salt, Imitation Vanilla, Nutmeg Ground, Onion Minced, Oregano Leaves, Paprika, Parsley Flakes

Spice Islands - Allspice, Alum, Anise Seed, Apple Pie Spice, Arrowroot, Basil, Bay Leaves, Caraway Seed, Cardamom, Cayenne Pepper, Celery Flakes, Celery Seed, Chili Powder, Chives, Cilantro, Cinnamon, Cloves, Coriander, Cream of Tartar, Crushed Red Pepper, Cumin, Curry Powder, Dill Seed/Weed, Fennel, Garlic Minced, Garlic Pepper, Garlic Powder, Garlic Salt, Ginger, Hickory Smoke Salt, Italian Seasoning, Jamaican Jerk Seasoning, Lemon & Herb, Lemon Pepper, MSG, Mace, Marjoram, Meat Tenderizer, Mint Leaves, Mustard, Nutmeg, Onion Minced, Onion Powder, Onion Salt, Orange Peel, Oregano, Oriental Five Spice, Paprika, Parsley, Pepper (All), Pepper Green Bell, Pickling Spice, Poppyseed, Poultry Seasoning, Pumpkin Pie Spice, Rosemary, Sage, Salt Free Original All Purpose Seasoning, Sesame Seed, Smokey Mesquite Seasoning

S

Spice Islands Specialty - Beau Monde, Crystallized Ginger, Garlic Pepper Seasoning, Italian Herb Seasoning, Saffron, Vanilla Bean

Steak Dance - Meat Seasoning & Tenderizer

Steitenbacher - Seasoning

Tones - Allspice, Alum, Anise Seed, Apple Pie Spice, Arrowroot, Basil, Bay Leaves, Caraway Seeds, Cardamom, Cayenne Pepper, Celery Flakes, Celery Seed, Chicken Seasoning, Chili Powder, Chives, Cilantro, Cinnamon, Cloves, Coriander, Cream of Tartar, Crushed Red Pepper, Cumin, Curry Powder, Dill Seed/Weed, Fennel, Garlic Minced, Garlic Powder, Garlic Salt, Ginger, Hickory Smoke Salt, Italian Seasoning, Jamaican Jerk Seasoning, Lemon & Herb, Lemon Garlic Seasoning, Lemon Pepper, Lime Pepper, MSG, Mace, Marjoram, Meat Tenderizer, Mint Leaves, Mustard, Nutmeg, Onion Minced, Onion Powder, Onion Salt, Orange Peel, Oregano, Oriental Five Spice, Paprika, Parsley, Pepper (All), Pepper Green Bell, Pickling Spice, Poppyseed, Poultry Seasoning, Pumpkin Pie Spice, Rosemary, Sage, Seasoned Pepper, Sesame Seed, Tarragon, Thyme, Turmeric

Trader Joe's - Spices of the World (21 Seasoning Salute, Garlic Powder, Savory 4 Pepper Blend)

Tropical - Chopped Onion, Cinnamon Powder, Garlic (Powder, Salt), Ground (Bay Leaves, Black Pepper, Cloves, Coriander, Cumin, Oregano), Onion Powder, Paprika, Parsley Flakes, Sweet Basil, Whole Oregano

Wegmans - Cracked Pepper Blend, Fleur De Sel (Sea Salt), Herbes De Provence, Lemon Pepper Seasoning, Pepper Black

Whole Pantry - Anise Seed, Extra Fancy Spanish Thyme, Freeze Dried Chives, French Tarragon, Garam Masala, Ground Coriander, Ground Ginger, Ground Nutmeg, Guatemalan Cardamom, Marjoram, Muchi Curry Powder, Oregano, Organic (Dill Weed, Ground Cumin, Minced Garlic, Orange Peel, Paprika, Vanilla Bean), Poppy Seed, Spanish Saffron, Tellicherry Black Peppercorns, Turmeric, Vietnamese

S

Cinnamon, Whole (Bay Leaf, Cardamom, Cinnamon Sticks, Cumin Seed, Fennel Seed, Nutmeg, Sage, White Peppercorns)

Winn Dixie - Basil Leaves, Bay Leaves, Caraway Seed, Cayenne Pepper, Celery (Flakes, Salt, Seed), Chives, Chopped Onion, Cinnamon (Powder, Sugar), Coarse Grind Black, Cream of Tartar, Crushed Red Pepper, Curry Powder, Dill (Seed, Weed), Fine Grind White Pepper, Garlic & Parsley Salt, Garlic (Pepper, Powder, Salt), Ground (Allspice, Bay Leaves, Black Pepper, Cinnamon, Cloves, Coriander, Cumin, Ginger, Mace, Marjoram, Nutmeg, Oregano, Red Pepper, Sage, Thyme, White Pepper), Imported Oregano, Instant Minced Garlic, Italian Seasoning, Meat Tenderizer (Gravy Pack), Minced (Garlic, Onion, Seed), Onion (Powder, Salt), Oregano, Oregano Leaves, Paprika, Parsley Flakes, Peppermill Black Pepper, Poppy Seed, Pumpkin Spice, Rosemary Leaves, Rubbed Sage, Salt & Pepper Twin Pack, Sesame Seed, Sweet Basil, Thyme Leaves, Turmeric, Whole (Allspice, Bay Leaves, Black Pepper, Celery Seed, Cinnamon Sticks, Cloves, Nutmeg, Oregano, Oregano Leaves, Pickling Spice)

Seasoning Mixes

McCormick -

Fajita

Guacamole

Hickory BBQ Buffalo Wings

Italian Chicken

Salsa

Sloppy Joes

Taco Seasoning Mix (30% Less Sodium, Chicken, Hot, Mild, Regular) *(Except Cheesy Taco Seasoning Mix)*

Tex-Mex Chili

Seaweed

Nagai's - Sushi Nori Roasted Seaweed

Yaki - Sushi Nori Roasted Seaweed

S

Seeds
> **365 Every Day Value** - Whole Sesame Seeds
> **365 Organic Every Day Value** -
>> Organic Ray Pumpkin
>> Organic Sunflower Kernels (Roasted & Salted, Unsalted)
>
> **Arrowhead Mills** -
>> Flax
>> Golden Flax
>> Mechanically Hulled Sesame
>> Sunflower
>> Unhulled Sesame
>
> **Astor** - Caraway, Celery, Dill, Poppy, Sesame,
> **Durkee** - Anise, Celery, Dill, Poppy, Sesame
> **Eden** - Pumpkin (Regular, Spicy), Sunflower
> **Frito Lay** - Sunflower, Sunflower Kernels
> **Laura Lynn** - Sunflower
> **Meijer Brand** - Sunflower (Plain, Salted In Shell)
> **Pumpkin** - Seasoned Pumpkin
> **Safeway** - Sunflower Kernels
> **Spartan Brand** - Sunflower Kernels
> **Spice Island** - Anise, Caraway, Celery, Dill, Poppy, Sesame
> **Tones** - Anise, Caraway, Celery, Dill, Poppy, Sesame
> **Trader Joe's** -
>> Pumpkin (Dry Roasted Salted, Organic)
>> Pumpkin & Pepitas
>> Sunflower (Dry Roasted, Organic)
>> Wundflower
>
> **Whole Pantry** - Anise, Poppy, Whole Cumin, Whole Fennel
> **Winn Dixie** - Caraway, Celery, Dill, Poppy, Sesame

Sesame Oil ...see Oil

Shakes

Atkins - Chocolate, Strawberry, Vanilla

GeniSoy -
Powder/Shakes
Chocolate
Natural Unflavored
Strawberry
Vanilla
Ultra XT
Chocolate
Natural Unflavored
Vanilla

Glucerna - Shakes (All Varieties)

Grainaissance -
Almond Shake
Amazing Mango
Banana Appeal
Chocolate Almond
Chocolate Chimp
Cool Coconut
Gimme Green
Go Go Green
Go Hazelnuts
Oh So Original
Rice Nog
Tiger Chai
Vanilla Gorilla
Vanilla Pecan Pie

Hy-Vee - Diet Strawberry, French Vanilla Diet, Milk Chocolate Diet, Strawberry

Kashi - Chocolate & Vanilla, GoLean Shake

S

      Odwalla - All Drinks *(Except Super Protein Vanilla Al Mondo & Superfood)*

      Ruth's - Protein Powders (All Flavors)

      Safeway - Nutritional Shakes (Plus, Regular) (All Flavors)

      Worldwide - Pure Protein Shakes

Shortening

      Albertsons

      Crisco - Butter Flavor, Regular

      Earth Balance - All Varieties

      Hy-Vee - Vegetable (Oil Shortening, Shortening-Butter Flavor)

      Laura Lynn - #3 Vegetable

      Meijer Brand

      Midwest Country Fare - Pre-Creamed Shortening

      Price Chopper

      Shaw's

      Smart Balance

      Spartan Brand - Vegetable (All Canister, Butter Flavor)

      Stop & Shop Brand - Meat Fat/Vegetable Shortening, Vegetable

      Wegmans - Vegetable

Shrimp... *All Fresh Seafood Is Gluten-Free (Non-Marinated, Unseasoned)*

      B&J - Cooked Extra Colossal Sized Shrimp, Cooked Shrimp, Raw Shrimp, Shrimp Platter w/Sauce, Uncooked Shell-On Shrimp

      Captain's Choice - Cooked Tail On Shrimp

      Chicken Of The Sea - All Varieties

      Crown Prince - Shrimp (Broken, Tiny)

      Trader Joe's - Shrimp Scampi, Shrimp Stir-Fry

Shrimp Sauce... see Cocktail Sauce

Sloppy Joe/Sloppy Joe Sauce

      Hormel - Not-So-Sloppy-Joe, Sloppy-Joe Sauce

Hy-Vee - Sloppy Joe

Laura Lynn - Sloppy Joe Sauce

Meijer Brand

Safeway- Sloppy Joe

Spartan Brand - Sloppy Joe Sauce

Smoke Flavoring

Wright's - Hickory Liquid Smoke, Mesquite Liquid Smoke

Smoked Sausage... see Sausage

Smoked Turkey... see Turkey

Smoothies

Cascade Fresh Cascaders - Acai, Peach, Raspberry, Strawberry

Hansen's - All Smoothie Flavors

Hy-Vee - Yogurt Smoothie (Peach, Raspberry, Strawberry, Tropical)

Lifeway - All Products

Lucerne - All Varieties

Silk Live! Smoothies - All Smoothies

Tillamook - All Yogurt Smoothies

Tropicana Fruit Smoothies - All Varieties

V8 Splash - All Varieties

Whole Soy & Co. - All Varieties

Wildwood Harvest- Soyogurt Smoothies - All Varieties

Snacks

365 Every Day Value -

Angel Fluffs White Cheddar

Cheese (Curls, Puffs)

Organic Fruit Strip (Blueberry, Cherry, Cranberry, Peach, Strawberry, Very Berry)

Organic Honey Roasted (Cranberry Delight, Trail Mix)

Amaranth - Mini Ridges Cheddar, Snackers (BBQ Sweet Sassy, French Onion)

S

B&J - Fruit & Nut Mix, Healthy Blend Mix, Trail Mix

Baffles - Snack Clusters (BBQ, Caramel, Cheddar, Chocolate, Cinnamon)

Barbara's Bakery - Cheese Puffs (Jalapeno, Original, Original Bakes, White Cheddar Bakes)

Betty Lou's - Nut Butter Balls (Chocolate Walnut, Coconut Macadamia, Peanut)

Carole's - Soycrunch (All Varieties)

Cheetos -

Asteroids (Flamin' Hot Mini, Mini, Xxtra Flamin' Hot Mini)

Baked! (Crunchy, Flamin' Hot)

Butter Flavored Puffcorn Snacks

Cheese Flavored Snacks (Cheddar Jalapeno, Crunchy, Flamin' Hot, Flamin' Hot Limon

Jumbo (Puffs, Puffs Cheezy Pizza, Puffs Flamin' Hot), Natural White Cheddar Puffs, Reduced Fat, Twisted)

Cracker Jack - Butter Toffee Clusters

Doritos Rollitos - 3D's Nacho Corn Snacks, Tortilla Snacks (Cooler Ranch, Nacho Cheesier, Queso Picante!)

Eden - All Mixed Up (Regular, Too), Wild Berry Mix

Food Club - Cheese Balls

French's - Potato Sticks (BBQ, Cheezy Cheddar, Original, Sticks To Go)

Frito Lay - Trail Mix (Original, Sweet Honey)

Funyuns - Flavored Rings (Mini Onion, Onion)

GeniSoy -

Potato Soy Crisps

Country Style Ranch

Parmesan & Roasted Garlic

Sea Salt & Black Pepper

Texas Roadhouse BBQ

Soy Crisps

    Apple Cinnamon

    BBQ

    Cheddar Cheese

    Creamy Ranch

    Deep Sea Salted

    Garlic & Onion

    Nacho

    Tangy Salt 'N' Vinegar

Herr's -

    BBQ Flavored Pork Rinds

    Cheese Curls (Honey, Hot)

    Crunchy Cheese Sticks

    Potato Sticks

Hy-Vee -

    Cheeze-eze

    Fruit Snacks (Dinosaurs, Rescue Heroes, Sharks, Variety Pack, Veggie Tales)

    Nut Trail Mix (Chocolate, Raisin)

    Strawberry Fruit Rolls

    Tropical Trail Mix

Kellogg's - Fruit Flavored Snacks, Yogos

Laura Lynn -

    Baked Cheese Curls

    Cheese Krunchy

    Fruit Snacks (Aliens, Animal, Creepy, Dinosaur)

Little Bear - Puffs

Masuya - Rice Sembei (Dijonnaise, Original Lightly Salted, Sun Dried Tomato, Tamari)

Meijer Brand -

    Fruit Rolls

        Justice League Galactic Berry

S

Rescue Heroes
Strawberry
Strawberry Garfield
Wildberry Rush
Fruit Snacks
Curious George
Dinosaurs
Heroes Big Box
Justice League
Peanuts
Rescue Mixed Fruit
Sharks
Variety Pack
Variety Pack-Big Boy
Snacks
Caramel Corn
Cheese Popcorn
Cheese Pops
Cheese Puffs
Cheezy Treats
Chicago Style Popcorn
Potato Sticks
Purple Cow Butter Popcorn
White Cheddar (Popcorn, Puffs)
Xtreme Snack Bars

Munchos - Regular Potato Crisps
Nu-World Foods - All Varieties
O'Day's - French Fried Potato Tater Puffs
Realfood - Corn, Flax & Soy, Multi-Corn, Sesame
Robert's American Gourmet -
Booty (Cocoa, Fruity, Girl Friend's, Pirate's, Pirate's

    w/Caramel, Veggie)

Dudes' Corn Chips

Peace Puffs

Pirate's Cannon Balls

Pirate's Swords

Potato Flyers (Original, w/Balsamic)

Power Puffs

Smart Puffs

Sunflower Tings

Super Veggie Tings

Tings

Safeway - Puffed Cheese Curls

Season's - Cheese (Curl Lite Cheddar, Puffs Cheddar)

Spartan Brand -

Cheese Puffs

Fruit Rolls (Strawberry, Wild Berry)

Fruit Snacks (Curious George, Dinosaurs, Justice League, Rescue Heroes, Sharks, Variety Pack)

Snack Corn Chips

Stop & Shop Brand -

Corn Cakes (Apple Cinnamon, Caramel)

Fruit Snacks (Curious George, Dinosaur, Justice League, Peanuts, Sharks, Tom & Jerry, Underwater World Fruit, Variety Pack, Veggie Tales)

Snacks (Build A Bear Fruit Snacks, Circus Peanuts, Crunchy Cheese Corn Snacks, Puff Cheese Corn Snacks, Simply Enjoy Fruit Medley)

Sun Snacks - White Cheddar Cheese Puffs

Trader Joe's - Organic Banana Chips

UTZ - Baked Cheese Curls & Balls, Crunchy Cheese Curls, Natural White Cheddar Cheese Curls, Puff 'N Corn (Caramel, Cheese, Plain)

S

Wild Oats Label - Organic Caramel Corn Kettle Cooked (Regular, w/Almonds)

Soda Pop/Carbonated Beverages

365 Every Day Value -

Soda

Black Cherry

Cherry Vanilla Crème

Cola

Ginger Ale

Italian (Lemon, Orange, Pink Grapefruit, Sparkling Cranberry, Tangerine)

Orange Crème

Raspberry

Root Beer

Key Lime

7up -All Varieties

A & W - Root Beer

Alta Springs - All Carbonated Flavors

Aquafina -

FlavorSplash (Citrus Blend, Raspberry, Wild Berry)

Sparkling (Berry, Lemon Lime, Original)

B&J Soda -

Cola (Classic, Diet)

Fruit Flavored Spring Water

Sparkling Water Flavors Variety Pack

Variety Pack Soda Cans

Boylan's - Soda

Canada Dry -

Club Soda (All Varieties)

Gingerale (Diet, Regular)

Tonic Water (All Varieties)

soda pop/carbonated beverages

S

Chek - All Carbonated Soft Drink Flavors

Coca-Cola -
  Caffeine Free Coca Cola Classic
  Caffeine Free Diet Coke
  Cherry Coke
  Coca Cola (C2, Classic, w/Lime, Zero)
  Diet Barq's Red Crème Soda
  Diet Coke (Regular, Sweetened w/Splenda, Vanilla, w/Lime)
  Diet Sprite Zero
  Fresca
  Minute Maid Light Lemonade
  Sprite
  Vanilla Coke

Crush - All Varieties

Dr. Pepper - All Varieties

Diet Rite - All Varieties

Hires - Root Beer

Hy-Vee Soda -
  Cherry Cola
  Club Soda
  Cola (Diet, Regular)
  Cream Soda
  Diet Tonic
  Dr. Hy-Vee
  Fruit Punch (Coolers, Regular)
  Gingerale
  Grape
  Hee Haw (Diet, Regular)
  Lemon Lime
  Orange
  Root Beer (Diet, Regular)

S

Seltzer Water Sour
Strawberry
I.B.C. - Root Beer
Mountain Dew -
Caffeine Free
Caffeine Free Diet
Code Red (Diet, Regular)
Diet
Live Wire
Pitch Black II
Regular
X (Diet, Regular)
Orangina - Sparkling Citrus Beverage
Pepsi -
Caffeine Free Pepsi (Diet, Regular)
Diet Pepsi Jazz
Pepsi (Diet, Regular)
Pepsi Lime (Diet, Regular)
Pepsi One
Pepsi Twist (Diet, Regular)
Pepsi Vanilla (Diet, Regular)
Sierra Mist (Free, Regular)
Wild Cherry Pepsi (Diet, Regular)
Prestige - All Carbonated Soft Drink Flavors
RC Cola - All Varieties
Reeds Ginger Beer - All
Safeway Select - Sodas (All Varieties)
Schweppes - All Varieties
Spartan Brand -
Cola
Ginger Ale

Grape

Lemon Lime

Mountain Blast

Orange

Red

Root Beer

Squirt - All Varieties

Stewarts - All Varieties

Sunkist - Diet, Regular

Superbrand - Fruit Punch, Lemon, Orange

Trader Joe's Fresh -

Grapefruit Italian Soda

Grapefruit Spritzer

Old Fashioned Sparkling Apple Cider

Organic (Sparkling Grapefruit, Sparkling Lemon, Sparkling Lime)

Sparkling (Apple Cider, Apple Juice, Blueberry, Cranberry Juice, Pomegranate)

Tropical - Drink (Fruit Punch, Grape, Orange)

Vernors - Diet, Regular

Villa Italia - Soda (Lemon, Orange)

Virgil's - Root Beer

Wegmans -

Aqua Mineral Water

Italian

Lemon Flavored Italian

Lemongrass Flavored

Lime Flavored

Soda

Black Cherry

Cherry

S

Club Soda
Cola (Caffeine Free, Caffeine Free Diet, Diet, Regular)
Cream Soda
Diet (Cherry Grapefruit, Grapefruit, Peach Grapefruit, Lemon, Lime, Orange)
Dr. W (Diet, Regular, Soda)
Fountain Root Beer (Diet, Regular)
Ginger Ale (Diet, Regular)
Grape Soda
Green Apple Sparkling Soda (Diet, Regular)
Merge Cola
Mt. W
Orange Soda
Tonic (& Diet)
Vanilla Cola (Diet, Regular)
W Red
W UP (Diet, Regular)
Wedge
Sparkling Beverage
  Black Cherry
  Cranberry Raspberry
  Cranberry Soda
  Key Lime
  Kiwi Strawberry
  Lemonade
  Mixed Berry
  Peach
  Peach Grapefruit
  Red Raspberry
  Strawberry
Sparkling Beverage w/Sweeteners

Strawberry

Tangerine Lime

White Grape

Sparkling Juices

Cranberry

Grape (Pink, Red, White)

Welch's - Sparkling Soda (All Varieties)

Wild Oats Label - Natural Italian (Lemon Soda, Pink Grapefruit Soda)

Winn Dixie -All Carbonated Soft Drink Flavors, Drink (Fruit Punch, Grape, Lemon, Orange)

Soup

A Taste of Thai -

Coconut Ginger Soup Base

Curry Rice Noodle Soup

Hot & Sour Rice Noodle Soup

Amy's -

Chunky Vegetable

Corn Chowder

Cream of Tomato (Light Sodium, Regular)

Fire Roasted Southwestern Vegetable

Lentil (Light Sodium, Regular)

Lentil Vegetable (Light Sodium, Regular)

Organic Soup (Black Bean Vegetable, Chunky Tomato Bisque (Light Sodium, Regular)

Potato Leek

Split Pea (& Light Sodium)

Thai Coconut

Tuscan Bean & Rice

Baxters -

Ambient

S

Medley of Country Vegetable
Smoked Bacon & Mixed Vegetable
Chilled
  Carrot & Orange
  Carrot Parsnip & Sweet Potato
  Curried Parsnip & West Country Apple
  Mushroom Risotto
  Potato Leek & Bacon
  Spanish Chorizo & Chick Pea
  Spicy Dhal
  Tomato Bisque
  Vegetarian Hungarian Goulash
Healthy Choice
  Chicken & Vegetable
  Spicy Tomato & Rice
Healthy Helpings
  Chicken & Vegetable Casserole
  Chunky Country Vegetable Pumpkin/Sweetcorn & Red
Pepper
  Smoked Bacon & Three Bean
Favorites
  Cock-a-Leekie
  French Onion
  Lentil & Bacon
  Pea & Ham
  Potato & Leek
  Scotch Vegetable
Luxury
  Beef Consomme
  Chicken Consomme
  Lobster Bisque

Pouch Soup
- Aromatic Chicken w/Thai Herbs
- Carrot Chilli & Mascarpone w/Parmesan
- Red Lentil & Pancetta
- Rustic Chunky Vegetable & Lentil

Vegetarian
- Carrot & Butterbean
- Country Garden
- Mediterranean Tomato
- Tomato & Butterbean

Campbell's Chunky Soup -
- Chicken Broccoli Cheese
- Healthy Request Condensed Chicken Rice
- Savory Lentil

Dinty Moore - Beef Stew

Dr. McDougall's - Big Cup (Black Bean & Lime, Pad Thai, Tortilla)

Edward & Sons - Miso-Cup (Golden Light, Organic Traditional w/Tofu, Reduced Sodium, w/Seaweed)

El Peto - All Varieties

Ener-G - Cream Of Mushroom

Fantastic World Foods -

Soup
- Baja Black Bean Chipotle
- Buckaroo Bean Chili
- Creamy Potato Leek
- Great Lakes Cheddar Broccoli
- Southwest Tortilla Bean
- Split Pea Soup
- Summer Vegetable

S

Soup & Dip Recipe Mix
  Creamy Potato Soup Mix
  Garlic Herb
  Onion
  Onion Mushroom
  Vegetable

Food Club - Beef Stew

Fungus Among Us - Soup Mixes (All Varieties)

Glutino - All Varieties

Health Valley -
  Fat Free (5 Bean Veggie, 14 Garden Vegetable)
  Organic (Potato Leek, Tomato, Vegetable)
  Organic Fat Free (Black Bean & Vegetable, Corn & Veggie, Lentil & Carrot, Pea & Carrot)
  Organic No Salt Added (Black Bean, Green Split Pea, Lentil, Tomato, Vegetable)

Hormel - Microwave (Bean & Ham)

Imagine -
  Crab Bisque
  Lobster Bisque
  Organic Bistro (Corn Chipotle Bisque, Cuban Black Bean Bisque)
  Organic Broccoli
  Organic Creamy (Butternut Squash, Portobello Mushroom, Potato Leek, Sweet Corn, Sweet Potato, Tomato, Tomato Basil)

Laura Lynn - Chicken & Rice, Soup Mix (Beefy Onion, Onion)

Lipton - Cup-A-Soup Cream of Chicken, Recipe Secrets Onion Soup Mix

Manischewitz -
  Soup
    Chicken Rice Cup of Soup

Soup Mix
- Hearty Bean Cello
- Homestyle Mediterranean Black Bean
- Split Pea Homestyle
- Split Pea w/Seasoning Cello
- Tomato Vegetable Homestyle

Mayacamas - Dark Mushroom, French Onion, Lentil, Potato Leek, Tomato

Meijer Brand - Condensed Chicken w/Rice, Homestyle Chicken w/Rice

Midwest Country Fare - Onion

Orgran - Garden Vegetable, Sweet Corn, Tomato

Pacific Natural Foods -
- Creamy Roasted Carrot
- Hearty Chicken Tortilla
- Organic (Creamy Butternut Squash, Creamy Tomato, French Onion)
- Roasted Red Pepper & Tomato

Progresso
- Healthy Favorites Garden Vegetable Soup (50% Less Sodium)
- Traditional Carb
  - Monitor Chicken Cheese Enchilada Flavor
  - Monitor Chicken Vegetable
- Traditional
  - Manhattan Clam Chowder
  - New England Clam Chowder
  - Potato
  - Broccoli & Cheese Chowder
  - Chicken & Wild Rice
  - Chicken Rice w/Vegetables

S

Southwestern Style Corn Chowder

Southwestern Style Chicken

Split Pea With Ham

Chicken & Wild Rice Soup (Microwaveable Bowl)

Lentil Soup (Microwaveable Bowl)

Rich & Hearty

New England Clam Chowder (Chunky Style, Traditional 99% Fat Free)

Chicken Corn Chowder

Creamy Chicken Wild Rice

Steak & Sautéed Mushrooms (Chunky Style w/Lean Beef))

Vegetable Classics

French Onion

Lentil

Green Split Pea w/Bacon

Creamy Mushroom

Garden Vegetable

Hearty Black Bean w/Bacon, Lentil

Safeway - Condensed Homestyle Chicken w/Wild Rice, Chicken w/Rice

Safeway Select -

Signature Soups

Baked Potato Soup

Fajita Chicken

Fiesta Chicken Tortilla

Toasted Corn Chowder

Soup Mix

Onion Soup Mix

Shari -

Organic

Cream of Tomato

French Green Lentil
Indian Black Bean & Rice
Italian White Bean
Split Pea
Tomato w/Roasted Garlic
Shelton's - Black Bean & Chicken, Chicken Rice
Stop & Shop Brand - Condensed Chicken w/Rice Soup,
 Ready To Serve (Chunky Vegetable Soup)
Spartan Brand - Soup Mix Dry Onion & Dip
Thai Kitchen -
 Instant Rice Noodle Soup
 Bangkok Curry
 Garlic & Vegetable
 Lemongrass & Chili
 Spring Onion
 Thai Ginger
 Soup Cans (Coconut Ginger, Hot & Sour)
Trader Joe's -
 Organic Soup
 Black Bean
 Creamy Corn & Roasted Pepper
 Creamy Tomato
 Lentil Vegetable
 Lentil-Microwaveable
 Tomato & Roasted Red Pepper
 Sweet Potato Bisque
 Regular Soup
 Butternut (Apple Squash)
 Carrot Ginger
 Creamy (Corn & Roasted Red Pepper, Corn Chowder
  Potbelly, Vegetable Medley Bisque)

S

Instant Rice Noodle Soup (Mushroom, Roasted Garlic, Spring Onion)

Lentil Soup w/Vegetables

Miso Soup

Portuguese Bean & Sausage

Rich Onion Potbelly

Stew (India Sambhar Lentil, Premium Chicken, Spanish Chicken)

Sweet Potato Bisque

Walnut Acres - Organic Savory Lentil

Wegmans - Lobster Bisque, New England Clam Chowder, Spicy Red Lentil Chili

Wild Oats Label - Natural (Butternut Squash, Creamy Tomato Basil)

Winn Dixie - Bean w/Ham

Sour Cream

Albertsons - Regular

Cabot - Lite, Regular

Cascade Fresh - Regular

Daisy Brand - Pure & Natural

Food Club - Lite, Regular

Friendship - Light, Nonfat, Regular

Hood - All Varieties

Horizon Organic - Regular

Hy-Vee - Regular

Laura Lynn - Regular

Lucerne - Lowfat, Nonfat, Regular

Nancy's - All Products

Shamrock Farms - Light, Regular

Shaw's - Fat Free

Spartan Brand - Sour Cream (Nonfat, Regular)

Stop & Shop Brand - Sour Cream (Light, Nonfat)

Tillamook - All Varieties

Trader Joe's - Regular

Wegmans - Fat Free, Light, Regular

Winn Dixie - Lowfat, Nonfat, Regular

Soy Beverage/Soy Milk

365 Organic Every Day Value -

Soy Beverage (Chocolate, Original, Vanilla)

Soy Original Refrigerated

Vanilla Soy Drink

Better Than Milk

Eden - EdenBlend, Edensoy (Unsweetened)

Ener-G - Soyquik

Full Circle - Soy Milk (Chocolate, Original, Vanilla)

Health Market Organic - Soy Milk (Chocolate, Original, Vanilla)

Hy-Vee -

Refrigerated Soymilk (Chocolate, Original, Vanilla)

Soy Milk (Chocolate, Original, Strawberry, Vanilla)

Laura Lynn / Harvest Farms - Soy Milk

Nature's Promise -

Chocolate Soymilk

Organic

1%, 2%

Chocolate Soymilk

Fat Free

Soymilk

Vanilla Soymilk

Whole

Odwalla - Soy Milk (Choc-ahh-lot, Plain, Vanilla Being)

Pacific Natural Foods - Organic Soy Unsweetened Original, Select Soy Low Vanilla, Ultra Soy Plain

S

Price Chopper - Soy Milk (All Varieties)
Safeway Select - Organic Soy Beverage
ShopRite - Soy Milk (Chocolate, Original, Vanilla)
Silk Soymilk (White Wave) - All Varieties (Silk Creamer, Silk Soymilk)
Soy Dream -
  Refrigerated Non-Dairy Soy Milk
    Classic Original
    Enriched Original
    Enriched Vanilla
  Shelf Stable Non-Dairy Soy Milk
    Classic Vanilla
    Enriched Chocolate
    Enriched Original
    Enriched Vanilla
SoySense - Chocolate, Original, Vanilla
Trader Joe's -
  Organic Soy Milk (Unsweetened)
  Soy Milk
    Chocolate
    Fat Free
    Original
    Organic Original
    Strawberry
    Unsweetened
    Vanilla
Vitasoy - Complete (Original, Vanilla), Holly Nog
Westsoy - 100% Organic Unsweetened Soy Beverage, Original
Wild Oats Label - Soymilk (Original, Vanilla)
Wildwood Harvest - Soy Milk (All Varieties)
Zensoy - All Varieties

Soy Burgers... see Burgers

Soy Chips... see Chips

Soy Crisps... see Crisps

Soy Flour... see Flour

Soy Sauce

    Eden Organics - Tamari Soy Sauce

    Food City

    Hy-Vee

    LaChoy - Lite, Regular

    Price Chopper

    San-J - Wheat Free Soy Sauce (Reduced Sodium, Regular)

    Save-A-Lot - Jade Dragon

    Spartan Brand - Original

Soy Yogurt... see Yogurt

Soybeans... see also Edamame
      *All **Fresh** Fruits & Vegetables Are **Gluten-Free***

    Wild Oats Label - Honey Toasted, Roasted & Salted, Roasted & Unsalted

Soymilk... see Soy Beverage

Spaghetti... see Pasta

Spaghetti Sauce... see Sauce

Spice... see Seasoning

Spinach... *All **Fresh** Fruits & Vegetables Are **Gluten-Free***

    365 Organic Every Day Value - Frozen Spinach

    Albertsons - Canned & Frozen

    B&J - Chopped Spinach

    Birds Eye - All Frozen Vegetables *(Except With Sauce)*

    Cascadian Farms - Chopped Spinach

    Del Monte - All Varieties

    Freshlike - Frozen Plain Vegetables *(Except Pasta Combos and Seasoned Blends)*

S

Green Giant - Frozen Vegetables (Creamed Spinach w/Artificial Cream Flavor, Cut (Leaf Spinach & Butter Sauce), No Sauce)

Hy-Vee - Frozen (Chopped, Leaf)

Laura Lynn - Canned

Marsh

Meijer - Frozen Spinach (Chopped, Cut Leaf, Leaf), Canned (Cut Leaf, No Salt, Regular)

Pictsweet - All Plain Vegetables (Frozen)

S&W - All Varieties

Stop & Shop Brand - Chopped, Cut, Leaf, No Salt Added, Regular

Tasty Bite - Kashmir Spinach, Spinach Dal

Wegmans - Whole Leaf Spinach

Sports Drinks

Gatorade - All Varieties (Performance Series, Propel Fitness Water, Thirst Quencher)

Powerade - Mountain Blast

Spartan Brand - Isotonic Sport Drink

Trader Joe's - Traderade

Wegmans -

MVP Sport Drink

Blue Freeze

Fruit Punch

Grape

Green Apple

Lemon Lime

Orange

Raspberry Lemonade

Velocity Fitness Water

Berry

Black Cherry

S

Grape
Kiwi Strawberry
Lemon
Winners Thirst Quencher
Amazon Freeze
Fruit Punch
Glacier Wave
Lemon
Lemon Ice
Lemon Lime
Orange
Tangerine Freeze
Tropical

Spread

365 Every Day Value -
Fruit Spread
Apricot
Black Cherry
Blackberry
Forest Raspberry
Strawberry
Wild Blueberry
Benecol - Light, Spread
Bett's - Cheddar Cheese & Horseradish Spread
Bionaturae - Fruit Spread (All Varieties)
Canoleo - 100% Canola Margarine
Earth Balance - All Varieties
Fleischmann's - All Varieties
Hy-Vee -
100% Corn Oil Margarine
Soft Margarine (Regular, Rich & Creamy)

S

Soft Spread
Vegetable Margarine Quarters
I Can't Believe It's Not Butter - All Varieties
Land-O-Lakes - Margarine
Laura Lynn -
Margarine (Lite, Quarters, Spread)
Peanut Butter & Grape Jelly Spread
Peanut Butter & Strawberry Jelly Spread
Squeezable Margarine
Taste Like Butter
Manischewitz - Apple Butter Spread
Maple Grove Farms of Vermont - Blended Maple, Honey
Maple Spread, Pure Maple
Meijer Brand -
Margarine Corn Oil Quarters
Margarine Soft (Sleeve, Tub)
Spread 48% Crock
Spread 70% Quarters
Spread No Ifs Ands Or Butter
Price Chopper - Margarine Spread
Safeway -
Vegetable Oil Spreads (37% Light, 70%)
Sticks (Homestyle)
Margarine
Shedd's Willow Run - Soy Bean Margarine
Smart Balance - All Products
Spartan Brand -
70% Quarters
Butter (Quarters, Solids)
Is It Butter 70%
Margarine (Corn Oil Quarters, Quarters, Soft Tub)

Margarine Soft Sleeve
Spread 52% Crock

Stop & Shop Brand - Simply Enjoy Smoked Salmon Dill
Sandwich Spread

Trader Joe's - Eggplant Garlic Spread, Natural Margarine,
Spicy India Spread

Walden Farms - Blueberry, Grape, Raspberry, Strawberry

Whole Kids Organic - Spread (Mixed Berry, Strawberry)

Wild Oats Label - Fruit Spread (Apricot, Blackberry, Blueberry,
Concord Grape, Raspberry, Strawberry)

Wegmans -

Margarine

Vegetable Oil Club Pack & Tubs (48%, 52 %, 80%)

Winn Dixie -

Vegetable Oil (48%, 68%, 80%)

Lite Vegetable Oil (40%, 52%)

Sprinkles... see Baking Decorations & Frostings

Squash... *All Fresh Fruits & Vegetables Are Gluten-Free*

Albertsons - Canned & Frozen

Cascadian Farms - Organic (Winter Squash)

Meijer Brand - Frozen Squash (Cooked)

Pictsweet - All Plain Vegetables (Frozen)

Stop & Shop Brand

Wild Oats Label - Organic Frozen (Chopped Spinach)

Starch

Argo - Corn Starch

Authentic Foods - Potato Starch

Bob's Red Mill - Arrowroot, Potato

Ener-G - Potato Starch

Glutino - Corn Starch, Potato Starch

Kingsford's - Corn Starch

S

    Laura Lynn - Corn Starch

    Manischewitz - Potato Starch

    Price Chopper - Corn Starch

    Safeway Brand - Corn Starch

Steak... *All Fresh Cut Meat Is **Gluten-Free (Non-Marinated, Unseasoned)***

    Trader Joe's - Australian Strip Steak

Steak Sauce

    Hargis House

    Hy-Vee - Classic

    Laura Lynn

    Lea & Perrins - Hot Pepper

    Meijer Brand

    Mr. Spice - Garlic Steak

    Safeway

    Shaw's

    Spartan Brand - Original

    Wegmans

Stew

    Dinty Moore - Beef, Chicken Stew, Microwave Meals Beef Stew

Stir-Fry

    365 Every Day Value - Asian, Texican Veggie Roundup

    Albertsons - Stir-Fry Vegetables

    Amy's - Asian Noodle, Thai

    Cascadian Farm - Organic (Chinese, Thai Vegetable Blend)

    Green Giant - Create A Meal! Stir-Fry (Sweet & Sour)

    Meijer - Stir-Fry

    Stop & Shop Brand - Japanese Stir-Fry Blend

    Trader Joe's - Shrimp Stir-Fry

Stir-Fry Sauce

    Mr. Spice - Ginger

S

Stock

Emeril's - Beef

Imagine - Organic Cooking Stock (Beef, Chicken, Vegetable)

Kitchen Basics - Beef, Chicken

Wegmans - All Natural Culinary Stock (Beef Flavored, Chicken, Thai, Vegetable)

Strawberries... *All Fresh Fruits & Vegetables Are Gluten-Free*

Hy-Vee - Frozen (Sliced Strawberries, Whole Strawberries)

Marsh Brand - Frozen Sliced Strawberries

Meijer Brand - Strawberries (Sliced, Whole, Whole Individually Quick Frozen)

Spartan Brand - Strawberries Mixed Fruit

Stop & Shop Brand - Sliced Strawberries (In Sugar, Regular, w/Artificial Sweetener), Strawberries

Trader Joe's - Freeze Dried Strawberries, Strawberries N Crème

Wegmans - Sliced (Strawberries w/Sugar), Strawberries

Wild Oats - Light Sliced Strawberries w/Aspartame, Organic Frozen Whole Strawberries, Sweetened Unsulphured Dried Strawberries

Stuffing

El Peto - All Varieties

Orgran - Coating & Stuffing Mix

Sugar

365 Every Day Value - Brown, Raw Turbinado

365 Organic Every Day Value

Dixie Crystals - All Varieties

Domino -

Brownulated

Cubes

Demerara Sugar Sticks

Demerara Washed Raw Cane

S

Organic

Sugar 'N Cinnamon

Superfine

Tablets

Food Club - Confectioners, Granulated, Light Brown

Hy-Vee - Confectioners Powdered, Dark Brown, Light Brown, Pure Cane

Imperial Sugar - All Varieties

Laura Lynn - Brown, Confectioners, White

Meijer Brand - Confectioners, Dark Brown, Granulated, Light Brown

Rapunzel - Powdered

Safeway - Brown, Granulated, Powdered

Spartan Brand - Confectioners, Granulated, Light Brown

Stop & Shop Brand - Granulated

Thrifty Maid

Tops - Light Brown

Trader Joe's - Brown, Organic, Turbinado

United Sugar Products - Crystal Sugar Products

Wegmans - Dark Brown, Granulated White, Light Brown

Wholesome Sweeteners - All Varieties

Winn Dixie

Sugar Substitute/Sweetener

Albertsons - Aspartame

B&J - Sweetener Sugar Substitute

Equal

Hy-Vee - Aspartame Sweetener, Saccharin Sugar Substitute

Safeway - Aspartame Sweetener

Splenda - Sugar Substitute

Sweet and Low

Wegmans - Sugar Substitute w/Saccharin, Sweetener w/Aspartame

Wholesome Sweeteners - All Varieties

Sunflower Seeds... see Seeds

Sweet & Sour Sauce

Contadina - All Varieties

LaChoy

Mr. Spice

Olde Cape Cod

Trader Joe's

Sweet Potatoes... *All Fresh Fruits & Vegetables Are Gluten-Free*

Green Giant - Frozen Candied Sweet Potatoes

Swiss Chard... *All Fresh Fruits & Vegetables Are Gluten-Free*

Syrup

365 Organic Every Day Value - Maple Syrup (Grade A
(Dark, Light, Medium), Grade B)

Albertsons - Chocolate

Astor - Chocolate, Strawberry

Aunt Jemima - All Varieties

B&J - 100% Pure Maple

Brer Rabbit - Full Flavor, Light

Flavorganics - All Syrup Varieties

Golden Griddle - Pancake

Grand Selections - 100% Pure Maple

Hershey's - Chocolate (Lite, Regular)

Hy-Vee -

Butter Flavor

Chocolate

Lite Pancake

Pancake

Pancake & Waffle

Strawberry

Kellogg's - Eggo Syrup

S

Laura Lynn - Pancake & Waffle (Lite, Regular)

Manischewitz - Chocolate

Maple Grove Farms of Vermont -

Maple

Apricot

Blueberry

Pure & Organic

Raspberry

Strawberry & Boysenberry

Sugar Free

Butter Flavor

Maple Flavor

Vermont

Maple Ridge - Buttery, White Corn

Marsh Brand - Pancake

Meijer Brand - Chocolate

Midwest Country Fare - Chocolate Flavored, Pancake & Waffle

nSpired - Ah!Laska - Organic Chocolate

Safeway Select - Butter Light, Chocolate, Light, Old Fashioned, Pure Maple

Shaw's - Lite Maple

Smucker's - All Fruit

Stop & Shop Brand - Chocolate

Trader Joe's - Maple

Vermont Maid - Light, Syrup

Walden Farms - Calorie Free Sugar Free Chocolate, Sugar Free Pancake

Wegmans -

Buttery Flavor

Light Reduced Calorie Pancake

Maraschino Cherry Flavored

    Pancake
    Pancake Lite
    Pancake Made w/ 2% Real Maple
  Regular
    Creamy Caramel
    Corn (Light, Regular)
    Maple
    Pure Maple (Dark Amber, Regular)
Whole Treat - Creamy Caramel, Dark Chocolate
Winn Dixie - Chocolate, Strawberry

T

Taco Sauce

Chi-Chi's - Taco Sauce
Hy-Vee - Medium, Mild
La Victoria - All Varieties
Laura Lynn - Regular
Old El Paso - Hot, Medium, Mild, Taco Toppers (Mild, Zesty Ranch)
Ortega - Taco Sauce (Mild, Spicy)
Taco Bell - Restaurant Sauce (Mild, Hot)

Taco Seasoning

Albertsons - Taco Seasoning Mix
Chi-Chi's - Fiesta Restaurante Seasoning Mix
Hy-Vee
Lawry's - Taco Seasoning Mix *(Chicken Only)*
Meijer Brand - Mild Taco Seasoning
Old El Paso - Mix (40% Less Sodium, Burrito Sea, Enchilada Sauce, Fajita, Mild, Regular)
Shaw's

T

Taco Shells
> **Food Club** - Taco Shells
> **Hy-Vee** - Taco Shells, White Corn Tortilla
> **Meijer Brand** - Taco Shells
> **Old El Paso** -
>> Stand 'N Stuff Taco Shells (Nacho, Regular, Salsa)
>> Taco Salad Shells (Yellow Corn)
>> Taco Shells (Super Stuffer, White Corn, Yellow Corn)
>> Tostada Shells
>
> **Ortega** - White Corn Taco Shells
> **Safeway** - Taco Shells (Jumbo, White Corn)
> **Tops** - Taco Shells

Tahini
> **365 Organic Every Day Value** - Tahini
> **Arrowhead Mills** - Sesame Tahini
> **Maranatha** - Organic (No-Salt Roasted Sesame, Raw Sesame)

Tamales
> **Costco** - Beef, Delimex Beef
> **Delimex** - Beef, Chicken & Cheese
> **Hargis House**
> **Hormel** - Beef
> **Sam's Club** - Beef
> **Schwan's** - Beef
> **Trader Joe's** - Beef, Cheese, Chicken, Chicken & Cheese, Handmade Green Chili & Cheese

Tangerines... *All **Fresh** Fruits & Vegetables Are **Gluten-Free***

Tapioca pudding
> **Let's Do...Organic** - Granulated, Small Pearl, Starch

Taquitos
> **365 Every Day Value** - Chicken
> **Costco** - Beef, Chicken

Delimex - Beef (Mexico Import), Beef / Deli-Pak, Chicken, Three Cheese,

El Monterey - Chicken Corn, Shredded Steak Corn

Mini Taquitos - Snacker Tray w/Salsa

Sam's Club - Beef

Schwan's - Beef w/Salsa

Smart & Final - Beef

Trader Joe's - Black Bean, Chicken

Whole Kids Organic - Organic (Bean & Cheese, Chicken)

Tartar Sauce

Baxters

Golden Dipt

Laura Lynn - Squeeze Tartar

Spartan Brand

Wegmans

Wild Oats - Organic Tartar Sauce

Tater Tots... see Potatoes

Tea

365 Every Day Value - Organic Tea (Berry Black, Black, Green, Green Mint, Green w/Lemon & Ginger, Lemon, White Jasmine, White Peach)

Arizona - Green Tea w/Ginseng (Diet, Honey)

Astor - Family Size, Instant

Authentic Food Artisan - Organic Rishi Tea (Silver Needle, Wile Tou Cha Pu-erth)

B&J - Iced Tea Mix (Decaf, w/Lemon)

Bigelow Tea - All Varieties *(Except Blueberry Harvest, Chamomile Mango, Cinnamon Spice, Take-A-Break)*

Celestial Seasonings -

Black Teas - Bali Black Raspberry, Black Cherry Pomegranate, Decaf Devonshire English Breakfast, Fast Lane, Golden Honey Darjeeling, Mango Darjeeling

T

Organic, Marrakech Express Vanilla Spice, Morning Thunder, Organic Black, Persian Mint Spice Decaf, Tuscany Orange Spice, Victorian Earl Grey (Decaf, Regular)

Chai Tea - Chocolate Caramel Enchantment, Decaf Original India Spice TeaHouse, Honey Vanilla White, Original India Spice TeaHouse, Sweet Coconut Thai Decaf, Vanilla Ginger Green

Green Tea - Antioxidant, Authentic, Blueberry Breeze, Decaf (Green, Honey Chamomile, Lemon Myrtle Organic, Mandarin Orchard, Mint Green), Goji Berry Pomegranate, Green Tea Sampler, Honey Lemon Ginseng, Lemon Zinger, Organic Green, Raspberry Gardens, Tropical Acai Berry

Herbal Tea - Acai Mango Zinger, Bengal Spice, Black Cherry Berry, Casein-Free, Candy Cane Lane Decaf, Chamomile, Cinnamon Apple, Classic Black Tea, Country Peach Passion, Cranberry Apple Zinger, Green Blueberry Breeze, Green Mint Decaf, Green Raspberry Garden, Fruit Tea Sampler, Herb Tea Sampler, Honey Vanilla Chamomile, Lemon Zinger, Mandarin Orange Spice, Mint Magic, Peppermint, Raspberry Zinger, Red Zinger, Sleepytime, Sweet Apple Chamomile, Sweet Clementine Chamomile Organic, Tangerine Orange Zinger, Tension Tamer, Tropic Of Strawberry, True Blueberry, Wild Berry Zinger

Holiday Tea - Candy Cane Lane, Nutcracker Sweet, Rudolph's Rockin' Raspberry Kids', Santa's Candy Sweet

Honeybush - Peach Apricot

Iced Tea - Blueberry Ice, Lemon Ice, Peach Ice, Raspberry Ice

Rooibos Tea - African Orange Mango African, Madagascar Vanilla Red, Moroccan Pomegranate Red, Red Safari Spice

Wellness Tea - Diet Partner, Echinacea Complete Care, Honey Peach Ginger, Metabo Partner, Sleepytime Extra, Tension Tamer, Throat Soothers, Tummy Mint

White Tea - Antioxidant Plum, Decaf China Pearl, Imperial White Peach, Perfectly Pear, Vanilla Apple Organic

Choice - Organic Green Jasmine Tea

Dixie Home - Tea

Fischer's - Family Size (Decaf, Regular), Tagless

Food Club - Green Tea, Southern Sweet Tea

Hansen's - All Products

Health Market - Green Tea Extract

Hy-Vee - Decaf (Green, Regular), Green Tea, Tea Bags, Thirst Splashers Raspberry Tea

Inko's - All Varieties White Tea

Kandia's Tea - All Varieties

Laura Lynn - Cold Brew, Decaf, Family, Family Decaf, Green, Tagless, Tea Bags

Lipton -

Diet Ice Tea Mix

Lemon-Decaf

Lemon-Regular

Peach

Raspberry

Tea & Lemonade

Regular

Calorie Free Ice Tea Mix (Lemon)

Decaf

Instant Ice Tea (100% Instant & Decaf)

Sugar Sweetened & Green Tea Bags (Regular, Jasmine)

Soothing Moments

Flavored Tea Bags (Blackberry Regular & Decaf, Mint, Orange & Spice Regular & Decaf, Raspberry)

Herbal Tea Bags (Cinnamon Apple, Country Cranberry, Gentle Orange, Ginger Twist, Moonlight Mint, Peppermint, Quietly Chamomile)

T

Meijer Brand - Iced Tea Mix

Midwest Country Fare - Tea Bags 100 Count

Nature's Promise - Organic Fair Trade Green Tea (Decaf, Lemon, Regular)

Newman's Own - Iced Tea, Lemon Aided Ice Tea, Lemonade Iced Tea

Numi - All Varieties

Oregon - Original Chai Tea Latte

Pacific Natural Foods - Organic Iced Tea (Black, Green, Lemon, Peach, Raspberry)

Price Chopper - Instant Iced Tea

Red Rose - All Varieties

Republic Of Tea - All Varieties

Rishi - All Varieties

Safeway Select - Green Tea, Herbal Tea (Chamomile, Evening Delight, Lemon, Peppermint), Iced Tea Mix (All Flavors)

Salada Tea - All Varieties

Save-A-Lot - Somerset Iced Tea Mix

Shaw's - Iced Tea Mix

SoBe - Black, Green, Lean Green, Oolang, Peach, Zen

Somerset - Iced Tea Mix, Instant Tea

Spartan Brand - Instant Tea, Tea Bags (Black, Decaf, Green)

Stash Tea - All Varieties

Suberbrand - Sweet Tea, Tea w/NutraSweet

Tazo Tea - All Varieties

Tejava - Unsweetened Tea

Trader Joe's - All Tea, Chai No Sugar Added, Green Tea-Unsweetened, Matcha Latte, Spicy Chai Latte

Twinings Tea - All Varieties

Wegmans -
Black Tea
Decaf (Black Tea, Green Tea)

Green Tea

Iced Tea (Diet, Regular)

Ice Tea Mix (Decaf, w/Natural Lemon Flavor & Sugar)

Orange Pekoe & Pekoe Cut Black Tea

Organic (Chamomile, Earl Grey, English Breakfast, Jasmine Green, Peppermint, Rooibos Strawberry Cream)

Pink Lemonade Ice Tea Mix (Decaf, w/Natural Lemon Flavor & Sugar)

Winn Dixie - Drink (Sweet Tea, Tea w/NutraSweet), Family Size (Decaf, Regular), Tagless

Teff

Bobs Red Mill - Whole Grain Teff

Tempeh

Lightlife - Flax, Garden, Soy, Wild Rice

White Wave - Original Soy, Soy Rice

Wildwood Harvest - All Varieties

Teriyaki Sauce

LaChoy

Premier Japan - Wheat Free

Tequila... *All Distilled* Alcohol Is **Gluten-Free**[2]

Tikka

Amy's - Indian Paneer Tikka

Stop & Shop - Simply Enjoy (Tikka Masala)

Tilapia... see Fish

Tofu

365 Organic Every Day Value - Extra Firm, Firm

Amy's - Indian Mattar Tofu

Lightlife - Tofu Pups

Mori-Nu -

Chinese Spice Seasoned

Japanese Miso Seasoned

T

Silken (Extra Firm, Firm, Lite, Soft)

Organic Silken Tofu All Varieties

Nasoya Foods - Firm Enriched, Organic (Extra Firm, Firm, Soft), Silken Tofu Enriched

Pete's Tofu - Italian Herb

Soya Nova Tofu - Garlic & Dill, West Coast Smoked

Stop & Shop Brand - Tofu (Extra Firm, Firm)

Trader Joe's - Tofu Organic (Extra Firm, Firm)

Wegmans - Tofu, X-Firm

White Wave - Extra Firm, Fat Reduced, Hard, Organic (Firm, Soft)

Wildwood Harvest - Plain

Tomatillos... *All Fresh Fruits & Vegetables Are **Gluten-Free***

Las Palmas - Crushed Tomatillos

Tomato Juice... see Drinks/Juice

Tomato Paste

365 Every Day Value - Organic Tomato

Albertsons - Regular

Amore - Paste All Varieties

Contadina - Tomato Paste (Regular, w/Pesto, w/Roasted Garlic) *(Except Contadina Italian Paste w/Italian Seasonings)*

Del Monte - All Varieties

Hy-Vee - Regular Tomato

Nielsen-Massy - Madagascar Bourbon Pure Vanilla Bean

Price Chopper - Regular Tomato

S&W Premium - Tomato

Shop & Stop Brand - Tomato

Spartan Brand

Wegmans - Tomato

Tomato Puree

Contadina

Price Chopper

    Progresso

    S&W

    Shaw's

    Wegmans

Tomato Sauce... see Sauce

Tomatoes... *All Fresh Fruits & Vegetables Are Gluten-Free*

    365 Every Day Value - Crushed w/Basil, Crushed & Rosemary, Diced, Peeled Whole

    365 Organic Every Day Value - Organic (Diced, Italian Whole Peeled w/Basil, No Salt Added, Whole Peeled)

    Albertsons - Canned

    B&J - Sun Dried Imported

    Bionaturae - All Tomato Products

    Contadina - All Varieties (Crushed, Diced, Stewed, Whole Tomatoes)

    Del Monte - All Varieties *(Except w/Flavored Meat)*

    Eden - Crushed (Regular, w/Basil, w/Onion), Diced (Regular, w/Chilies, w/Basil, w/Roasted Onion), Whole Roma, Whole w/Basil

    Hunts - All Varieties

    Hy-Vee - Crushed, Diced (Chili Ready, w/Chilies, w/Garlic & Onion), Italian Style (Diced, Stewed), Mild Diced & Green Chilies, Original Diced & Green Chilies, Petite (Cut, Diced), Stewed, Tomato Paste, Whole Peeled

    Laura Lynn - Tomatoes

    Pictsweet - All Plain Vegetables (Frozen)

    S&W - All Varieties

    Safeway - All Canned

    San Andrea - Sun Dried Tomatoes

    Shaw's - Canned

    Spartan Brand -

        Canned

            Crushed Specialty

T

    Stewed
    Stewed Italian
    Whole
  Diced
    For Chili
    Italian
    Mexican
    Regular
    w/Green Chilies
    w/Roasted Garlic & Onion

Stop & Shop Brand -
  Crushed (Italian Seasonings, No Added Salt, Regular)
  Diced (Italian Seasonings, No Added Salt, Regular)
  Stewed (Italian Seasonings, Mexican Style, No Added
    Salt, Regular)
  Whole Peeled (No Added Salt, Regular)

Trader Joe's - Dried Organic, Julienne Sliced Sun Dried, Sun-Dried Tomato Bruschetta

Wegmans -
  Crushed
  Diced (Chili Style, Italian Style, Roasted Garlic & Onion)
  Coarse Ground
  IC Crushed w/Herb
  IC Whole Roma
  Italian Style Stewed
  Kitchen Cut w/Basil
  Peeled Whole
  Stewed
  Whole (No Salt, Regular, w/Basil)

Tonic... see Soda Pop/Carbonated Beverages

Tortilla Chips... see Chips

Tortilla Soup... see Soup
Tortillas
>**Food For Life -** Brown Rice, Sprouted Corn
>**Manny's -** Authentic Corn Tortillas
>**Mission -** White Corn Tortillas
>**Que Pasa -** Corn Tortillas
>**San Carlos -** Corn Tortillas
>**Trader Joe's -** 100% Corn Tortillas
>**Winn Dixie -** Corn Tortilla

Trail Mix... see also Nuts
>**365 Organic Every Day Value -**
>>Cranberry
>>Chocolate Banana Trail Mix
>>Fruit-Chocolate & Nut Mix
>>Hulabaloo Mix
>>Organic Honey
>>Raw Trail Mix
>>Tropical Trail Mix
>
>**Enjoy Life -** Not Nuts!
>**Frito Lay -** Original
>**GeniSoy Trail Mix -** Happy Trails, Mountain Medley, Tropical Trails,
>**Hy-Vee -** Nut Trail Mix (Chocolate, Raisin), Tropical Trail Mix
>**Safeway -** Trail Mix w/Candy Pieces
>**Trader Joe's -**
>>Almond & Cherry Mix
>>Antioxidant Nut & Berry Mix
>>Cashews & Cranberries Trek Mix
>>Cranberry Trail Mix
>>Go Raw Trek Mix
>>Organic Trek Mix w/(Almonds, Chocolate Chips,

T

    Cranberries)

    Pistachio

    Rainbow Trail Mix

    Savory & Tart Trek Mix

    Simply Almonds

    Pistachio

    Simply The Best Trek Mix

    Sweet

    Tempting Trail Mix

Trek Mix... see Trail Mix

Truffles

    Safeway Select - Butterscotch, Chocolate/Raspberry, Milk Chocolate, Mocha

Tuna... *All Fresh Fish Is Gluten-Free (Non-Marinated, Unseasoned)*

    Albertsons - Canned Tuna

    Bumble Bee - All Varieties *(Crackers In Ready-to-Eat Salads & Crackers Is NOT Gluten-Free,)*

    Chicken Of The Sea - All Varieties *(Except Teriyaki Tuna Cups, Tuna Salad Kits)*

    Grand Selections - Solid White Albacore Tuna

    Hy-Vee - Light Chunk Tuna In (Oil, Water)

    Laura Lynn - Chunk, Solid White Albacore

    Midwest Country Fare - Light Tuna Chunks Packed In Water

    Portside - Chunk Light In Water

    Price Chopper - Canned (Chunk, Solid)

    Progresso - Albacore Tuna (Solid White Packed In Olive Oil), Solid Light Tuna (Yellow Fin Packed In Olive Oil)

    Safeway Select - Chunk Light, Chunk Light Tongol, Tuna

    Starkist -

      Starkist Tuna *(Except Crackers In Starkist Lunch To-Go)*

      Starkist Tuna Creations *(Except Herb & Garlic Variety)*

      Starkist Tuna Fillets (Pouch) *(Except Teriyaki Variety)*

  Tops - Solid White Tuna In Water
  Trader Joe's - Marinated Ahi Tuna Steaks, Tongol Chunk Light
     Tuna (& No Salt Added)
  Wegmans - Tuna In Water, Tuna Low Sodium
  Wild Oats -
     Albacore Solid (No Salt, w/Salt)
     Smoked Light Tuna Slices (Ginger & Sunflower Oil, In
        Water, Sunflower/Sesame Oil)
     Tongol Chunk (No Salt, Salt)
  Winn Dixie - Tuna In Water
Turkey... *All **Fresh** Meat Is **Gluten-Free (Non-Marinated,
     Unseasoned)**
  Applegate Farms - All Varieties
  B&J - Canned Turkey Breast Meat
  Boar's Head - All Varieties
  Butcher's Cut - Ground Turkey, Oven Roasted Turkey Breast
  Butterball -
     Honey Roasted
     Lemon Pepper
     Less Salt
     Mesquite
     Oven Roasted
     Turkey Ham & Turkey Pastrami
  D&W Vac Pack Meats - Black Pepper Turkey, Honey, Oven
     Roasted, Santa Fe
  Dietz & Watson -
     Bacon Lover's
     Black Forest (Regular, Smoked)
     Champagne Honey
     Gourmet Lite
     Homestyle Turkey Breast

T

London Broil

Pepper & Garlic

Peppered

Santa Fe

Eagle Valley -

Mesquite

Oven Roasted (Buffalo, Regular)

Salsa

Smoked BBQ

Zesty Turkey Breast

Healthy Choice - Golden, Honey Roasted

Heavenly Turkey - w/out Glaze

Honeysuckle - All Varieties *(Except Italian Style Meatballs, Teriyaki Tenderloin, Frozen Turkey Burger)*

Hormel -

Deli Sliced (Honey, Oven Roasted (Regular, Turkey Breast)

Canned Turkey Meats

Natural Choice (Honey Deli Turkey, Oven Roasted Deli Turkey, Smoked Deli Turkey)

Smoked (& Turkey Breast)

Hy-Vee -

Deli Thin Slices Turkey Breast (Honey Roasted, Oven Roasted)

Oven Roasted White Turkey

Smoked White Turkey

Thin Sliced Honey Turkey

Thin Sliced Turkey

Turkey (Natural & Moisture Enhanced)

Turkey Bologna

Isaly's - Breast of Turkey

Jennie-O -

Festive Tender Cured Turkey

Flavored Tenderloins (Lemon-Garlic, Seasoned Pepper, Tequila Lime)

Fresh Ground Turkey (Extra Lean, Italian, Lean)

Fresh Lean Turkey Patties

Fresh Tray (Breast Slices, Breast Strips, Tenderloins)

Frozen Turkey Breast *(Except Gravy Packet)*

Hickory Smoked Turkey Breast (Cracked Pepper, Garlic Pesto, Honey Cured, Sun Dried Tomato)

Oven Ready Turkey (Garlic & Herb, Homestyle)

Oven Ready Turkey Breast *(Except Gravy Packet)*

Oven Roasted Turkey Breast

Pan Roasts w/Gravy (White, White/Dark Combo)

Prime Young Turkey - Fresh or Frozen *(Except Gravy Packet)*

Refrigerated Quarter Turkey Breasts (Cajun-Style, Cracked Pepper, Hickory Smoked, Honey Cured, Oven Roasted, Sun-Dried Tomato)

Smoked Turkey Breast (Hickory, Honey Cured, Mesquite)

Smoked Turkey Wings & Drumsticks

So Easy

    Glazed Breast Filets (BBQ, Honey Glazed)

    Slow Roasted Turkey Breast

    Stuffed Breasts (Broccoli & Cheese, Pepper Cheese & Rice, Swiss Cheese & Ham)

Turkey Breast

    Apple Cinnamon

    Garlic Peppered

    Hickory Smoked

    Homestyle Pan Roasted

    Honey Cured Peppered

    Honey Maple

    Honey Mesquite

T

Hot Red Peppered

Italian Style

Maple Spiced

Mesquite Smoked

Oven Roasted

Smoked

Smoked Peppered

Tender Browned

Tomato Basil

Turkey Store (Barbecue Turkey Thighs, Frozen Ground Turkey (Regular, Seasoned))

Manor House - Turkey

Marval - Canadian Maple

Meijer Brand -

Meijer Sliced Chipped Meat (Corned Beef, Ham, Pastrami, Turkey)

Sliced Chipped Meat (Pastrami, Turkey)

Turkey Breast (Hickory Smoked, Honey Roasted, Zipper 97% Fat Free)

Norwestern - Deli Turkey (Hickory Smoked, Oven Roasted, Turkey Pastrami)

Perdue -

Carving Turkey Breast

Fresh Lean Ground Turkey

Oven Roasted

Pan Roasted (Cracked Pepper, Honey Smoked)

Smoked (Hickory, Honey, Mesquite)

Whole Turkey

Carving Whole Turkey

Healthsense Oven Roasted (Fat Free, Reduced Sodium)

Whole Turkeys (Seasoned Broth)

Safeway - Primo Taglio Turkey (All Varieties), Roasted Turkey Breast

Shelton's - Free Range Turkeys, Ground Free Range Turkey

Shaw's - Turkey Breast (Hotel Style, Natural Flavor)

SPAM - Smoked & Oven Roasted Turkey

Stop & Shop Brand - Turkey Breast (Oven Roasted Fat Free, Smoked)

Tops - Whole Young Turkeys

Trader Joe's - Mequite Smoked Turkey Breast Sliced

Wegmans - Thin Sliced Turkey Breast (Oven Roasted, Smoked, Smoked Honey)

Wellshire Farms - All Natural Turkey Breast (Pan Roasted, Smoked), Sliced Turkey Breast (Oven Roasted, Smoked), Turkey Breast Oven Roasted

Turkey Bacon... see Bacon

Turkey Burgers... see Burgers

Turkey Ham... see also Ham

Jennie-O - Honey Cured Turkey Ham, Refrigerated Turkey Ham

Turkey Jerky... see Jerky

Turkey Lunch Meat... see Deli Meat

Turkey Sticks... see Jerky

Turnips... *All Fresh Fruits & Vegetables Are **Gluten-Free***

Pictsweet - All Plain Vegetables (Frozen)

U

V

Vanilla Extract... see Extract

Vegenaise

Follow Your Heart - Expeller Pressed

V

Vegetable Juice... see Drinks/Juice
Vegetable Oil... see Oil
Vinegar

    365 Every Day Value - Balsamic 5 Years Old
    365 Organic Every Day Value - Balsamic
    Albertsons - Apple Cider, Balsamic, Rice, White Distilled
    Authentic Food Artisan (AFA) - Lorenzi Balsamic
    Bionaturae - Balsamic
    Bragg - Apple Cider
    Di Lusso - Red Wine
    Eden - Organic (Apple Cider, Brown Rice, Red Wine, Ume Plum)
    Grand Selections -
        Balsamic Vinegar of Modena
        Red Wine Vinegar
        White Wine Vinegar
    Heinz -
        Apple Cider Vinegar *(Heinz Apple Cider Flavored Vinegar*
            DOES contain gluten)
        Distilled White Vinegar
        Red Wine Vinegar,
    Hy-Vee - Apple Cider Flavored Distilled, White Distilled
    Meijer Brand -
        Balsamic Aged (4 Yr, 12 Yr)
        Cider
        Red Wine
        White Distilled
        White Wine
    Price Chopper - Apple Cider, Red Wine
    Progresso - Balsamic Vinegar
    Regina -
        Balsamic

Raspberry Balsamic
Red Wine (Regular, w/Natural Garlic Flavor)
White Wine
Safeway Select - All Varieties *(Except Malt Vinegar)*
Save-A-Lot - Estcott White
Spartan Brand - Cider, White
Spectrum - Organic (Balsamic, Red Wine, Unfiltered Apple
Cider, White Wine)
Stop & Shop Brand -
Cider
Simply Enjoy (Balsamic of Modena, White Balsamic)
White
Wine
Tops - Apple Cider, White
Trader Joe's -
Apple Cider
Balsamic (Genuine, Of Modena-Gold Quality)
Orange Muscat Champagne
Seasoned Rice
White Balsamic
Wegmans -
Apple Cider
Balsamic (Aged Up To 3 Yrs, 8yr, 12yr)
Chianti Red Wine Vinegar
Red Wine Tuscan
Vinegar Cider
White Distilled
White Wine
Westcott - Apple Cider, White
Whole Pantry - Organic Raspberry Red Wine

V
W

Vitamins... *see Gluten-Free OTC Pharmacy Guide*
Vodka... **All Distilled Alcohol Is Gluten-Free*[2]

W

Wafers... see Cookies
Waffles/Waffle Mix... see Pancakes
Walnuts... see Nuts
Wasabi
> **French's GourMayo** - Wasabi Horseradish
> **Hime** - Japanese Horseradish Powder Sushi Wasabi
> **Ka-Me** - Wasabi Powder
> **S & B** - Prepared Wasabi in Tube
> **Spectrum** - Artisan Wasabi Mayonnaise (Organic)

Water
> **Alta Springs** - All Carbonated Flavors
> **Aquafina** -
>> FlavorSplash (Citrus Blend, Raspberry, Wild Berry)
>> Purified Drinking Water
>> Sparkling Berry
>> Sparkling Lemon-Lime
>> Sparkling Original
>
> **B & J** - Simply H2O Water
> **Crystal Geyser** - Alpine Spring
> **Dasani** - Regular, w/Lemon
> **Deja Blue** - Purified Drinking Water
> **Evian**
> **Fiji** - Natural Artesian
> **Ice Mountain**
> **Panafiel** - Mineral Water
> **Poland Spring** - Sparkling Spring

San Pelligrino - Sparkling Water

Spartan Brand - Water (Distilled, Drinking, Spring)

Trader Joe's - Sparkling, Spring

Wegmans -

Aqua Mineral Water (Italian, Lemon Flavored Italian, Lemongrass Flavored, Lime Flavored)

Baby Water

Purified Water w/Fluoride

Sparkling Water (Raspberry, Tangerine Lime, Lemon, Lime, Mineral, Mixed Berry)

Wild Oats - Sparkling Water

Watermelon... *All **Fresh** Fruits & Vegetables Are **Gluten-Free***

Whipping Cream

Albertsons - Whipping Toppings

Garelick - Naturals Extra Heavy

Hy-Vee -

Frozen Lite Whipped

Frozen Whipped Topping (Extra Creamy, Fat Free, Regular)

Real Whipped Cream (Lite, Regular)

Kraft - Cool Whip

Laura Lynn - Whipping Cream

Lucerne -

Aerosol Whipping Cream (Light, Non-Dairy)

Whipping Cream (Heavy, Light, Regular)

Marsh Brand - Aerosol Whipped Cream

Meijer Brand -

Frozen Whipped Topping (Fat Free, Lite, Original)

Ultra Pasteurized Heavy Whipping Cream

Ultra Pasteurized Whipped Cream Aerosol (Dairy, Non-Dairy)

Safeway - Lactose Free, Light, Regular

W

Spartan Brand - Frozen Whipped Topping (Light, Regular)

Stop & Shop Brand - Whipped Topping (Fat Free, French Vanilla, Lite, Non-Dairy, Regular)

Wegmans - Extra Creamy, Fat Free, Lactose Free, Lite, Whipped Light Cream

Winn Dixie - Non-Dairy Whip Topping

Whiskey... *All **Distilled** Alcohol Is **Gluten-Free**[2]

Wine... *All wine made in the **USA** is **Gluten-Free**[2]

Wing Sauce

Butcher's Cut - Jazz N Spicy Buffalo Wing Sauce

Di Lusso - Buffalo Wing Sauce

Frank's - RedHot - Buffalo Wing, Original, Xtra Hot

Mr. Spice - Hot Wing!

Wingo - Regular

Wings... *All **Fresh** Meat Is **Gluten-Free (Non-Marinated, Unseasoned)**

Jennie-O - Smoked Turkey Wings & Drumsticks

Perdue - Buffalo Chicken Wings (Hot n Spicy), Individually Frozen Chicken Wings

Stop & Shop Brand - Wings (Buffalo Style, Honey BBQ)

Trader Joe's - Chicken Wings

Worcestershire Sauce

French's

Giant

Hargis House

Hy-Vee

Lea & Perrins - Original

Marsh Brand

Price Chopper

Safeway

Save-A-Lot

Spartan Brand

> **The Wizard's -** Wheat-Free Vegan Worcestershire
> **Thrifty Maid**
> **Winn Dixie**

X

Xanthan Gum
> **Deli Bulk Pack** - Xanthan Gum

Y

Yeast
> **Fleischmann's**
> **Gayelord Hauser** - 100% Natural Brewers Yeast
> **Hodgson Mills -** Yeast
> **Red Star -** Active Dry, Bread Machine, Quick Rise

Yellow Squash... see Squash

Yogurt
> **Albertsons -** All Flavors
> **Cascade Fresh -** All Varieties
> **Colombo** - All Yogurt (Classic, Light)
> **Dannon -** Plain (Low Fat, Natural, Non-Fat)
> **Food Club -** All Varieties
> **Hy-Vee -**
>> Fat Free (Key Lime Pie, Plain)
>> Low-Fat
>>> Black Cherry
>>> Blueberry
>>> Cherry-Vanilla
>>> Lemon
>>> Mixed Berry
>>> Plain

Y

      Raspberry
      Strawberry
      Strawberry Banana
   Nonfat
      Banana
      Blueberry
      Cherry
      Lemon Chiffon
      Peach
      Raspberry
      Strawberry
      Strawberry Banana
      Vanilla
   Regular Peach Yogurt
   Whipped Low Fat
      Cherry
      Key Lime Pie
      Orange Cream
      Peaches N Cream
      Raspberry
      Strawberry
   Yogurt To Go
      Strawberry
      Strawberry & Blueberry
      Strawberry/Banana & Cherry

Imagine Foods - Soy Dream Organic Frozen Yogurt (Butter Pecan, Green Tea, Mocha Fudge)

Laura Lynn - Low Fat Yogurt

Lucerne - All Varieties (Fat Free, Pre-Stirred Low Fat, Yo Cups, Yo On The Go), Frozen Yogurt (Fat Free Vanilla)

Marsh Brand - Plain Yogurt

Meijer Brand -

Y

Blended
  Boysenberry
  Strawberry
  Strawberry-Banana
  Tropical Fruit
Fruit On The Bottom
  Blueberry
  Peach
  Raspberry
  Strawberry
Lite
  Banana Crème
  Black Cherry
  Blueberry
  Cherry-Vanilla
  Coconut Cream
  Lemon Chiffon
  Mint Chocolate
  Peach
  Raspberry
  Strawberry
  Strawberry-Banana
  Vanilla
Lowfat Blended
  Blueberry
  Cherry
  Mixed Berry
  Peach
  Pina Colada
  Raspberry

Y

Lowfat Vanilla
Nancy's - All Products
Price Chopper - All Varieties
Shaw's - All Varieties
Silk Soy (White Wave) - All Varieties
Stoneyfield Farm - Plain Yogurt (Low Fat, Nonfat, Whole Milk)
Stop & Shop Brand -
Grab'ums Yogurt To Go
Cotton Candy/Melon
Strawberry/Blueberry
Tropical Punch/Raspberry
Lowfat Blended
Blueberry
Peach
Raspberry
Strawberry
Vanilla
Lowfat Fruit On The Bottom
Blueberry
Peach
Raspberry
Strawberry
Strawberry/Banana
Nonfat Light
Banana
Blueberry
Cherry
Cherry Vanilla
Coffee
Peach
Raspberry

Y

    Strawberry

    Strawberry/Banana

    Vanilla

  Nonfat Plain Yogurt

Tillamook - All Varieties

Trader Joe's -

  All Varieties (Dairy Yogurt)

  Non-Dairy Yogurt Cultured Soy Yogurt (Peach, Raspberry, Strawberry)

Wegmans -

  Blended Lowfat

    Blueberry

    Cherry

    Coffee

    Key Lime

    Lemon

    Mixed Berry

    Orange Cream

    Peach

    Raspberry

    Strawberry

    Vanilla

  Blended Strawberry Banana

  Fruit On The Bottom Fat Free

    Black Cherry

    Blueberry

    Lemon

    Mixed Berry

    Peach

    Raspberry

    Strawberry

Y

Strawberry/Banana
Light Blended Nonfat
Blueberry
Keylime
Mixed Berry
Orange Cream
Peach
Raspberry
Strawberry
Strawberry Banana
Vanilla
Lowfat
Apricot Mango
Blueberry
Cherry
Cherry Vanilla
Lemon
Mixed Berry
Peach
Pina Colada
Pineapple
Plain
Raspberry
Strawberry
Strawberry Banana
Strawberry Kiwi
Vanilla
Nonfat Plain Yogurt
YoGo
Raspberry & Tropical Punch

Strawberry & Blueberry

Watermelon & Strawberry Banana

WholeSoy & Co. - All Products (Frozen Yogurts, Smoothies, Yogurts)

Wildwood Harvest - All Varieties

Winn Dixie - All Varieties (Lowfat, Nonfat, Regular) *(Except Frozen Yogurts)*

Yoplait -

All GoGurts

All Yogurt (Light, Kids, Original, Smoothie, Thick & Creamy (Light, Regular), Nouriche, Whips)

Z

Zuchini... *All **Fresh** Fruits & Vegetables Are **Gluten-Free***

Del Monte - All Varieties

Stop & Shop Brand

Gluten-Free
Over The Counter (OTC)
Pharmacy Guide

Rx   Allergy/Sinus/Cold /Flu Relief

Actifed - Tablets

Afrin - Nasal Spray

Alka Seltzer - Plus Night Time Cold Medicine Tablets

B&J - Cold & Sinus Caplets

B&J - Complete Allergy Medicine

B&J - Daytime Cold/ Flu Medicine Softgels

B&J - Loratadine Allergy Relief

Benadryl - Softgels Dye Free

Children's Tylenol - Cold Night Suspension Grape

Children's Tylenol - Plus (Cold Chewable Tablets, Cold & Cough Chewable Tablets Cherry, Cold & Cough Suspension Cherry)

Children's Motrin - Cold Suspension (Berry, Dye-Free, Grape)

Claritin - Reditabs

Diabetic - Tussin (Maximum Strength, Night Time)

Dibromm DM - Grape Elixir

Dimetapp - Infant Decongestant + CG

Infant's Tylenol - Plus Cold Drops

Meijer - Apap Cold Child Suspension Grape

Meijer - Apap Cough Cold (Child Suspension Cherry, Infant Drops Cherry)

Meijer - Apap PE Allergy Sinus Caplets

Meijer - Apap PE Cold Flu Day Cool Caplets

Meijer - Apap PE Cold Severe Congestion Caplets

Meijer - Day-Nite 6hr (Liquid Gels)

Meijer - Daytime 6hr (Liquid, Liquid Gels)

Meijer - Dibromm (DM Grape Elixir, Grape Elixir)

Meijer - Diphedryl (Capsules, Cherry Elixir, Tablets)

Meijer - Effervescent Cold Tablets

Meijer - Ibuprofen Sinus (Brown Caplets)

Rx

Meijer - Loratadine (Allergy Daily Tablets, D 24hr Tablets)

Meijer - Naproxen Sodium Sinus Cold Caplets

Meijer - Nasal Spray (Extra Moist Liquid, Liquid, Multi Symptom Liquid, No Drip Pump Liquid)

Meijer - Nitetime 6 hr (Cherry Liquid, Liquid Gels, Original Liquid)

Meijer - Nitetime Cough 6 hr (Cherry Liquid)

Meijer - Pedia Cough Decongestion Drops

Meijer - Pseudoephedrine Adult Decongestion Liquid

Meijer - Pseudoephedrine Sinus Nondrowsy Liquid Gel

Meijer - Tussin (CF Liquid, CS Liquid, Cough Cold Softgels, DM Liquid, Pedia Cough Cold Liquid)

Meijer - Tri-acting Nitetime Grape Liquid

Meijer - XP Day-Nite 6hr Original Liquid

Motrin - Cold & Sinus Caplets

Robitussin - Drops Menthol / Eucalyptus, Liquid Regular

Safeway Select - 24 Hour Allergy Relief (Regular, With Loratadine)

Safeway - Allergy Relief

Safeway - Allergy Diphenhydramine Hydrochloride Anti-Histamine

Safeway - Benehist Allergy

Safeway - Cough & Cold Decongestant

Safeway - Day Time Cold & Cough

Safeway - Maximum Strength Suphedrine

Safeway - Multi Symptom Nasal Spray

Safeway - Night Time Cold Medicine

Safeway - Suphedrine Severe Cold

Simply Cough - Liquid Cherryberry

Simply Stuffy - Liquid Cherryberry

Sudafed - Cold/Allergy Soft Capsules

Sudafed - Cold Tablets

Top Care - Allergy Relief Loratadine Tablets

Top Care - Daytime 6hr Liquid

Rx

Top Care - Dibromm Grape Elixir

Top Care - Diphedryl (Capsules, Cherry Elixir, Tablets)

Top Care - Nasal Spray (Liquid, Saline Liquid, Sinus Liquid, Multi Symptom Liquid, X-moist Liquid,)

Top Care - Nitetime (6hr Cherry Liquid, 6hr Cough Cherry Liquid, 6hr Original Liquid, 6hr Liquigels)

Top Care - Pseudoephedrine (Liquigels, Sinus Nondrowsy Liquigels, Tablets)

Top Care - Tussin (CC MS Liquid, CF Liquid, CS Liquid, DM Clear Liquid, DM Liquid, MS Liquid, Pedia CC Liquid)

Tylenol - Cold (Daytime Caplet, Severe Cold & Flu Daytime Liquid, Severe Cold & Flu Nightime Liquid, Severe Congestion Caplets)

Tylenol - Sinus (Allergy Sinus Caplets, Day Caplets, Severe Congestion)

Waldryl - Dye Free Softgels

Walgreens - Allergy Sinus (Caplets, Gelcaps)

Walgreens - Allergy Sinus Headache Caplets

Walgreens - Apap Cold (Caplets, Child Suspension Grape, Infant Drops Bubblegum)

Walgreens - Apap Flu (Child Suspension Bubblegum, Daytime Gelcaps)

Walgreens - Apap Sinus (Caplets, Gelcaps)

Walgreens - Congestion

Walgreens - Cough FM Decongestant Liquid

Walgreens - Daytime (Liqui-gels, Liquid)

Walgreens - Dayhist Allergy Tablet

Walgreens - Decongestant FC Tablets

Walgreens - Diphedryl (Cherry Elixir, FC Minitabs, Sleep Capsules, Sleep Tablets, Tablets)

Walgreens - Diphedryl/ Pseudoephedrine Tablets

Walgreens - Flu CC Maximum Strength (Non Drowsy Pouch, Regular Strength Pouch Tablets)

Walgreens - Ibuprofen Sinus (Caplets Brown)

Rx

Walgreens - Loratadine (D 24 Tablets, Liquid, 24 hr Tablets)

Walgreens - Maximum Strength Day/Nite Combo (Allergy/Sinus, Cold , Sinus)

Walgreens - Maximum Strength Day/Nite Flu Combo

Walgreens - Nasal Spray Multi Symptom Liquid

Walgreens - Naproxen Sodium (Caplets, Tablets)

Walgreens - Nitetime Cough Child Cherry Liquid

Walgreens - Nitetime Child Liquid (Cherry, Original)

Walgreens - Nitetime Liqui-gels

Walgreens - Non-Aspirin Maximum Strength Cold Caplets

Walgreens - Nose Drops Decongestant Liquid

Walgreens - Pedia Cough Decongestant Drops

Walgreens - Phenlyephrine HCL Tablets

Walgreens - Pseudoephedrine (Child Decongestant Liquid, HCL Tablets, Maximum Strength Non Drowsy Tablets, Plus Tablets, Severe Cold Non Drowsy Caplets, Tablets, 12 hr Tablets)

Walgreens - Tri-Acting Cold Allergy (Liquid, Nitetime Grape Liquid)

Walgreens - Tussin (CC Maximum Strength Liquid, CF Liquid, CS Liquid, Cold/Cough & Flu Softgels, Cough Liquigels, DM Clear Liquid, DM Liquid, Pedia CC Liquid)

Waltussin - Liquigels

Vicks - Nyquil

Antacids

B&J - Acid Reducer Famotidine

B&J - Antacid (Extra Strength Assorted Berry, Regular Strength Peppermint)

B&J - Pink Bismuth

Children's Mylanta - Tablets Bubblegum

Gaviscon - Antacid XS

Lactaid - Ultra Caplets, Fast Acting Caplets

Rx

Meijer - Antacid Calcium (Peppermint Chewables, XS Berry Chewables, XS Chewables, XS Fruit Chewables, XS Tropical Chewables, XS Wintergreen Chewables, Ultra Fruit Chewables)

Meijer - Antacid Fast Acting Liquid (Regular Strength Original, Maximum Strength Cherry, Maximum Strength Original)

Meijer - Cimetidine Tablets

Meijer - Dairy Digestive Extra Strength, Regular Strength, Ultra Caplets)

Meijer - Effervescent Antacid Pain Tablets

Meijer - Famotidine Tablets

Meijer - Milk Of Magnesia (Cherry Liquid, Mint Liquid, Original Liquid)

Meijer - Pink Bismuth (Chewables, MS Liquid, RS Liquid)

Meijer - Ranitidine

Mylanta - Liquid Original Flavor, Maximum Strength Liquid Original Flavor, Ultra Tablets Cool Mint

Pepcid - AC Tablets, Complete Chewable Berry Tablets, Complete Chewable Mint Tablets

Pepto Bismol - Caplets, Cherry Tablets, Liquid Cherry, Maximum Strength Liquid, Original Liquid, Tablets

Pepto Bismol - Children's Tablets (Bubblegum, Watermelon)

Prilosec - OTC

Rolaids - Multi Symptom (Berry, Mint)

Safeway - Antacid (Fruit, Peppermint, Plus Double Strength, Wintergreen)

Safeway - Milk Of Magnesia (Mint)

Tagamet - HB

Top Care - Cimetidine Tablets

Top Care - Dairy Digestive Ultra Caplets

Top Care - Effervescent Antacid Pain Tablets

Top Care - Famotidine

Top Care - Milk Of Magnesia (Mint Liquid, Original Liquid)

Rx

Top Care - Pink Bismuth (Chewables, Maximum Strength Liquid, Regular Strength Liquid,)

Top Care - Ranitidine Tablets

Tums - Antacid (Regular)

Walgreens - Antacid (Comfort Gel Cherry, Fruit, Mint, Mint Liquid, XS Original)

Walgreens - Antacid Fast-acting Regular Strength Liquid (Mint, Original)

Walgreens - Dairy Digestive Caplets (Regular, Ultra)

Walgreens - Effervescent Antacid Pain Tab

Walgreens - Magnesium Hydroxide Tablets

Walgreens - Milk Of Magnesia (Cherry, Mint, Original)

Walgreens - Pink Bismuth (Cherry, Maximum Strength Liquid, Regular Strength Liquid)

Antibiotic Ointment

Hy-Vee - First Aid - (Allergy Creme 2%, Antibiotic Ointment, Hydrocortisone Cream 1%)

Anti-Diarrhea

B&J - Pink Bismuth

Imodium - AD Caplets, Advanced Chewable Tablets

Meijer - Loperamide (Caplets, Liquid)

Meijer - Pink Bismuth (Chewables, MS Liquid, RS Liquid)

Pepto Bismol - Caplets, Cherry Tablets, Liquid Cherry, Maximum Strength Liquid, Original Liquid, Tablets

Pepto Bismol - Children's Tablets (Bubblegum, Watermelon)

Safeway - Anti Diarrheal Tablets

Top Care - Loperamide Caplets

Top Care - Pink Bismuth (Chewables, Maximum Strength Liquid, Regular Strength Liquid)

Walgreens - Loperamide (Tablets, Caplets, Liquid, NCRC Caplets)

Rx Walgreens - Pink Bismuth (Cherry, Maximum Strength Liquid, Regular Strength Liquid)

Antifungal Relief

Hy-Vee - Foot Care / Antifungal Creme

Meijer - MiconazoleCream

Meijer - Miconazole Foot Spray Liquid

Meijer - Tioconazole Ointment

Meijer - Tolnaftate Spray (Liquid, Powder)

Top Care - Miconazole 3 Day Cream Preapp.

Top Care - Miconazole 3 Day Disapp. Combo Pack

Top Care - Miconazole 7 Day Cream Disapp.

Top Care - Tioconazole 1 Day Ointment (Disapp., Preapp.)

Anti-Gas

Beano - Gas Relief Tablets

Gas-X - Antacid Tablets Extra Strength, Cherry Creme Extra Strength, Fast Tablets Wild Berry, Softgels Extra Strength)

Infant's Mylicon - Drops Non-Staining

Lactaid - Fast Acting Caplets, Ultra Caplets

Meijer - Gas Relief Ultra Softgels

Meijer - Simethicone Drops

Mylanta - Gas (Liquid Original, Maximum Strength, Maximum Strength Mint Tablet, Regular Strength, Tablet Mint, Ultra Mint Tablet)

Phazyme - Gas Relief Softgels, Ultra Strength Softgels

Top Care - Dairy Digestive Ultra Caplets

Top Care - Gas Relief XS Softgels

Top Care - Simethicone Drops

Walgreens - Dairy Digestive Caplets (Regular, Ultra)

Walgreens - Gas Relief (Extra Strength Capsules, Extra Strength Softgels, Regular Capsules, Regular Softgels)

Cough Drops/ Sore Throat Spray/ Lozenges

Rx

Halls - Sugar Free Menthol

Hy-Vee - Cherry Eucalyptus Flavor Drops, Honey Lemon Cough Drops, Sugar Free Black Cherry Drops

Meijer -Sore Throat Spray Cherry

Safeway - Cough Drops (Honey Lemon & Vitamin C Citrus)

Top Care Cough Drops (Honey Lemon Bonus, Ice Blue, Menthol Cherry, Menthol Eucalyptus, Menthol Sugar Free)

Walgreens - Sore Throat Spray Liquid (Cherry, Menthol)

Vicks - Chloroseptic Sore Throat Spray

Diabetic Products

Cinnabetic II - Diet Supplement

Diabetic - Tussin (Maximum Strength, Night Time)

Diabetx - Snack Bars (Chewy Nut Caramel, Peanut Butter Crunch, Pecan Delight, Toffee Square)

Enterex - Diabetic (Chocolate, Strawberry, Vanilla)

Glucerna - Shake (Butter Pecan, Chocolate, Strawberry, Vanilla)

Glucerna - Snack Bar Caramel Nut

Glucerna - Weight Loss (Chocolate, Vanilla)

Hair Care

California Baby - Body Wash & Shampoo

California Baby - Detangler Hair Spray

California Baby - Hair Conditioner

California Baby - Shampoo & Body Wash

California Baby - Super Sensitive Baby Shampoo

California Baby - Super Sensitive Hair Conditioner

California Baby - Tea Tree & Lavender Shampoo & Body Wash

Meijer - Minoxidil 5% Liquid

Rx
Safeway - Baby Shampoo
Safeway - Baby Wash

Laxatives/ Hemorrhoidal Relief

B&J - Fiber laxative (Regular, Sugar Free)

B&J - Optifiber Fiber Supplement

B&J - Stool Softener

Bisacodyl - Enteric Coated Tablets

Citrucel - Caplets, Clear Mix

Docusol - Mini Enema

Dulcolax - Stool Softener

Dulcolax - Suppository

FiberCon - Caplet

FiberLax - Tablets

Fleet - Babylax

Meijer - Fiber Therapy Caplets

Meijer - Hemorrhoidal (Cream, Ointment, Suppository)

Meijer - Laxative Tablets (Natural MS, Senna, Women's)

Metamucil - Capsules, Capsules Plus Calcium, Original Regular Strength Powder, Smooth Orange Flavor Powder, Smooth Sugar Free Orange Flavor Powder

Safeway - Fiber Therapy

Safeway - Senna Laxative Tablets

Top Care - Hemorrhoidal (Ointment, Suppositories)

Top Care - Laxative (Bisacodyl, Chocolate, Fiber Caplets, Natural Maximum Strength, Senna, Women's)

Walgreens - Enema For Children

Walgreens - Fiber Therapy Orange Powder

Walgreens - Liquid Glycerin Suppository

Walgreens - Natural Fiber Capsules

Walgreens - Stimulant Laxative Tablets

Rx

Wal-dult - Glycerin Suppositories
Wal-gentle - Laxative Suppositories
Wal-infants & Children - Glycerin Suppositories

Misc. Products

B&J - Baby Wipes (Soft Cloth Scented, Soft Cloth Unscented, Unscented)
Bausch & Lomb - Moisture Drops
Blistex - Ointment
Chapstick - Lip Balm Regular
Crayola - Classic Markers
Elmers - Carpenter Wood Glue
Meijer - Hair Skin Nail
Meijer - Heat Therapy (Back Wrap)
Meijer - Nicotine Gum (Mint, Regular)
Pedialyte - Oral Electrolyte
Pediasure - Vanilla Reclosable Bottle
Safeway - Lip Balm
Safeway - Foam Adhesive Bandages
Safeway - Sam-E
Top Care - Pregnancy Test
Walgreens - Urinary Pain Relief
Whole Foods - Lip Balm (Peppermint, Tangerine, Vanilla Honey)

Motion Sickness

Dramamine - Original Formula Tablets
Walgreens - Dimenhydrinate
Walgreens - Meclizine Tablets

Rx ## Oral Hygiene

Anbesol - Baby Grape Teething Gel

Aquafresh - Toothpaste Extreme Clean

Crest - All Toothpaste Varieties

Hy-Vee - Antiseptic Mouthwash/Rinse (Anti Plaque Rinse, Mint Anti Cavity Fluoride, Mint Anti-Plaque Rinse, Blue Mint, Peppermint, Spring Mint)

Gerber - Tooth / Gum Cleanser

Listerine - Antiseptic Mouthwash

Safeway - Waxed Dental Floss (Mint)

Toms - Toothpaste Spearmint

Pain Relief

Advil - Caplets, Gelcaps, Liqui-gels, Tablets

Advil- Migraine Liqui-gels

Aspirin - Enteric coated (Caplets, Cherry Chewable Tablets, Tablets)

B&J - Acetaminophen (Extra Strength Caplets, Extra Strength Gelcaps)

B&J - Aspirin (Adult Low Strength Enteric Coated, Enteric Coated Tablets, Tablets)

B&J - Headache PM Tablets

B&J - Ibuprofen (Caplets, Children's Oral Suspension Liquid Berry, Liquid Softgel Capsules, Tablets)

B&J - Naproxen Sodium

B&J - Nite-time PM

Bufferin - Tablets

Children's Tylenol - Flavor Packets (Apple, Bubblegum, Chocolate, Strawberry)

Children's Tylenol - Meltaways (Bubblegum Burst, Grape Punch, Wacky Watermelon)

Rx

Children's Tylenol - Suspension (Bubblegum, Cherry Blast, Grape, Strawberry)

Children's Motrin - Chewables Grape, Chewables Orange, Suspension Berry, Suspension Bubblegum, Suspension Dye-Free, Suspension Grape

Children's Motrin - Junior Strength Chewable Tablets (Grape, Orange)

Infant's Motrin - Drops (Berry, Berry Dye-Free, Dye-Free, Regular)

Infant's Tylenol - Drops (Cherry, Grape)

Junior Tylenol - Meltaways (Bubblegum Burst, Grape Punch)

Meijer - Apap (Caplet Red, Caplet White, ES Caplet, ES Tab, ES Gelcap, ES Geltab)

Meijer - Apap Child (Bubblegum Suspension, Cherry Suspension, Grape Suspension)

Meijer - Apap Infant Cherry Suspension

Meijer - Aspirin Enteric Coated (Adult Orange Tablets, Child Orange Chewables)

Meijer - Headache Tablets

Meijer - Ibuprofen (Caplets Brown, Caplets Orange, Child Suspension Bubblegum, Junior Caplets, Junior Chewables Orange, Tablets Brown, Tablets Orange)

Meijer - Naproxen Sodium (Caplets, Tablets)

Meijer - Migraine Caplets

Motrin IB - Caplets, Gelcaps, Tablets

Orudis KT - Tablets

Safeway - Acetaminophen

Safeway - Acetaminophen Extra Strength Rapid Release Gelcaps

Safeway - Aspirin (Coated Enteric, Coated Micro, Regular Strength, Low Strength)

Safeway - Children's Chewable Non Aspirin (Grape, Fruit)

Safeway - Ibuprofen (Caplets Brown, Liquid Softgels)

Safeway - Migraine Relief Capsules

Rx

Safeway - Non Aspirin Extra Strength (Capsules, Gel Capsules)

St. Joseph - Adult Chewable Tablets, Enteric Coated Tablets

Top Care - Apap (Caplets, Tablets, Child Chewables Bubblegum, Child Suspension Bubblegum, Child Suspension Cherry, Child Suspension Grape, Infant Drops Cherry, Infant Suspension Cherry, Junior Chewables Fruit, Junior Chewables Grape, PM Caplets)

Top Care - Aspirin (Buff Tablets, Child Orange Chewables, Enteric Coated Tablets)

Top Care - Headache Tab

Top Care - Ibuprofen (Caplets Brown, Caplets Orange, Child Suspension Berry, Child Suspension Grape, Infant Suspension Berry, Tablets Brown, Tablets Orange)

Top Care - Naproxen Sodium (Caplets, Tablets)

Top Care - Pain Relief Aspirin Tablets

Top Care - Pain Relief Non Aspirin PM (Gelcaps, Geltabs)

Tylenol - Arthritis Pain Relief (Caplets, Extended Release Arthritis Caplet)

Tylenol - Extra Strength Caplets, Extra Strength Gelcaps, Extra Strength Geltabs, Extra Strength Tablets, Regular Strength Tablets, 8hr Caplets, 8hr Geltabs)

Walgreens - Apap (Arthritis Caplets, Caplets, Gelcaps, Tablets, 8 hr Caplets)

Walgreens - Apap Child (Chewables Bubblegum, Chewables Grape, Chewables Fruit, Suspension Bubblegum, Suspension Cherry)

Walgreens - Apap Fast Melts Tablets (Bubblegum, Grape)

Walgreens - Apap Headache Relief Tablets

Walgreens - Apap Infant Drops (Cherry, Grape)

Walgreens - Apap Junior Strength Chewable Tablets (Bubblegum, Grape)

Walgreens - Ibuprofen (Caplets, Dye Free Tablets, Tablets)

Walgreens - Ibuprofen Child Suspension (Berry, Bubblegum, Fruit, Grape)

Walgreens - Ibuprofen Infant Berry Drops
Walgreens - Menstrual Maximum Strength (Caplets, PM Gelcaps)
Walgreens - Migraine Caplets
Walgreens - Non-Aspirin Menstrual Caplets
Walgreens - Teri-Buffered Aspirin Tablets

Rx

Sleep Aids

Meijer - Apap PM (Caplets, Gelcaps, Geltabs)
Meijer - Sleep Aid Nitetime (Caplets, Tablets)
Simply Sleep - Caplets
Top Care - Sleep Aid (Nitetime Caplets, Tablets)
Tylenol - PM Caplets
Unisom (Sleep Aid Tablets, Sleep Gel Maximum Strength)
Walgreens Apap PM (Caplets, Gelcaps, Tablets)

Soap

365 Every Day Value - Glycerin Soap -(Chamomile, Lavender, Olive & Aloe, Rosemary Mint, Unscented, Vitamin E)
B&J - Clear Antibacterial Hand Soap
B&J - Moisturizing Hand Soap
Dove - Sensitive Skin Bath Bar
Hy-Vee - Antibacterial Dish Detergent (Green Apple, Original)
Hy-Vee - Original Ultra Dish Detergent
Hy-Vee - Sparkly Clean Detergent (Fresh Scent, Lemon Scent)
Hy-Vee - Sparkly Clean Dishwasher Detergent (Fresh Scent, Lemon Scent)
Sun & Earth - Liquid Soap Pump
Whole Foods Market - Milled Soap (Lavender French, Lemon Verbena, Milk French, Sandalwood French)

Rx ## Stay Awake

Meijer - Stay Awake Tablets
Top Care - Stay Awake Tablets
Vivarin - Tablets

Supplements

365 Every Day Value - Evening Primrose Oil
365 Every Day Value - Fish Oil
365 Every Day Value - Folic Acid
365 Every Day Value - Glucosamine Sulfate
365 Every Day Value - Psyllium Husk Powder
365 Every Day Value - St. John's Wort
365 Every Day Value - Vanilla Whey Protein Powder
B&J - Co Enzyme Q Softgels
B&J - Concentrated Odorless Garlic
B&J - Fish Oil (Concentrate, Enteric Coated, Extra Strength)
B&J - Gingko Biloba
B&J - Glucosamine & Chondroitin (Regular, Plus MSM)
B&J - Green Tea Complex
B&J - Oyster Shell Calcium
B&J - Saw Palmetto Caplets
Health Market - Valerian Extract
Health Market - Soy Isoflavones
Health Market - St. John's Wort Extract
Health Market - Stress (B With Zinc, Form + Iron Tablets, Tablets)
Health Market - Cranberry Extract
Health Market - Daily Amino Acid 6
Health Market - Digestive Enzymes
Health Market - Echinacea Extract
Health Market - Ace Antioxidant

Rx

Health Market - Acidophilus
Health Market - Alpha Lipoic Acid
Health Market - Enteric Coated Triple Omega Complex
Health Market - Beauty Gelatin
Health Market - Bilberry
Health Market - Black Cohosh with Soy
Health Market - Chitosan
Health Market - Chromium Picolinate
Health Market - Co Q
Health Market - Evening Primrose Oil
Health Market - Ferrous Sulfate
Health Market - Flaxseed (Meal, Oil)
Health Market - Folic Acid 4
Health Market - Garlic Extract (Odorless)
Health Market - Ginkgo Balboa Extract
Health Market - Ginseng Extract
Health Market - Glucosamine
Health Market - Glucosamine & Chondroitin
    (Regular, Maximum, TRP)
Health Market - Grape Seed Extract
Health Market - Hair, Skin & Nails
Health Market - Healthy Eyes Extra Vision
Health Market - Herbal Energizer
Health Market - Lecithin
Health Market - L-Lysine (Regular, Natural)
Health Market - Lutein
Health Market - Lycopene
Health Market - Melatonin
Health Market - Milk Thistle Extract
Health Market - MSM
Health Market - Saw Palmetto Extract

Rx

Health Market - Oyster Shell Calcium (Regular, + D)
Health Market - Papaya Enzymes Chewable
Health Market - Norwegian Cod Liver Oil
Health Market - Olive Leaf Extract
Health Market - Omega Softgels
Health Market - Omega 3 Fish Oil Enteric Coated
Meijer - Acidophilus Bifido RS
Meijer - Anti-oxidant
Meijer - Astaxanthin 30
Meijer - Biocosinol
Meijer - CLA (Conjugated Linolenic Acid)
Meijer - Chromium Picolinate
Meijer - Cod Liver Oil
Meijer - Cranmax
Meijer - DHA
Meijer - EPA (Eicosapentaenoic Acid)
Meijer - Estroplus Extra Strength
Meijer - Fish Oil (Concentrate, Enteric Coated, Extra Strength,
Extra Strength Enteric Coated)
Meijer - Focus smart
Meijer - GLA (Gamma Linolenic Acid)
Meijer - Glucosamine Chondroitin (3X, Extra Strength,
+ MSM, Regular)
Meijer - Glucosamine + Collagen + HA
Meijer - Glucosamine Sulfate
Meijer - Green Tea
Meijer - Ginseng
Meijer - Menopause Complex AM PM
Meijer - L-Arginine
Meijer - Lutein
Meijer - Lycopene

supplements

Rx

Meijer - MSM 1500
Meijer - Memory + Mood Supplement
Meijer - Odorfree Garlic
Meijer - Phytosterol Esters
Meijer - Saw Palmetto
Meijer - Soy Isoflavones
Meijer - Super Omega
Meijer - Vision Formula w/Lutein
Nutrition Now - Rhino Acidophilus
Nutrition Now - Rhino Dippin' Pops Echinacea and Vitamin C
Nutrition Now - Rhino Echinacea
Nutrition Now - Rhino Veggie-Fruit Bears
Nutrition Now - Rhino Wigglers
Nutrition Now - Rhino Zinc
Nutrition Now - Warm Herbal Relief
Nutrition Now - Yeast Defense
Safeway - Docusate Sodium
Safeway - Famotidine Tablets
Safeway - Glucosamine Chondroitin
Safeway - Glucosamine Sulfate
Safeway - One Tablet Daily Vitamin
Top Care - Vitamin Cod Liver Oil Softgels
Top Care - Vitamin Co-Enzyme Q Softgels
Top Care - Vitamin Fish Oil Softgels Extra Strength
Top Care - Vitamin Flax Seed Oil Natural
Top Care - Vitamin Herbal (Echinacea, Ginkgo Biloba, St. John Wort Caplet)
Whole Foods Market - Acerola C With Bioflavonoids Chewables
Whole Foods Market - Acetyl L-Carnitine
Whole Foods Market - Alpha Lipoic Acid
Whole Foods Market - Astralagus

Rx

Whole Foods Market - B Daily Essentials

Whole Foods Market - Bilberry

Whole Foods Market - Biotin

Whole Foods Market - Carnitine

Whole Foods Market - Chelated Iron

Whole Foods Market - Complete Multivitamin
(Regular, Without Iron)

Whole Foods Market - DHA

Whole Foods Market - Daily (W/ Iron, Without Iron)

Whole Foods Market - Echinacea & Goldenseal

Whole Foods Market - Folic Acid

Whole Foods Market - Ginkgo

Whole Foods Market - Glucosamine Chondroitin
Double Strength Complex

Whole Foods Market - Glucosamine, Chondroitin
& MSM Complex

Whole Foods Market - Glucosamine With MSM

Whole Foods Market - Grape Seed Extract

Whole Foods Market - Hair, Skin & Nails

Whole Foods Market - Hi Potency Multivitamin

Whole Foods Market - Kelp

Whole Foods Market - L-Carnitine

Whole Foods Market - L-Glutamine

Whole Foods Market - L-Lysine

Whole Foods Market - L-Tyrosine

Whole Foods Market - Lecithin

Whole Foods Market - MSM

Whole Foods Market - Magnesium Chelate

Whole Foods Market - Nettles

Whole Foods Market - Niacin, Flush Free Formula

Whole Foods Market - Nutritional Yeast

Whole Foods Market - Organic Evening Primrose Oil

Rx

Whole Foods Market - Organic Flax Seed Oil
Whole Foods Market - Papaya Chewable
Whole Foods Market - Potassium, Sustained Release
Whole Foods Market - Pycogenol
Whole Foods Market - Quercetin With Bromelain
Whole Foods Market - Selenomethionine
Whole Foods Market - Soy Isoflavones
Whole Foods Market - St. John's Wort
Whole Foods Market - Stress B-Complex with Vitamin C
Viactiv - Soft Calcium Chews

Skin Care

California Baby - Botonical Moisture Cream
California Baby - Moisturizing Cream
Hy-Vee - Acne Power Wing
Hy-Vee - Foaming Face Wash
Hy-Vee - Gentle Skin Cleanser
Hy-Vee - Oil Of Beauty Lotion SPF 15
Hy-Vee - Pore Cleanser
Hy-Vee - Skin Cream

Vitamins & Minerals

365 Every Day Value - Adult Multi Vitamin
365 Every Day Value - B Complex Vitamin
365 Every Day Value - Calcium Magnesium
365 Every Day Value - Vitamin C Chewable
365 Every Day Value - Vitamin E Softgels
365 Every Day Value - Zinc Lozenges
AlphaBetic - Multivitamins
B&J - AF Multivitamin & Minerals Supplement W/ Lycopene

Rx

B&J - Calcium (Chocolate Chews W/ Vitamins D & K, Citrate, Coral, + Vitamin D)

B&J - Children's Chewable Multivitamins & Minerals

B&J - Daily Performance Multivitamin & Mineral Supplement

B&J - High Energy Health Pack Vitamin & Mineral Supplement

B&J - Mens Daily Vitamins

B&J - Mature Daily Vitamins

B&J - Vitamin B Complex Tablets

B&J - Vitamin C (Chewables, Tablets, W/ Rose Hips)

B&J - Vitamin E Softgels

Caltrate - 600-D, Colon Health, Original, Plus Chewables, Plus Chewables Assorted, Plus Tablets, W/ Soy

Carlson - Vitamins (All Varieties)

Centrum - Chewables, Junior W/ Extra, Kids Complete, Kids Nicktoon Complete, Kids Spongebob Complete, Liquid, Performance, Silver

Health Market - 50 Plus Multiple Vitamins

Health Market - Beta Carotene Natural

Health Market - Calcium (+ D, Citrate, Citrate + D, Coral, Hi Potency Plus, Liquid Plus D, Regular, Plus)

Health Market - Calcium, Magnesium, & Zinc Plus D

Health Market - Century Vitamins (Regular, Senior)

Health Market - Children's Vitamins (Animal Shapes, Animal Shapes Plus Vitamin C, Animal Shapes w/Extra C, Animal Shapes w/Iron, Complete Animal Shapes, Complete Chewables)

Health Market - Essential Multiple Vitamin Tablets

Health Market - Ester-C

Health Market - Iron

Health Market - Magnesium

Health Market - Maximum Multiple Vitamin Tablets

Health Market - Multiple Vitamins (Mega Men's, Mega Women's, Men's)

Rx

Health Market - Niacin (Natural, Regular)

Health Market - One Daily (Active Vitamins, Active Woman, Maximum, Men's, Weight Control, Women's)

Health Market - Potassium

Health Market - Prenatal Vitamins

Health Market - Sentry (Performance, Senior, Vitamins)

Health Market - Therapeutic M Vitamins

Health Market - Vitamin-A

Health Market - Vitamin B (BI, B6, BI2, Balanced B, Natural Balanced B)

Health Market - Vitamin C (Chewables, Regular, Synthetic, Time Released)

Health Market - Vitamin C Natural With Rose Hips (Chewables, Regular)

Health Market - Vitamin D

Health Market - Vitamin E (Blended, Natural, Regular, Water Soluble)

Health Market - Women's Multiple Vitamins

Health Market - Zinc Gluconate

Health Market - Zinc Lozenges With Vitamin C & B6

Hy-Vee - Chocolate Soft Calcium Chews

Hy-Vee - Vitamins

Meijer - 50 Plus With Ester

Meijer - Advanced Formula With Ester

Meijer - Calcium (+ D, Citrate Chewable, Coral, Phosphorus + D)

Meijer - Ester-C

Meijer - Men's With Ester

Meijer - Slow Release Iron 30

Meijer - Women's With Ester

Meijer - Vitamin A

Meijer - Vitamin BI2

Meijer - Vitamin E

Rx

Meijer - Vitamin E + Vitamin C

Meijer - Vitamin E Oil

Meijer - Vitamin E + Fish Oil

Natrol - Vitamins (All Varieties, Except Oatbran And Ultra-Carb Intercept)

Nature's Answer - Vitamins (All Varieties)

Nutrition Now - Calcium Soft Chews (Chocolate)

Nutrition Now - Rhino Beanie Vites

Nutrition Now - Rhino Calcium Chews (Assorted Fruit, Chocolate)

Nutrition Now - Rhino Chewy C Plus Echinacea

Nutrition Now - Rhino Chewy Vites

Nutrition Now - Rhino Daily Grubs

Nutrition Now - Rhino Ester-C

Nutrition Now - Rhino Swirlin' Calci-Bears Chewables

Ocuvite - (Extra Vitamin, Preservision EC Tablets, Preservision Tablets, Vitamin/ Mineral)

Polyvisol - Vitamins Drops + I

Pioneer Nutrition - Chewable Vitamins/ Minerals

Pioneer Nutrition - Ipriflavone Calcium Magnesium

Safeway - B Complex

Safeway - Calcium/ Magnesium/ Zinc

Safeway - Calcium (Coral, Plus D, W/ Vitamin D)

Safeway - Central Vitamin (Multi Card)

Safeway - Central Vitamin/Multi Vitamin

Safeway - Central Vitamin W/ Lutein

Safeway - Children's Chewable Vitamins (All)

Safeway - Prenatal Vitamins

Safeway - Super Men's Multi Vitamin

Safeway - Woman's One Tablet Daily

Top Care - Adult Nutritional Supplement (Chocolate, Chocolate Plus, Strawberry, Strawberry Plus, Vanilla, Vanilla Plus)

Rx

Top Care - Vitamin A (Natural, Natural Beta Carotene)

Top Care - Vitamin B (B-100 Balanced Natural, B Complex w/C Natural, B-6 Synthetic, B-12 Natural)

Top Care - Vitamin C (Chewable Multi Flavor, Chewable w/Rose Hips, Children's Chewable Jungleland, Children's Jungleland Complete, Drop Supplement, Regular, W/ Rose Hips)

Top Care - Vitamin Calcium (Chews Caramel, O.S.)

Top Care - Vitamin Chewable Iron Jungle

Top Care - Vitamin E (Blend Natural, Regular Natural, Regular Synthetic)

Top Care - Vitamin Magnesium

Top Care - Vitamin Multi Century (Senior w/Lutein, w/Lutein)

Top Care - Vitamin Multi (Daily, Daily Diet Support, Max, Men's, Natural, Prenatal, Women's)

Top Care - Vitamin NBE (Calcium Citrate, Glucosamine / Chondroitin Double Strength, Glucosamine / Chondroitin Regular Strength, Hi Potency Calcium + D, OS Calc + D, Ferrous Sulfate)

Top Care - Vitamin Potassium Gluc. Natural Caplets

Top Care - Vitamin Supplement (Garlic Natural, Glucosamine Sufate Complex, L-sysine)

Top Care - Vitamin Zinc Gluc. Natural Caplet

Walgreens - Multibetic Vitamins

Whole Foods Market - Vitamin B-1

Whole Foods Market - Vitamin B-2

Whole Foods Market - Vitamin C

Whole Foods Market - Vitamin C with Bioflavonoids

Whole Foods Market - Vitamin D

Whole Foods Market - Vitamin E with Mixed Tocopherols

Whole Foods Market - Vitamin K

INDEX

index

index

index

index

NOTES

NOTES

NOTES

Making Gluten-Free Living Easy!

Cecelia's Marketplace

Kalamazoo, Michigan

www.ceceliasmarketplace.com

Quick Order Form

 Online Orders: www.ceceliasmarketplace.com

✉ **Mail Orders:** Kal-Haven Publishing
P.O. Box 20383
Kalamazoo, MI 49019
U.S.A.

	Quantity	Price	Total
Cecelia's Marketplace Gluten-Free Grocery Shopping Guide	_____	(x $24.95) =	_____

Sales Tax: Michigan residents please add 6% sales tax _____

Sub Total: _____

Shipping: (quantities 1-2 add $4.05)
(quantities 3-6 add $8.10) _____

Total: _____

*Please make check or money order payable to Kal-Haven Publishing

Name: _____

Address: _____

City: _____ State: _____ Zip: _____

Email address: _____

Making Gluten-Free Living Easy!

Cecelia's Marketplace

Kalamazoo, Michigan

www.ceceliasmarketplace.com

Quick Order Form

Online Orders: www.ceceliasmarketplace.com

✉ **Mail Orders:** Kal-Haven Publishing
P.O. Box 20383
Kalamazoo, MI 49019
U.S.A.

	Quantity	Price	Total
Cecelia's Marketplace Gluten-Free Grocery Shopping Guide	_____	(x $24.95) =	_____
Sales Tax: Michigan residents please add 6% sales tax			_____
Sub Total:			_____
Shipping: (quantities 1-2 add $4.05) (quantities 3-6 add $8.10)			_____
Total:			_____

*Please make check or money order payable to Kal-Haven Publishing

Name: _____

Address:_____

City:_____State:_____Zip:_____

Email address:_____

Making Gluten-Free Living Easy!

Cecelia's Marketplace

Kalamazoo, Michigan

www.ceceliasmarketplace.com

Quick Order Form

 Online Orders: <u>www.ceceliasmarketplace.com</u>

✉ **Mail Orders:** Kal-Haven Publishing
P.O. Box 20383
Kalamazoo, MI 49019
U.S.A.

	Quantity	Price	Total

Cecelia's Marketplace Gluten-Free
Grocery Shopping Guide _____ (x \$24.95) = _____

Sales Tax: Michigan residents please add 6% sales tax _____

Sub Total: _____

Shipping: (quantities 1-2 add \$4.05)
(quantities 3-6 add \$8.10) _____

Total: _____

*Please make check or money order payable to Kal-Haven Publishing

Name: _____

Address: _____

City: _____State: _____Zip: _____

Email address: _____